D1190163

Judaic Ethics
For a Lawless World

Volume XII in the **Moreshet Series,** Studies in
Jewish History, Literature and Thought

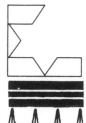

A CENTURY OF ACHIEVEMENT

1886–1986
תרמ"ו–תשמ"ו

Judaic Ethics
For a Lawless World

by
ROBERT GORDIS

A Centennial Publication of
THE JEWISH THEOLOGICAL SEMINARY OF AMERICA
NEW YORK
1986

COPYRIGHT © 1986
ROBERT GORDIS

Library of Congress Cataloging-in-Publication Data

Gordis, Robert, 1908-
  Judaic ethics for a lawless world.

  (Moreshet series; v. 12)
  Bibliography: p.
  Includes index.
  1. Ethics, Jewish. I. Title. II. Series.
BJ1280.G67 1986b   296.3'85   86- 7430
ISBN 0-87334-034-5

Manufactured in the United States of America

For Fannie,
my heart's delight

Contents

Foreword

It is no secret that we live in an age of crisis careening toward catastrophe. The crisis is worldwide, deep-seated, and multiform, threatening the survival of the race. As the effort is made to shore up the dike of civilization at one point, the floodwaters threaten to crash through the breach at another. With the growing sense of helplessness in the face of these massive problems comes a variety of deeply disquieting states of mind in our generation, particularly among our youth, despair, cynicism, callousness to human suffering, aggressiveness, and violence.

This volume seeks to discover how this condition came into being and to suggest what can be done to pull mankind back from the precipice of disaster. It is maintained that these problems—social, economic, political, and cultural, both at home and abroad—are ultimately moral in origin.

Chapter 1 begins with a brief survey of the dimensions of our multiple crises. We have been told that our age is pragmatic, marked by "the death of ideology"; actually it is the decay of idealism that is the root of all our ills.

Our society is ostensibly governed by an ethical consensus, deriving from a coherent worldview. Actually that conception of life has long been shattered, and we have been operating with the bits and pieces of a moral code that no longer commands the allegiance of the individual and is therefore only fitfully enforced by society.

Chapter 2 suggests that the crisis has been a long time in the making, being the end result of a process going back to the Renaissance. The progress of the last five hundred years has left man with his powers immeasurably enlarged and with his sense of self-worth drastically attenuated.

The character of the malady suggests the nature of the cure—there is need to find a moral basis for the life of the individual and society. In such a quest one naturally turns to two major enterprises of the human spirit, religion and science. Chapter 3 explores their mutual relationship, concerning which misunderstanding is rife. Chapter 4 examines their possible value in establishing a basis for morals and concludes that their role is limited.

Chapter 5 then turns to the examination of another resource that has been available for many centuries, the doctrine of natural law, which goes back to Greco-Roman civilization and reaches its apogee in the Middle Ages. Unfortunately, natural law, as traditionally expounded, possesses major drawbacks from the modern perspective; it has, therefore, been largely dismissed in the modern age as irrelevant and useless. I suggest that these defects can be remedied if our perspective is broadened to include another source for natural law—the Hebraic component. Though this aspect of natural law was well known and appreciated by scholars and thinkers in the seventeenth and eighteenth centuries, it has been almost totally neglected in modern times. Yet the Judaic tradition can supply dynamism and a sense of historical growth and development, hitherto lacking in natural law.

Chapter 6 then presents some of the major biblical sources available for a revitalized system of natural law.

Chapter 7 focuses upon a central element in Hebraism, the opening chapter of Genesis, the overarching significance of which has been lost in a maze of theological exegesis. Within the brief compass of the Creation narrative may be found an all-inclusive concept of the nature of the world and of man's role in it. Nor is this all. The ancient rabbis deduced from the biblical account of Adam's creation a succinct yet comprehensive set of ethical norms that are the foundations of a civilized society.

Natural law is not based on any specific dogma or creed, but it does assume some axioms and postulates. It is predicated upon the presence of rationality in the universe and in human nature. In traditional terminology, natural law builds upon a faith in a righteous God who is the Creator of the universe and the Governor of history. This faith has been shaken to its foundations in our day by the Nazi Holocaust. Chapter 8 seeks to demonstrate that even in the face of the horrors of Nazism, we need not follow the path trodden by untold numbers of our fellow human beings, who have been driven to despair or have sought asylum in illusion. The alternatives that they have chosen are entirely comprehensible in view of the agonies they have borne. Nevertheless, there is another way. Biblical thought offers several significant insights that make it possible for our post-Nazi generations to face life with insight, courage, and compassion.

Chapter 9 discusses another path through the maze of our current crises, the one that has been elected by "born-again" Christians and Jewish "returnees." They have chosen to oppose the modern spirit in virtually all its manifestations. Claiming to return to the religion of the "good old days," they wrap themselves in a mantle of personal piety, concentrating on their own salvation and disregarding the massive social, economic, and international problems that cry out for solutions. In essence, they have eliminated ethical concerns from the area of religion or reduced them to the vanishing point. Thus our age is witness to what would in the past have seemed a paradox or an impossibility— the decay of ethics in the face of the revival of religion.

Chapter 10 deals with a far more sophisticated attempt to sever the nexus between religion and ethics—Kierkegaard's famous theory of the teleological suspension of the ethical, which he found at the base of Abraham's sacrifice of Isaac, narrated in the Book of Genesis. In spite of the popularity of the idea in many circles, it is argued that Kierkegaard's interpretation rests on a total misreading of the biblical text and a basic distortion of biblical thought.

Several of the contributions that the Judaic tradition can make to natural law and contemporary ethics are set forth in the four concluding chapters in greater detail. In an age when pollution of air, water, and food is on the increase, the Hebraic attitude toward ecology, including elements hitherto unrecognized, is both interesting and significant. In an age when hostility among various traditional religions is sparking violence and bloodshed, the doctrine of freedom of conscience evolved by the Jewish tradition may help set the pattern for other creeds to follow. Today democracy seems to be in retreat; a discussion of the dimensions of democracy—its problems and potential—is therefore apposite. The final chapter treats of the most fundamental issue of our time—that of world peace—upon which the survival of the human race and of civilization depends.

Throughout my life I have loved the Bible and sought to contribute to the understanding and appreciation of its contents and form by my research and teaching. I was actuated not only by the intrinsic beauty and truth of the Bible, but by my ever-growing conviction that the Hebrew lawgivers, historians, prophets, and sages, particularly in conjunction with the postbiblical Jewish tradition, have a valuable contribution to make to the modern world. The present work represents an installment on my debt to this rich heritage, which, I profoundly believe, has the power to bless mankind by its message of righteousness, truth, and beauty.

My grateful acknowledgment is extended to the editors and publishers of the following journals for permission to use material that originally appeared in their columns: *Christian Century,* published by Christian Century Foundation, *Judaism,* published by American Jewish Congress, *Midstream,* published by the American Zionist Federation, and SIDIC, (Sources Internationales de Documentation Judeo-Chrétienne) published by the Soeurs de Sion in Rome for the Roman Catholic Commission on Christian-Jewish Relations. This material has been thoroughly revised and integrated into the contents and structure of this book.

Many of the ideas here presented were exposed to the tender mercies of my students at Temple and Columbia Universities, the Hebrew University in Jerusalem, the Jewish Theological Seminary of America in New York, and audiences throughout the United States and Canada, whose comments and criticisms helped improve and clarify the views I presented to them.

I am deeply grateful to Beatrice Snyder, Ina Lipkowitz, and the late Trude Kramberg, who suffered with my execrable handwriting and labored with exemplary devotion and patience over the manuscript, typing and retyping it times without number.

For all its imperfections, this book has had the benefit of a gifted and scholarly editor. My good friend, Dr. Robert Milch, has prepared the manuscript for publication with meticulous care and devoted concern.

I am thankful for the opportunity given me here to express publicly my life-long gratitude to my dear friend, Bernard Scharfstein, who has published half a dozen of my books. Through the unique publication program of KTAV Publishing House, headed by him and his brother Sol, he has made an extraordinary contribution to the advancement of Jewish scholarship and letters, the full scope of which is yet to be fully recognized.

This book appears as a Centennial Volume of the Jewish Theological Seminary in its hundredth anniversary year. It is a source of profound gratification to me that it is being published during the historic administration of Chancellor Gerson D. Cohen, an eminent Jewish leader and scholar whom I am proud to call my friend. I bespeak for him many more years of well-being and creative achievement.

In the sunset years of our lives, Fannie and I are more conscious than ever of how greatly the Giver of life has blessed us. Our three distinguished sons, their gifted and charming wives and our richly endowed grandchildren, continue to be an ever deeper source of pride and joy to us. I have been blessed, far beyond my power to deserve, by the boundless understanding, devotion, and love of my dear wife. Each day of our life together has revealed new facets of Fannie's wisdom and goodness. With God's continued blessing, "hand in hand we'll go."

Robert Gordis

New York City
Ḥanukkah, 5746

Part I

The Years of Discontent

Chapter 1

The Root of All Our Evils

EVERY GENERATION since Adam seems to derive a melancholy satisfaction from believing that it is living in the most dangerous of times. Nevertheless, our own age may well have the best claim. Ours is an era of multiple crises with every nation confronted by towering problems at home and abroad, embracing all aspects of its life—political, economic, social, and cultural.

In America, the breakdown of accepted norms of conduct has brought us to the brink of ethical nihilism. The catalogue of catastrophes is awesome—the widespread corruption in government and public service, in business and academic life; the irruption of violence, not only in the cities, but in the countryside; the drug-and-drink culture; the deterioration of education; the collapse of accepted standards of personal and family morality in favor of instant gratification; the escalating polarization of economic, ethnic, and racial groups; and the legitimization of lying and cheating on all levels of society.

Corruption and inefficiency are accepted as the normal way of life in politics and government, public service, business and academic life. Promises by candidates running for office are not taken seriously, either by them or by their constituencies, either before or after the election. That the millions spent on political campaigns will be recouped by the successful candidate from various "sources," white, black, and gray, is taken for granted.

More and more of our urban population find life in the cities intolerable, in view of the mounting filth in the streets, the overcowding of people, the noise, the traffic, and the escalation of violence. Because the criminals have fled to suburbia and beyond, the filth, crime, and crowding of the cities have all spilled over into the countryside.

3

For decades the public school system served to create and cement a sense of national unity among the various ethnic and religious groups comprising the American population. The physical deterioration of the schools and the decline of teaching in the face of student violence, alcoholism, and drug use have encouraged the creation of independent school systems for the rich and for some sections of the middle class. In addition to the private schools, denominational schools, Catholic, Protestant, and Jewish, have proliferated.

In many respects, the growing self-awareness of the various religious and ethnic groups in the national population has been salutary. It has helped to develop a sense of self-respect and loyalty to specific traditions. At the same time, a high price is paid by the larger society, because of the existence of separate and unrelated school systems, in each of which the personal contacts of the pupils are limited to members of their own group. Inevitably there is a rise in group parochialism and a sense of alienation from others who differ in appearance, behavior, or outlook. What is unfamiliar becomes a subject of fear, suspicion, and hatred. Here is the breeding ground of hostile group stereotypes. The end result is a weakening of the sense of community and the ascendancy of competing pressure groups.

The drug-and-drink culture is today universal in the Western world and is rapidly corrupting other sections of the planet. The goal of instant gratification, when it is not achieved among the underprivileged, leads to sullen resentment and bears within it the seeds of hostility and crime. On the other hand, when instant gratification is achieved among the overprivileged, it leads to a sense of ennui, listlessness, and cynicism, the loss of any sense of purpose in life or any concern for others.

All but destroyed today are such antiquated notions as the sense of the common weal, the concept of professional conduct, the standard of *noblesse oblige*. To cite a relatively minor instance, the connection between the ideal of sportsmanship and the practice of sports has almost disappeared. Professional sport in America today is an amalgam to the nth degree of greed and mayhem that are the staples of the sports pages and the sports newscasters.

Perhaps the most far-reaching area of decay lies in the personal relationships of men and women. The institution of marriage as a permanent living arrangement for a man and a woman is under major challenge by "alternative life-styles." The rising rate of divorce, with one divorce for every three marriages, has doubled in the last decade. The trend suggests that the term "marriage" is often a euphemism for renting a spouse and bedfellow for a fixed period of time—and not necessarily on an exclusive basis.

One out of every five children, for a total of 12.2 million, up 4 million from 1970, lives with one parent. In ninety percent of cases the single parent is the mother, either divorced or separated. Twenty-three percent of all households in the United States consist of one person living alone, according to the United States Census Bureau. The number of unmarried couples has tripled in the ten years between 1970 and 1980, rising to 1,560,000 from 523,000. These represent, however, only two percent of all households in the nation. Divorce is not a sin, but it is a tragedy, for every divorce is a tombstone on the hopes of two people who had once looked forward to happiness together.

Moreover, we are receiving bad news from financial experts, lawyers, and psychiatrists. They inform us that the alternative life-styles of unmarried couples living together have not avoided all the ills of traditional marriage, but are producing the same kinds of interpersonal stresses. The Lee Marvin "palimony" case highlighted the persistence of the battles over money, and the Tarnower-Harris murder trial revealed the ravages of jealousy and violence that the new, free, and enlightened "relationships" were expected to eliminate.

As a result, a vast chorus of purveyors of nostalgia have arisen to glorify the old order and insist that the traditional system of family morality was ideal. The truth is that the "good old days" were not good when they were not old. The subjection of women and the suppression of children under the old order were widespread evils, crying out for redress. Untold numbers of men, women, and children lived lives of quiet desperation under the old dispensation.

But whatever our philosophic position may be, whether one has greeted the new morality with joy or viewed it with alarm, one cannot deny the existence of massive ills that the sexual revolution has not cured. Pornography and prostitution, involving the corruption of children, are on the increase. The growth of venereal disease has reached epidemic proportions.

Today there are hundreds of thousands of abortions every year. One may well oppose the tactics and the goals of the Right to Life movement, but no one possessing sense and sensitivity can help seeing abortion as a tragedy, involving physical danger as well as psychological trauma for the woman. That it poses major ethical and religious problems, bringing in its wake an attitude of indifference to the value of human life is all too clear from the polarization and controversy the issue has introduced into American society. Teenage pregnancies now reach the astounding figure of one million a year, offering the unpleasant alternatives of abortion on the one hand and unwanted children doomed to penury and neglect on the other.

For decades, the explicit philosophy of the age has been "bigger is better." The litmus test in every area of society is "growth," abetted by the introduction of newer and more sophisticated electronic equipment to handle the multiplying mass of detail. Now the problems have outstripped the capacity to solve them. The computers may be ready, but the computer programmers are not. As banks and other businesses grow larger and more complex and become cogs in conglomerates, callousness, inefficiency, and disregard of the public become accepted and expected patterns of response from corporation and government offices on all levels.

Since the "Americanization" of the world is proceeding apace, the disease is worldwide. To cite one instance, Sweden was long held up to the world as having achieved a nearly ideal solution to the tension between security and freedom, blending the best features of socialism and capitalism into an effective and responsible "middle way." The system continues, on the whole, to work pretty well, but the human material has been proving recalcitrant. The eroding of traditional norms of conduct, particularly among the young, has been accompanied by grave psychological traumas manifesting themselves in alcoholism, drugs, violence, apathy, and suicide.

Once more, the temptation to succumb to nostalgia for a past that never was must be resisted. To speak of the moral vacuum of our times does not mean to assume that earlier traditional values in past societies were free from grave weaknesses. The pages of history and literature bear testimony to the widespread oppression and injustice, compounded by moral obtuseness and hypocrisy, that overlaid much of the conventional modes of behavior and speech in the past.

If we must single out one word to describe the temper of our age it would be "lawlessness." Today, there is more crime and more corruption than in the past, or so we think. But the difference is not merely quantitative; it is qualitative. It is the erosion of standards which were previously recognized as binding, not only by the law-abiding majority, but also by the law-violating minority. La Rochefoucauld's famous epigram, "Hypocrisy is the homage that vice pays to virtue" was ironic, but it expresses a truth probably not intended by the author. The hypocrite is himself a moralist *manqué*, who recognizes the validity of the standards he is violating. Our age has progressed beyond hypocrisy to "honesty." But though often hailed as an ethical advance, the new mores do not represent a greater devotion to the truth. People no longer feel it necessary to offer even the shoddy tribute of hypocrisy to traditional standards of conduct. Frankness in speech and in the delineation of sex and violence on the printed page, the screen, the stage, television, is free from inhibition. Obscenity and pornography have become respectable because they are profitable—and as their history demonstrates, impervious to legal definition and prosecution.

Finally, the massive social and economic problems of the age must be seen against the mounting terror of nuclear annihilation. For several years people comforted themselves with the doctrine of terror as a deterrent. The unspeakable horror of the prospect that the human race might be exterminated, it was felt, would of itself be the surest guarantee that nuclear bombs would never be used. It has been quickly forgotten that when Alfred Nobel invented dynamite at the end of the last century he triumphantly announced that world peace was now assured, since no nation would dare use so lethal a weapon in war. Today there is talk of "clean bombs," "limited nuclear conflicts," and "pinpoint bombing" against military targets only. Our Communist adversary presumably would sit idly by and learn the lesson while his population was being wiped out. It is all a matter of "game plans" and "scenarios." High-powered research institutes offer scientific projections demonstrating that only sixty million or eighty million Americans would be exterminated by a nuclear bomb falling in the United States.

Many experts believe that the casualties of the first nuclear attack would be considerably higher. Meanwhile, what was "unthinkable" only a decade ago "may not be undesirable," a high official in Washington has assured us, because a nuclear war is "thinkable, do-able and winable."

Wearing the perpetual smile which is obligatory for all high-level officials, the American government continues to provide "anti-Communist" and "moderate authoritarian" states like Guatemala and Saudi Arabia with weapons and planes of the most sophisticated variety; nuclear arms are not too far off. In this process, the American armament makers, who will presumably not be ungrateful, demonstrate how profit and patriotism go hand in hand until the ultimate catastrophe overtakes the human race.

It is probably true that most men and women today, particularly the adults who grew to maturity before the atomic age, have succeeded in putting the threat of nuclear annihilation out of their conscious thought, but it remains a potent element in their subconscious. They are able to continue the habits of thought and action bred in them during their youth. But the younger people, who have always lived in the shadow of sudden death, have adopted the stance of despair described by the Hebrew prophet two millennia ago: "Let us eat and drink, for tomorrow we die" (Isa. 22:13).

Faced by the massive problems, perils, and perplexities of today, modern men and women believe or have become convinced that they lack the power to solve their problems. Violence, greed, and cynicism are the dominant features of the age. These phenomena are not to be attributed to a sudden upsurge of viciousness in human nature, which tends to be fairly stable through the ages. Nor are they to be explained as due to the unleashing of demonic and uncontrollable forces in the hearts of man—an explanation which has been offered as the key to the understanding of the Nazi Holocaust. Actually, the temper of our times is the end result of a process extending over centuries. All these aspects of contemporary society, however variegated, suggest a diagnosis that may be simply put—the loss of a system of values, the lack of a basis for telling right from wrong, and the absence of responsibility for oneself or for others.

However, we need not stand by helplessly as the structure of civilization weakens and collapses. We must embark on the task of finding a new basis for morals that will command much the same degree of allegiance and support enjoyed by the traditional codes in past generations. The adoption by society of a consensus on ethical standards will not *ipso facto* eliminate wrongdoing and elevate the level of human behavior. But the acceptance of ethical standards is a prerequisite for any significant improvement in ethical conduct.

The first step in the process is to recognize that the erosion of moral standards has proceeded *pari passu* with the progress of Western civilization. Our first task is to discover the factors that have created man's present condition and brought him to the brink of disaster.

Chapter 2

The Paradox of Modern Man

"DO NOT SAY, 'What has happened, for the earlier days were better than these?' for not wisely have you raised the question" (Eccles. 7:10). In these words the biblical sage Koheleth warned against the common tendency to glorify the dead past and denigrate the present. Nostalgia for the good old days, artificial or genuine, has become a popular article of commerce, a stock-in-trade of politicians and preachers. The old standards left much to be desired even in their time; changing conditions and new insights have made some of them irrelevant or harmful. But for all their drawbacks, traditional morals are far better than none, as the multiple problems of our age demonstrate.

I believe that our contemporary crisis is the end result of a process going back half a millennium and extending from the Renaissance to our own day. Like all great movements in history, the Renaissance, which marked the transition of the Western world from medievalism to modernism, cannot be dated with precision. It began in Italy in the thirteenth century and reached its height in the fifteenth. From the fifteenth to the middle of the seventeenth century, its influence radiated throughout Western Europe: in France, the German states, the Low Countries, Spain, Portugal, and England.

Basically, the Renaissance stressed the role of the individual and made his worldly experience the touchstone of meaning in life. It served to unleash unsuspected capacities among men and women that enriched every aspect of human activity. Within a few centuries the Renaissance produced a galaxy of genius and talent in every department of thought and activity. Michelangelo and Rembrandt, Galileo and Newton, Molière, Shakespeare, and Bach, and hundreds of lesser figures stimulated a growing sense that man's powers were virtually limitless. The arts of painting and sculpture rivaled the Golden Age of Greece, while the achievements in literature and music were unparalleled in history. The far-reaching scientific discoveries and technological inventions laid the groundwork for the discovery of the New World and the Industrial Revolution. In the person of Leonardo da Vinci, scientific and artistic creativity reached an apogee.

These intellectual achievements led to major progress in the practical realm. In the fifteenth and sixteenth centuries the great voyages of discovery opened up a vast New World to exploration and exploitation by Europeans. In the seventeenth and eighteenth centuries the Industrial Revolution made available new and far more efficient forms of energy, the first of which was steam, to be succeeded in ever rapidly growing momentum by electricity and finally by nuclear power. As a result, a cornucopia of goods and services, both necessities and luxuries, poured forth, which the ancients and medievals could have conceived of only as the result of some Faustian compact with the devil. Perhaps this is precisely what happened!

In the twentieth century the tempo of progress becomes ever more dizzying and dismaying. The discoveries of nuclear physics unleashed new sources of energy that have radically transformed the pattern of living and increased the prospects of dying for our generation. The beneficial effects of nuclear power are indeed extensive, but they are dwarfed by comparison with their potential for evil. For the first time in human experience, man is sufficiently powerful to obliterate the human race and wipe the earth clean in a flood of fire. Moreover, the pygmies sitting in the seats of power almost everywhere on the planet give every indication of being hell-bent on doing just this.

The past four hundred years have marked an incredible growth in man's ability to control and manipulate the world of nature. Man's sway extends from the microcosm of the sub-atom to the macrocosm of stellar space. But this fantastic expansion of man's capacities has set a dialectic in motion that was not originally evident.

Together with this trend toward ever greater control and mastery of the world about him, another tendency, parallel to it yet diametrically opposed, has been making itself felt—a steady decline in man's sense of his own self-worth, a growing feeling of his unimportance in a vast universe. Beset by impersonal forces and automatic processes that seem to defy control, man sees himself reduced to helplessness, his hopes and dreams turning to ashes.

The negative view of man's place in the world did not emerge in the heyday of the Renaissance. On the contrary, that period marked the pinnacle of man's self-confidence. The high conception of man's significance was nurtured by the extraordinary achievements in the arts and sciences, as well as by the biblical doctrine of man as created in the image of God, little less than the angels. It finds superb expression in Hamlet's soliloquy:

> What a piece of work is a man! How noble in reason! How infinite in faculties!
> In form and moving how express and admirable! In action how like an angel!
> In apprehension how like a god! The beauty of the world, the paragon of animals!

While man's high sense of self-esteem continued to hold sway and indeed seemed to grow with his achievements, it was being quietly undermined by a series of major scientific discoveries that attenuated the role and importance of the human species—or were so perceived. In the sixteenth century, the Copernican discoveries in astronomy did more than give a new, simpler, and therefore "truer" concept of the solar system than the Ptolemaic theory. Not only man's view of the heavens was revolutionized; his view of himself was transformed. Previously the earth was conceived of as the center of creation, with the sun, the moon, and the stars having been made for man's benefit: in the words of Genesis, to "serve as signs both for festivals and for days and years" (1:14). Now the earth was reduced to the role of a lesser planet revolving around the sun, with man becoming a brief sojourner on a minor astronomical speck in the universe. A few centuries later, scientists were to demonstrate that the entire solar system was only one galaxy among an almost limitless number. But the major blow to man's self-esteem had already been inflicted by Copernicus. Man had become physically insignificant in the cosmos. Theoretically, one could still hold fast to the old faith that man is created to glorify God, but his hosannahs tended to be drowned out in the vast reaches of interstellar space.

Then came the second blow at man's self-esteem. Against the background of new theories in mathematics and physics, Spinoza, in the seventeenth century, saw the universe as a vast mechanism governed by immutable laws. As part of nature, man was locked into the iron law of causation, automatic, immovable, and inescapable. Hence, Spinoza denied man's freedom of will. Human beings may think that they are free to choose one course of action over another, but, Spinoza insisted, they were laboring under an illusion. Three times Moses had emphasized that the people were free to choose between life and death, the blessing and the curse (Deut. 11:26; 30:15, 19). Spinoza declared that the only true freedom lay in recognizing and submitting to the law of necessity, recognizing that each human act is a link in the iron chain of causation.

Actually, Spinoza was grappling with the perennial paradox of man's free will versus determinism—he had by no means conquered the problem or resolved the paradox. In opting for determinism as against freedom, he had chosen one horn of the dilemma. On the other hand, religious thinkers have, with relatively few exceptions, taken hold of the other horn and maintained the principle of freedom of the will. As a philosopher, Spinoza was concerned with the rigorous logic of his thought; the major thinkers and teachers of Judaism and Christianity were more concerned with the consequences for men's actions. That no one is totally master of his fate was, of course, self-evident, but they felt it essential to insist upon man's freedom of will, even at the cost of philosophic inconsistency. "Everything is in the hand of God—except the fear of God," the Talmud taught (*B. Barakhot* 33b). While all else that befalls us, health or sickness, richness or poverty, even wisdom or stupidity, may be determined by factors outside our control, the choice between right and wrong is in our power to decide.

Acutely conscious of the paradox, the second-century sage Rabbi Akiba boldly seized hold of both horns of the dilemma. "Everything is foreseen [by God], but free will is given [to man]" (*Abot* 3:15). Akiba clearly recognized the difficulty, if not the impossibility, of resolving the contradiction between free will and determinism, and he boldly made human needs and actions paramount. In doing so, he anticipated by a millennium and a half the judgment of the eighteenth-century English writer Samuel Johnson, who declared, "All theory is against the freedom of the will; all experience for it."

Spinoza's philosophic genius notwithstanding, he had actually placed a time bomb under the structure of society by insisting on the iron law of causation. If all action is predetermined, by what right can anyone be rewarded for positive deeds and punished for negative ones? If our sense of free will is an illusion, how can the doctrine of human responsibility survive? With its disappearance, the fabric of a society governed by law would come apart at the seams. To be sure, he had taught—and practiced—the ideal of virtue for its own sake, without the desire or the hope of reward—a doctrine preached by the noblest exemplars of traditional religion before him. But this rarefied doctrine could appeal only to the chosen few. Once the idea of man's life being governed by necessity had permeated all levels in society, there would be no compelling reason for being accountable for one's acts. Whether the reasoning was air-tight and irrefutable was of little moment. It meant that human beings had been denuded of their moral responsibility and society had been stripped of its moral authority.

The full consequences of Spinoza's thought, and that of his successors both in science and philosophy, were not to become apparent for decades and even for centuries, but the process had been set in motion. The mechanistic view was popularized by the English theologian William Paley in his enormously influential book *Natural Theology; or, Evidence of the Existence and Attributes of the Deity*, published in 1802. Paley sought to buttress faith in the traditional God of Christianity by invoking his famous metaphor of the world as a cosmic clock, the existence of which presupposes a Clock-Maker. Though he sought to defend belief in a Deity, his mechanistic analogy implicitly undermined the concept of man's moral freedom and responsibility.

Thus, others, like the seventeenth-century poet, the Earl of Rochester, drew far less optimistic conclusions from the mechanistic view of the universe. His attitude is described by James Sutherland in his book *English Satire* in these words: "He expressed the moral crisis of Western Europe at the time when the new philosophy had shattered the old, unified world-picture and man was seen as an isolated unit, miserable and insignificant in a hostile and indifferent world."

However, even more devastating challenges were to emerge from sciences yet unborn. The most important steps in the deflation of man, because they were most directly related to him, were destined to be taken in the name of the life sciences, economics, sociology, biology, and psychology.

As the nineteenth century wore on, the mounting social and economic problems of an industrial society and the widespread suffering of the masses became evident. As a result, there emerged a variety of proposals for social reform on the one hand and passionate calls for revolution on the other. Incomparably, the most influential was the voice of Karl Marx, the patron saint of all the shades and varieties of socialism and communism today. The story is told that when Lenin died and came to heaven, St. Peter deputized Karl Marx to meet his most famous and successful disciple and to escort him to his seat. As they walked through the various heavenly chambers, Lenin saw large crowds standing far off, making obeisance to Marx, and he asked, "Who are these, Master?" Marx replied, "Son, I do not know. They are too few to be my followers, but too many to be my readers."

The precise contours of Marx's doctrines are not our present concern. As with all Scriptures, the later exegesis proved more influential than the original text—what was read into it has proved more important than what can be read out of it. Basic to Marx's worldview was his insistence that the most important forces in society are economic. The ownership and control of the instruments of production and of the mechanisms for the distribution of goods and services—these are the determining factors in human existence. All the other, nonmaterial aspects of life, such as literature, music, art, science, philosophy, and above all religion, are merely "cultural compulsives," designed to mask the economic realities of life, and thus further the material interests of the ruling classes.

Marx's two basic contributions were the economic interpretation of history and his call for social action, the latter flowing out of the former. The economic interpretation of history is a scientific theory; the call for social revolution, a pragmatic program. Karl Marx was the first social scientist to recognize with perfect clarity that the economic conditions of society are the fundamental factors in human affairs and take precedence over all others. This insight is independent of social philosophy or religious preconceptions. Perhaps the most lucid exposition of Marx's thesis was written by a leading conservative economist, the late Professor E. R. A. Seligman of Columbia University.

Unfortunately, Marx's brilliant contribution to the science of history was obscured, because it was exaggerated, by his followers. Marx had said that the primary motivation for human activity is the desire for food, shelter, and security; what is more, the economic facts of a given society, such as the distribution of wealth, the living standards, the workers' wages, and the stage of technological advance, *condition* the other elements of civilization: the moral codes, scientific research, literature, art, and religion. Marx's followers took this to mean that economic forces *determine* the culture of society.

The difference between "condition" and "determine" is elementary, but it was coolly ignored by the most militant and articulate of Marx's disciples. If the economic order *determines* the culture and is found to be untenable, then both must be destroyed root and branch, for all cultural manifestations are merely the hypocritical masks of selfish vested economic interests. Morality is nothing but bourgeois hypocrisy; scientific research, the slave of the propertied classes, and religion, the instrument for keeping the masses contented in their slavery.

If, however, it be recognized that while economic forces condition the culture, they do not determine it, the consequences are radically different. Then it follows, indeed, that economic interests may exploit science, religion, and morality for their own use, but these and all other expressions of the human spirit have a genuine, independent *raison d'être*. Culture needs to be redeemed from its economic shackles, not destroyed, if civilization is to endure. The failure to recognize the true dimensions and limits of the economic interpretation of history has been a disaster. It is the cause for the Communist oppression of religion and the suppression of all forms of intellectual and artistic freedom in the Soviet Union and among its satellites. A starving musician hungrily snatches at food; but once he has eaten, he reaches for his instrument. This truth the Marxist interpretation of history ignored.

Nevertheless, whether Marx himself indicated clearly enough the limits of the economic factor in history is a moot question. It is clear that the message the masses of men derived from him—or from his disciples—was that economics is all-powerful, that mankind is completely at the mercy of material factors. The sovereignty of man—his claim to being a rational creature of God—had been struck another telling blow. The groundwork had been laid for the omnipotent rule of the Almighty Dollar.

Contemporaneously with Marxism, a challenge to man's freedom arose from another quarter. Building upon the work of their predecessors, the nineteenth-century biologists Charles Darwin and A. R. Wallace presented a new view of life on this planet in their theory of the evolution of species, which challenged the biblical account in Genesis that all living things were created separately and within a six-day period of time. Darwin, Wallace, and their coworkers held that the animals, including man, had evolved slowly during aeons from one another by a process of "natural selection." The popular perception of the place of mankind now suffered another major setback—man was now only the most highly developed of the primates on earth, a little higher than the apes, and not a little lower than the angels.

Though evolution was a scientific theory designed to explain a very important segment of reality, it had important links to "natural theology," which sees the hand of God in the world of nature. Far from excluding God from the universe, Darwin concluded *The Origin of Species* with the sentence: "There is grandeur in this view of life, with its several powers, having been originally breathed by the Creator into a few forms or into one; and that, whilst this planet has gone cycling on according to the fixed law of gravity, from so simple a beginning endless forms most beautiful and most wonderful have been and are being evolved." In his letters, Darwin repeated his belief that evolution does not exile God from his world.

But both the advocates and the opponents of evolution were bitterly engaged in converting—and perverting—a scientific hypothesis into a philosophical pronouncement, negative or positive as the case might be. For the mythical man on the street, the human species was only the cleverest of the animals—and the most dangerous. What was worse, by his actions, man proceeded to prove it.

The closing decades of the nineteenth century and the entire twentieth witnessed another far-reaching revolution in man's perception of his nature. This time the challenge, coming from the field of psychology, was direct and unmistakable. Sigmund Freud, whose towering genius overshadowed even his greatest disciples and opponents, Carl Jung and Alfred Adler, discovered a new and unsuspected world in the human spirit, in which reason was a minor element at most. Freud's followers and dissenters differed widely in their description of these unknown components of the human psyche. But they were at one in creating the popular perception that man's conscious thought and the use of reason were only the tip of the iceberg and that the subconscious and the irrational played a dominant role in human activity. Freudian psychoanalysis revealed that man's conscious reason is contaminated and manipulated by sexual drives, licit or illicit as they may be. Alfred Adler gave a position of primacy to the inferiority complex or the thirst for power. Carl Jung emphasized archetypal racial memories and impulses buried deep in the human psyche.

Most practitioners of psychology and psychiatry have been eclectic, adopting and adapting elements from the various schools. This is not only sound procedure pragmatically, but also theoretically. It avoided the dangers of a monolithic approach to the human spirit and recognized the complexity within the psyche.

But the view of man that emerged in the marketplace made a shambles of Hamlet's soliloquy, "How noble in reason, how infinite in faculties." Man saw himself as lacking in nobility, bereft of reason, limited in his faculties, at the mercy of dark forces both within himself and in his environment that were all basically beyond his control.

The shocks to man's perception of his place in the world have continued to come with increasing frequency. The second half of the twentieth century has brought new and far-reaching discoveries in the field of biogenetic research. Scientists have begun to penetrate the secrets embedded in the genes and are learning how to manipulate and recombine these bearers of life to produce new, unknown forms, the character of which cannot even vaguely be imagined. The need for safeguards in this area is widely recognized, and efforts are being made to establish standards. It is, however, a new continent that has come within man's ken. It is noteworthy that the feeling of exhilaration at the discovery is exceeded by a widespread sense of foreboding before the perils of the unknown.

Atomic research, which like all branches of science is ethically neutral, has produced extraordinary results. But they have been far more evident in the invention of weapons of annihilation than in the creation of new sources of plenty and well-being.

The same period has also witnessed the birth and proliferation of the computer. Through progress in computer science, the most complicated analyses of existing data and projections for the future have become commonplace. Man, to be sure, is the creator of the computer, but he is both awed and cowed by the Golem, who threatens to make his creator superfluous.

Our brief survey of the contributions of Copernicus, Darwin, Marx, Freud, and their successors has done far less than justice to the magnitude of their achievements and the extent of their influence. They have transformed our understanding of our world and of ourselves and revolutionized the objective conditions of human life nearly everywhere on this planet. Unfortunately there is an unwritten law in history that the greater a man's influence upon his fellowmen, the greater the degree of misunderstanding and distortion of his ideas and goals. While this melancholy truth is demonstrated preeminently in the lives of the great religious leaders of mankind, it is equally valid for scientists and philosophers. The all-but-universal price of popularity is vulgarization. The achievements of these great minds remain among the proudest possessions of the race. But the popular perception of their ideas and discoveries—and this has been far more influential—has been much less of a blessing. It is this aspect of their lives and careers with which we are concerned here.

The impact of their contributions has been dual in character, one proximate and direct, the other more remote and subtle. The direct consequences are in evidence everywhere in our culture, but the subtler effects of these ideas on man's understanding of reality are of more fundamental and abiding importance.

Copernicus had shown that the earth was not the center of the universe; hence man was reduced in his own estimation to being one creature on a tiny and unimportant planet from which God had been expelled. As the Russian astronaut triumphantly announced, he did not find God in outer space.

Darwin's "survival of the fittest" became a scientific "license" for the untrammeled exercise of greed and cruelty in exploiting weak and defenseless elements in society. Highly sophisticated versions—or perversions—of the doctrine created "social Darwinism," the rationale for the neoconservatives' fierce defense of the social and economic status quo.

Marx's "class struggle" offered an ideological base for the breakdown of the sense of brotherhood linking all human beings in a common bond and provided a justification for class antagonism and the practice of the terrorism of the left. The siege mentality of Communist regimes led to the suppression of all forms of personal freedom on a "temporary" basis, which has lasted seventy years in the Soviet Union, in spite of the guarantees of the Constitution. Totalitarianism is the only acceptable form of government in Communist and pro-Communist countries.

Freud's stress upon the importance of sexuality (which had a far broader meaning than the vulgar understanding of the term) and upon the psychic dangers of the suppression of the instincts served as *carte blanche* for one of the most pervasive aspects of our society—the unlimited exploitation of sex, ranging from child pornography and sexual abuse to its subliminal use in advertising.

Undoubtedly, the new astronomy of Copernicus and his successors, as well as the philosophical demonstrations of Spinoza, affected men's perception of themselves only indirectly, but it influenced the outlook of other, second-level thinkers who in turn had a direct impact upon their contemporaries. The self-image of modern man may be described as follows: The human race today is the result of the convergence of several major forces that determine its existence. Man's physical and psychological equipment has come to him from the lower animals, as modified by his heredity and environment (praise be to Darwin and Galton), transformed by the economic forces that control his environment (courtesy of Marx), and always at the mercy of the irrational impulses warring in his soul (thanks to Freud, Adler, and Jung).

All these influences have united to produce the tragic paradox confronting mankind on the threshold of the twenty-first century—an ever-expanding power over the external universe and a constantly shrinking sense of control over his inner world, accompanied by an abysmal decay in his feeling of self-worth, and consequently, an erosion of his sense of moral responsibility. In a mysterious and malevolent world, he feels alone and alienated, caught in the grip of instincts and lusts that he cannot control and which he is driven to gratify, so that every other human being is his potential or actual enemy.

Franz Kafka has given a superb expression to modern man's conception of his place in the world in his tale *The Trial*. The one character, K, is charged with a crime that he cannot discover by powers that he cannot identify, and he waits as a virtual prisoner for a decision that never comes. On one level, the most obvious, Kafka has prophetically presented a parable of the horror of Nazism in its heyday. On a deeper level, Kafka is describing the tragic predicament of modern man and by that token the condition of modern society.

The two readings of *The Trial* are not far apart. The gap between Nazism and our world is constantly narrowing. Less than four decades after the overthrow of Hitler, a worldwide recrudescence of anti-Semitism is taking place. A far-flung campaign is underway to "revise" history and to deny that the extermination of six million Jews in the gas chambers and crematoria of Europe ever took place. The United Nations, created as an instrument for amity among peoples and world peace, has been prostituted through Arab petrodollars and Communist machinations and become a forum for hypocrisy and aggression. Through a campaign of calumny and terror, disguised in the language of diplomacy and legality, the Nazi campaign to annihilate the Jewish people has been revived. That the new barbarism was first discernable in the onslaught on Jews and the isolation of Israel should occasion no surprise in view of the historic role of the Jew as the scapegoat *par excellence* for the ills of mankind. In the thirteenth century the philosopher Judah Halevi declared: "As the heart among the organs of the body, so is Israel among the nations." When Arab terrorism began to prey upon Jewish civilians in Israel or elsewhere, the world remained indifferent. Now the practice of terrorism has become worldwide, from Ireland to Guatemala, from London to Capetown, and the free world cowers in fear and trembling, feeling itself helpless before the enemy. There is something prophetic in the rabbinic dictum: "Any trouble that attacks Israel alone is no problem; the trouble that attacks both Israel and the nations is truly a problem" (Midrash Devarim Rabbah 2:22).

Guerilla terrorism is at present an obvious evil. But we are being assured that nuclear terror is a blessing, preserving peace among the superpowers by the "deterrence of terror"! The prospect of mass extermination by nuclear means, it is argued, is of itself the surest guarantee that nuclear bombs will never be used again. It is conveniently forgotten how often in modern history some new instrument of destruction, whether high explosive, bombing plane, or poison gas, has been hailed as inaugurating an era of world peace because no nation would dare to use so lethal a weapon.

Fundamentally, the moral regeneration of mankind is called for. The worldwide apathy, despair, and savagery that are abroad in the land are the end result of man's loss of confidence in his capacity to face and overcome his problems. The erosion of his sense of responsibility has destroyed his traditional basis of morality. To rebuild his moral defenses will be a long and difficult process, but nothing less can save humanity from self-annihilation.

There is a desperate need for articulating a system of values based on a consensus in society on the parameters of human action and relationships. We need to utilize all the findings of science to bring us as accurate a description of the external world and of human nature as is available. Only on that basis is there hope that the promise and the vision held out by the world's great religious and ethical teachers will find fulfillment. Can a firm basis for morals in the new and unfamiliar age of technology be found in religion? What contribution can science make to this enterprise? How are these two major pursuits related to each other? Upon what foundation can an all-inclusive system of ethics be established that will command the allegiance of modern men and women? All these issues need to be explored, for what we are seeking is not a temporary shelter but a permanent home for the body and the soul of mankind.

Part II

A Basis for Morals: Where Can It Be Found?

Chapter 3

Religion and Science: Their Mutual Relationship

AS WE SET OUT on the quest for a basis for morality in the twentieth century and beyond, two prerequisites are indispensable, its acceptability, and its adequacy. First, it must command a sufficient consensus among men and women to win general adherence by the various elements in modern society. Second, it must be sufficiently comprehensive to offer guidance and direction in all the major areas of human activity and concern.

In setting out on this quest, we are not compelled to begin from scratch. There are two major enterprises of the human spirit that would seem to be available as sources of morality. One, religion, goes back to the earliest emergence of man on this planet. The other enterprise, science, though its roots go back to antiquity, is essentially a modern phenomenon; its major achievements and its technological fruits are of comparatively recent vintage. Advocates of religion often claim, in view of its presence in every society we know, that man is a religious animal. Science cannot make a similar claim for itself, but it does command all-but-universal respect bordering on adulation, because of its vast contributions to human life. What is more, it has one other crucial advantage. While religion has been marked throughout its history by incredible diversity and mutual hostility, science possesses a broad consensual basis, its major attitudes and discoveries being recognized and accepted among all nations and social systems. Science is the universal language of mankind.

However, before turning to a consideration of the possible contribution either or both can make to a viable ethical system, we must reckon with the problems posed by their respective roles and by the relationship they bear to each other. The fact cannot be ignored that hostility and conflict have prevailed between them for centuries. Are religion and science inherently competitive and mutually exclusive, or does each have a distinctive role to play without which human life would be the poorer? If so, what are the elements of a relationship between them?

Nearly a century ago, in 1896, Andrew D. White published his *History of the Warfare of Science with Theology in Christendom.* Today, the book would need to be updated with several new chapters. In 1925 Tennessee enacted a law that forbade the teaching of evolution in the public schools on the explicit ground that it contradicted the creation narrative in the first chapter of Genesis. It led to the worldwide sensation of the Scopes trial. In that famous encounter, William Jennings Bryan's defense of the biblical creation account against the theory of evolution was not so much refuted by Clarence Darrow as laughed out of court.

A half century later, another chapter in the struggle is being written and we are learning anew the uses of language to obfuscate one's meaning. Being more sophisticated than their predecessors, the present-day opponents of science are not attempting to outlaw the teaching of evolution in the schools as contradicting Genesis. The statutes adopted in Arkansas and Louisiana, like those pending in other states, are not trying to introduce religion into the public schools. They ask only that "creationism" be presented as an alternative scientific "theory" to that of evolution, a "balanced treatment" of two scientific explanations competing with one another on their own merits. That creationism coincides with the narrative in the first chapter of Genesis is purely coincidental.

The Arkansas law was declared unconstitutional by Federal Judge William Overton, who declared that the law violated the First Amendment to the Constitution by breaching the principle of the separation between church and state. But that does not mean that the campaign has been abandoned, it has merely been postponed. For the latter-day fundamentalists are determined as well as sophisticated. The next step is already in view. In Texas, Mel and Norma Gabler have waged a vigorous campaign at the statewide textbook-adoption hearings which determine all textbook purchases for the state. Their goal is to have the term "evolution" and the name "Darwin" deleted from all approved texts. Some publishers are surrendering to this economic pressure by setting up a system of self-censorship in advance.

More important than the immediate outcome are the consequences for the long term. The simplistic approach of TV and radio, abetted by the expertise and the financial resources available to the advocates of creationism, makes the issue appear to be a choice between religion and science, in which everyone must take his place either on one side of the barricades or the other. This would be a disaster either way. The latest skirmish should lead to a careful analysis of the true relationship of science and religion.

At the outset, a basic difference in the relative status of religion and science should be noted. Ours is a scientific age, in which science is dominant, affecting every other aspect of life. Though its origins are to be sought in antiquity, science—with its offspring, technology—as an effective, organized, and creative enterprise is the hallmark of the modern age. Religion, on the contrary, belongs to man's ancient past. All the great seminal spirits in religion, Moses, Zoroaster, Buddha, Confucius, Jesus, and Mohammed, are separated from our day by millennia.

When, at the end of the Middle Ages, religion began to lose its dominant position, science emerged in the human arena as a young David, vigorous and self-confident, confronting an aged Goliath, weighed down by the encrusted armor of centuries. For many years, both sides conceived of the relationship between religion and science as one of antagonism.

Defenders of the faith maintained that science was man's endeavor to discover the truth through the imperfect instruments of reason and observation and hence was tentative and partial. On the other hand, they held that religion represented God's perfect revelation of His truth to His children and was therefore infinitely to be preferred. Consequently, when the accepted teachings of religion were challenged by science, science deserved to be suppressed. The history of the warfare of science with theology, to use the title of Andrew D. White's work, is the story of fruitless attempts to crush the burgeoning efforts of science to break the fetters of outworn notions of reality. Galileo, Giordano Bruno, Copernicus, Mendel, Darwin, Freud, and hundreds of lesser figures each had to encounter the hostility and even the persecutions of the religious Establishment and its allies.

As science continued its triumphant march, and technology showered its material blessings upon the world, the roles of victor and vanquished were reversed. To be sure, lip service continues to be paid to religion, especially by politicians and the recipients of honorary degrees. But it is widely believed, though rarely stated, that in the contest between the farrago of superstition and ignorance which is religion, on the one hand, and the proud product of man's intellect and knowledge which is science, on the other, only one outcome is possible—science must conquer and religion withdraw ignominiously from the field of battle.

Today the strategy of confrontation has largely fallen out of favor. The fracas in the South notwithstanding, the smoke of battle has largely cleared away. Except for extremist groups at both ends, the recognition has been growing that religion and science are both indispensable enterprises in the good society and therefore that a reconciliation between science and religion is essential as well as desirable.

How, however, is this peace, or at least an armistice, to be achieved? Here a variety of strategies have been proposed.

One view once widely held, advocated by Herbert Spencer and others, tries to separate the two antagonists and assigns to each a different sphere of influence. At any given time, man's universe consists of two areas: the Unknown, which is the domain of religion, and the Known, which is the field of science. It follows that as science continues its research, the realm of the Known grows at the expense of the Unknown, and the empire of science annexes more and more territory from the kingdom of religion. It is as though two men were sharing a pie between them; the more one takes, the less remains for the other. The implication left unstated is clear. The ultimate end is the peaceful expiration of religion and the total triumph of science.

Increasingly, it is becoming clear that this conception of the relationship of religion and science is too simplistic to be true. The theory is based not merely upon a failure to understand religion, but also upon a misconception of the nature of science. Twentieth-century scientific research has revealed the paradox that the increase of knowledge means the increase of ignorance, for each discovery reveals new and unsuspected vistas on the horizon. As the frontiers of man's knowledge in the fields of astronomy, physics, and psychology have broadened, he has attained to a far better knowledge of reality, to be sure, but with it has come a correspondingly greater understanding of how much more he does not know.

At the beginning of this century, the atom, as the etymology of its name, "uncut," indicates, was regarded as the ultimate and indivisible element of matter, beyond which there was nothing to investigate. Today we know that the atom represents a microcosm—an entire universe of dazzling and baffling complexity. Obviously, we know infinitely more about the constitution of the atom than did our grandfathers, but we are far more aware than they of how much more is unknown.

At the turn of the century, human psychology had no conception of the subconscious and its ramifications, as revealed by the research of Freud, Adler, Jung, their disciples and their successors. Today we know much more about the psychological constitution of human beings, but our knowledge has, at the same time, revealed unplumbed depths in the human soul.

The relatively simple solar system of Laplace, with the sun at the center and the planets circling about it, has today been superseded by an astronomical conception of multiple galaxies, each of limitless dimensions.

Our growing knowledge in every field is accompanied by an ever deeper sense of ignorance in what an astronomer has rightly called "the mysterious universe." Every branch of science illustrates this truth, which has rendered naive—and obsolete—the nineteenth-century hope that as man's knowledge grew his ignorance would correspondingly diminish. Ignorance is no temporary state that man will transcend in time. It remains, and must remain, a permanent feature of the human condition.

Another attempt to separate religion and science posits that science deals with the facts, with the world as it is, while religion is concerned with values, with life as it should be. This distinction is by no means totally mistaken, but it cannot successfully separate the "antagonists." On the one hand, science rests upon a system of values. To cite only two, the dedication to the search for truth and the insistence on freedom of thought and expression. On the other hand, religion cannot maintain values that fly in the face of reality, and contradict the facts of the physical world or the realities of human nature. As experience has shown time and again, the attempt to create values that ignore facts is a prescription for disaster. If there is no free flow from facts to values and from values to facts, both science and religion are stultified.

Another and far older method of dealing with the problems has come back into favor in our day, when mysticism has undergone a rebirth. Science and philosophy, it is maintained, utilize the intellect as their instrument of discovery, depending on observation and rational deduction to arrive at their conclusions. Religion lies entirely beyond the domain of the intellect, depending only upon an inner light that reveals the true nature of reality to the religious believer by a process that can neither be explained nor communicated. Hence, the truths of religion can be caught, not taught; they certainly cannot be proved. Reason is useful enough in the mundane concerns of life, but not on the great fundamental issues of life and death, suffering and salvation, with which religion is concerned.

Thus the church father Tertullian justified his belief in the dogmas of Christianity by the affirmation, *Credo quia impossibile*—"I believe because it is impossible." He thus lifted the tenets of his faith beyond the reach of reason, so that it is impervious to analysis and rational criticism. As for the chosen few who experience the mystical encounter with God, the event is not merely beyond reason, it is generally ineffable, beyond the power of speech, so that only metaphors can transmit something of the believer's experience.

Another approach also derives from medieval thought. In the Middle Ages, when religious dogma posed difficulties for the intellectuals, some thinkers evolved the theory of the "two truths" in religion, one level for the masses and another for the elite. Since the language of the Bible is susceptible to different interpretations, the simpleminded believer and the educated philosopher could read the same biblical text, practice the same rituals, and recite the same prayers, but read a different meaning into the identical words. Indeed, as Leo Strauss pointed out, the ambiguities of language were often consciously used by medieval writers to convey different meanings to different groups of readers. This served to avoid persecution at the hands of the established authorities of church or state, or to keep esoteric doctrines limited to special groups.

Today the doctrine of the two truths operates differently—it lodges in the same person, who is able to develop the faculty of a compartmentalized mind. Through this attribute the individual preserves the simple faith of the "old-time religion" by sealing it off hermetically from any contact with the conclusions or implications of the natural and social sciences with which he may well be familiar. By refusing to subject their religious beliefs and practices to rational examination, many gifted and able practitioners of various scientific disciplines are thus able to remain within the ranks of religious fundamentalism, Christian or Jewish. The president of an Orthodox-sponsored university once explained that while the students are taught both religion and science, it is not intended that their religion influence their science or that their science affect their religion—only that the same person know both religion and science.

No doubt this arrangement works for some, but for most modern people this intellectual schizophrenia is fraught with acute psychic discomfort. A spirit divided against itself cannot survive.

Even for those who cultivate the compartmentalized mind, there is a heavy price to pay. In circles which have adopted this method of "safeguarding" religion, fanaticism and hostility toward all those outside the charmed circle are rampant, traits which are essentially manifestations of inner turmoil, of helpless frustration and gnawing doubts that cannot be totally and successfully suppressed.

The tensions between religion and science must be resolved, but in a more fruitful and satisfying manner. Religion has been defined as philosophy suffused by emotion, but it is not on that account hostile to reason. Because religion is concerned with matters beyond our normal range of observation and experience, its view of the total universe must go beyond reason, but it cannot go against reason. Vital religion is supra-rational, not anti-rational. That reason is a partial and an imperfect guide to life and the world is self-evident. For a fleeting hour we walk through a mysterious and beautiful universe, carrying the lamp of reason that casts weak shafts of light into the surrounding darkness. But our journey would be more perilous still if we extinguished the lamp and groped our way in total night.

What is more, since the world is a *uni-verse* and not a *pluri-verse*, the known is organically related to the unknown, and sheds light upon it. Man's discoveries through observation and reason, partial and imperfect though they be, offer significant clues to those aspects of existence that lie beyond the powers of observation and reason to fathom. In their parables and injunctions the great teachers utilized the mundane, everyday experiences of the "here-and-now" to convey their insights into the "then-and-there." To borrow and drastically modify a well-known pronouncement: "Faith is the substance of things hoped for, resting on evidence of things seen."

Clearly no iron curtain, or even a silken screen, can be interposed between religion and science, if either is to be true to its role in human life. Neither a war to the death nor a sterile armistice with a no-man's-land between science and religion can suffice. Instead, the realization has been growing that both are basic human enterprises, and that, necessarily, there must be a peaceful working relationship between them.

Based upon this approach, several varied solutions have been proposed. Some advocates of traditional religion argue that religion and science teach the same truths about the world. Thus, it is often maintained that the first chapter of Genesis, when properly understood, actually contains the fundamentals of evolution. The six "days" of creation refer to long eras of time; as the psalmist says, "A thousand years in Thy sight are but as yesterday when it is past." The order of creation in Genesis resembles the sequence postulated by evolution: fish, birds, reptiles, land animals, and, finally, man. Thus, these proponents of traditional religion declare, there is no contradiction between the Bible and science.

This harmonization of religion and science simply won't work. That Genesis takes "day" to mean a twenty-four-hour period is clear from the reference to "evening" and "morning" each day of the creation week and to the establishment of the Sabbath on the seventh day. Besides, one might ask, why did no one "discover" the theory of evolution in the opening chapter of Genesis before Darwin enunciated his views? It is clear that for nearly thirty centuries, the alleged teaching of evolution in Genesis was hardly effective! Moreover, the most important aspect of evolution—the recognition that each species evolved from its predecessor on the evolutionary ladder—is, of course, nowhere stated or even implied in the biblical narrative; Genesis clearly refers to the special creation of each category of living creatures.

There is a more fundamental question: If religion and science teach the same body of truth, what need is there today for both disciplines? Saadia, the medieval Jewish philosopher, who presented a similar defense of the role of religion as against philosophy, argued that most persons were slow to learn and imperfect in their understanding, and therefore that religious tradition gave them, in brief and easily comprehensible form, those truths which it would have taken them a lifetime to achieve through the processes of reason. But even if this contention were accepted, one could argue that today, when scientific truths are widely taught, there is no longer any need for religion. Like an aged retainer in a family, religion can be thanked for past services rendered and escorted to the door.

If the relationship of science and religion cannot be one of antagonism, neither can it be that of identity. If they both have value, it must be because they complement, not reduplicate, each other.

At the very outset, we may note the similarity in the approach of both science and religion to reality. As Morris Raphael Cohen pointed out, it is a vulgar error to assume that the scientist begins with the indiscriminate observation of phenomena. Actually, he begins with an idea, a "hunch," or, to use a more respectable term, a hypothesis, which serves as his handle for grasping the segment of the world which he is investigating. Without a working theory, he would be overwhelmed by the mass and the complexity of the data before him. As Darwin stated, "All observation must be for or against some view, if it is to be of any service." What distinguishes the true scientist from the counterfeit is the former's willingness to modify and, if need be, to scrap his theory in favor of another view, if the objective facts decisively demand it. Yet the history of science is replete with examples of the obstacles which new ideas have encountered in making headway against accepted notions. Religious beliefs are held, as a rule, with greater tenacity, and changes are even more painful. But, essentially, the steps in the process are similar: an original belief, its confrontation with reality, and the consequent modification of the idea.

In an even more fundamental sense as well, religion and science resemble each other. Both rest upon a substratum of faith in a world which is intelligible because it reflects the operations of an intelligence (whether with a capital I or a small letter is immaterial here). Underlying all scientific activity is the spirit which Einstein described in these words: "What a deep faith in the rationality of the world and what a longing to understand even a small glimpse of it, which makes it worthwhile for a man to spend years of lonely work upon scientific research!"

Faith in the rationality of the world *precedes* scientific research and in turn is supported by it. When for example, a biologist begins to study an organism, his first question is, What is the function of this particular organ? He takes it for granted that the existence of an organ postulates an activity. In fact, when he finds an organ which seems to be useless, such as the appendix, he assumes that it must have possessed a function in the past, and that today it is a vestigial remains. The chemist Mendeleieff, in his Table of Atomic Numbers, positioned all the various chemical elements known in his time, and did not hesitate to postulate that the empty places in his table would ultimately be filled in. His prophecy was fulfilled. But as significant as his foretelling of the few missing elements was the underlying faith that the blocks out of which the universe is built fall into a pattern. That his assumption proved to be true is important for our understanding of the nature of the world; that it was made at all reveals the nature of the scientific process.

Belief in the rationality of the world has as its corollary the faith in the uniformity of nature, the universality of its laws. Thus when a chemist publishes the results of his experiments in his laboratory, he is expressing his conviction that what he has discovered in one corner of the earth applies everywhere else, and that what is true today held true yesterday and will be valid tomorrow, and hence is subject to verification.

Even more fundamental than the faith in the rationality and the uniformity of nature is the assumption that what man sees really exists, that the world about him is not simply an illusion, a fantasy of the imagination. No one can prove that in his waking state man is not asleep, and that what he sees about him is not a dream. Yet all human activity, scientific and practical, is predicated on the belief that, allowing for the distortions and imperfections of man's observation and reason, the real world exists. Solipsism, the view that nothing really exists in the world but I, is universally rejected as a fallacy, not because of any logical demonstration, but because all life and activity would be impossible on that assumption.

Thus science in general rests upon articles of faith of the most far-reaching character. In addition, each science has its own body of special assumptions or articles of faith. It is therefore literally true that *no significant proposition can ever be proved* unless it rests upon a foundation of beliefs which are not susceptible of proof. A striking example is afforded by Euclidean geometry, where every proposition is proved

Q.E.D. Yet, as any elementary student of the subject knows, before the first theorem can be demonstrated, a whole series of axioms and postulates must be assumed, none of which can be "proved." Obviously, they are accepted as reasonable, because they seem plausible, but they cannot be demonstrated, as is clear from non-Euclidean geometry that does not accept them. Yet unless these unproved axioms and postulates are taken for granted, the entire superstructure of Euclidean geometry is impossible.

Obviously, religion, too, rests upon a series of beliefs which are not subject to logical demonstration, but which its devotees believe to be reasonable and true. The process of conviction is thus not very dissimilar in both enterprises. Undoubtedly, the beliefs of religion are not the same as the assumptions made by science. The body of "undemonstrable" beliefs may be more extensive in religion than in science. In part, the reason lies in the fact that religion is concerned with the entire universe, rather than with the segment which man has succeeded in exploring. Since in the very nature of things, all the "evidence" on the meaning of life is not in—and never will be—different human beings will arrive at different conceptions of life. Finally, because the beliefs of religion are concerned with the perennial issues of life and death, they will be held with passion and surrendered only after considerable anguish and struggle. Yet in all these respects, the contrast between religion and science, while very real, is a difference of degree rather than of kind.

It is true that religion attributes the truths which it cherishes to Divine communication, a process of revelation, the product of an encounter between God and the prophet, who is then bidden to teach: "Thus saith the Lord." Yet even this ineffable experience is not altogether dissimilar to what science calls intuition. Jung argued that "no scientific discovery has ever been achieved except by intuition." Einstein wrote: "At times I feel certain that I am right without knowing the reason. When the eclipse of 1919 confirmed my intuition, I was not in the least surprised." Intuition represents that mysterious inner burst of light which comes to the most gifted and favored of human spirits.

Thus both religion and science begin with assumptions, with acts of faith. Armed with its respective body of belief, each enterprise goes forth to observe the world about us. Various reasonable conclusions will emerge, constituting the content of science on the one hand, and the teaching of religion on the other. It is, therefore, clear that Tertullian's aphorism cited above, *Credo quia impossibile*, "I believe because it is impossible," is far better replaced by the affirmation of Anselm, *Credo ut intelligam*, "I believe in order that I may understand." Faith must nurture understanding, as surely as understanding ultimately flowers into faith.

The similarities in approach between religion and science must not obscure the far-reaching and significant differences between them. First and foremost is the fact that each branch of science is concerned with some single aspect of reality. For the purpose of understanding the complex world in which we live, scientific research divides it into specific segments, such as astronomy, geology, physics, chemistry, biology, and psychology. Each segment, having thus been demarcated for the purpose of analysis, is then subjected to rigorous scrutiny and study. It is this capacity to subdivide which makes it possible for science to master its subject matter. Religion, on the other hand, is concerned with a view of reality as a whole.

From this difference, far-reaching consequences flow. When science is confronted with an insoluble problem, even in its own area, it can afford to confess its ignorance and wait for future discoveries. On the other hand, religion, when faced by the mystery of evil, must have a word for the anguished soul walking in darkness, and it must speak out *now*. For living and suffering men and women it must offer a world-view that encompasses the whole of life, the unknown as well as the known, the chaos as well as the cosmos. Religion must have a response to the elements of chaos, of evil and meaninglessness in the world, as well as to the aspects that reveal meaning and order. It must help man to face suffering and death as well as teach him to savor the beauty and gaiety of life. What is more, men must be shown how to enjoy life's pleasures without having them turn to gall and wormwood through surfeit or misuse. An ancient rabbi declared, "This world from which we depart is a wedding feast" (B. Erubin 54a). Religion must educate human beings not to be grasping or complaining, but rather to be grateful and gracious at God's table. In short, a valid religious worldview cannot ignore the vast segment of reality that science has comprehended and interpreted, but neither can it overlook the limitless elements of the universe which science has not yet mastered.

Nor is this a temporary condition. There are many aspects of life in the world that are forever beyond the power of scientific method. There are more things in heaven and earth than can be weighed and measured; the things that count often cannot be counted.

We are becoming increasingly aware of the reality of that which is beyond the material. As the atom of matter dissolves into the electron of energy, so we are discovering that all the components of human nature, such intangibles as human aspiration, fear, and frustration are realities, concrete forces in their impact on the world of nature and man. What is more, we are aware of the fallacies of "reductionism." The psychologists may analyze and classify the elements of human nature, but the whole is greater that the sum of its parts. Man is more than sixty-seven cents worth of carbon, oxygen, hydrogen, and nitrogen. Bettelheim has recently reminded us that for Freud *die Seele*, "the soul," is a reality of the human personality, encompassing far more than "the mind" and "mental processes."

Nevertheless, the scientific enterprise of observation, analysis, and classification must come first, if the injunctions of religion are not to do violence to human capacities and aspirations. Unfortunately, it has happened all too often, especially in past eras when the prior activity of science was forbidden or ignored, that established religion has demanded of men adherence to norms that were impossible, unworthy, or both.

An even more fundamental difference between religion and science has a direct bearing on the agonizing searching of soul that many contemporary scientists have undergone since the atomic bomb descended on Hiroshima and Nagasaki. Working on nuclear bombs, space missiles, and biological warfare has proved a traumatic experience for many ethically sensitive men and women in the scientific community. Strictly speaking, however, this is a problem not for science, but for the scientist, because he is also a human being and a member of society, and therefore concerned with its well-being.

Science *per se* is concerned with the discovery of facts, not with passing judgments on what is right or wrong, beautiful or ugly, good or evil. The objectivity of science is basic to its function; every aspect or reality is of equal and neutral value for scientific research. Whatever the field of research, it is legitimate so long as it seeks the truth as honestly as possible. What society does with the discovery, whether it uses it for life or for death, is no longer a scientific question, but an issue in ethics, in which religion plays—or should play—a central role. For religion is fundamentally concerned with value judgments, with a scale of ideals and commandments which it sets before people. Science, in other words, deals with the means and not with the ends of life, except in the negative sense—and it is important—of ruling out certain proposed goals as running counter to the facts of man's nature and of the world. But when there are several possible alternatives, none of which contradicts the facts, science *per se* is neutral.

To recognize that facts are the area of science and that values are the province of religion does not mean to isolate the protagonists from each other, but, on the contrary, to make it clear that tension between religion and science is both inevitable and necessary. Vital religion, being concerned with reality, must always build upon the facts as disclosed by scientific research. When science changes its understanding of the universe, religion must necessarily adjust its vision of the world, as well as the conclusions which it has drawn from it.

Does this mean that religion is perpetually at the mercy of science? The answer is both yes and no. Most scientific progress consists of minute changes in our body of knowledge that do not affect our overall view of the universe. But any basic, far-reaching change in the field of science must ultimately affect the worldview upon which religion is based.

When the Ptolemaic view of the earth as the center of the universe, with the sun rising in the east and setting in the west, gave way to the Copernican conception of the earth as one of several planets revolving around the sun, the change had tremendous repercussions upon religion's conception both of God and of the role of man in His plan. No wonder the medieval church fought so bitterly against the ideas of Galileo and Copernicus.

The evolutionary hypothesis of the origin of species by Darwin, Wallace, and their coworkers had to transform radically the conception of God's role in creation, man's place in the world, and his relation to inanimate and animate nature. The implications of evolution thus went far beyond the contradictions that it offered to the details of creation in the opening chapter of Genesis.

Modern psychology, particularly in the psychoanalytical schools, is still too fluid for any degree of assurance or any real consensus as to its abiding results. Yet it has already drastically affected our conception of the nature of man, his impulses, his capacities, his vices, and his virtues, as well as the role of rational and irrational factors in human character.

In sum, a rethinking of religious fundamentals becomes an inescapable duty, however painful at the outset, when any major scientific discovery transforms our conception of reality.

There will be cases, of course, where science itself will be noncommittal with regard to competing theories, or the conclusions which may be drawn from them that go beyond the objective evidence. Professor R. A. Millikan, the famous physicist, maintained that the more he read and studied, the more he was sure about the existence of God. His colleague, Dr. Linus C. Pauling, confessed, "My experience has been different, in a sense almost opposite that of Professor Millikan." The knowledge of the physical universe by both men is of the highest order; they diverge in their interpretation of the phenomena.

Millikan and Pauling, Einstein and Watson in their role as scientists have to be ready to submit their scientific views to critical examination by their colleagues on the basis of objective phenomena. But what meaning—or lack of meaning—each reads into the facts with which he deals is subjective and cannot be verified or disproved in the laboratory. The theory of evolution, as preached by some of its early protagonists, was hailed by Ernst Haeckel and others as "disproving" God. Freud's view of religion as an illusion and his conception of God as a transformation of the father-image—ideas such as these represented incursions by a great scientist into areas beyond the legitimate sphere of science. Every scientist has a perfect right to have his own religion, theistic, agnostic, or atheistic as it may be. But when he speaks on the issues of life, he should be aware of the fact that it is as a man and not as a scientist that he speaks.

Thus, it has been argued that the biologic and geologic evidence of evolution simply indicates that one species was derived from another, but does not disclose any direction in the process. Does the scroll of evolutionary development give any evidence of design? There have been scientists on both sides of the question. Finding design in the evidence is an interpretation of the data of science which will impress the observer as more or less plausible, depending on nonscientific factors in his personality.

In such instances, religion is free to choose that particular approach which is most congenial to its own thinking and for which it believes the evidence is strongest. Religious faith has a right and a duty to read the book of life through its own lenses, particularly whenever, as is often the case, science itself offers only partial and tentative clues to reality.

A parable all too congenial to our war-ridden age may serve to illustrate the true relationship of religion and science. Let us imagine an army commander confronting a powerful enemy in a far-flung campaign. In preparing for battle, General Headquarters sends out scouts to bring back reports concerning the disposition of the enemy forces, the nature of the terrain, the quantity and the quality of his supplies, and, if possible, the battle plans of the foe. When the intelligence reports are brought back, the commander-in-chief must coordinate all the material, evaluate it, and then plan his strategy. His task is admittedly hazardous and uncertain, because the reports which he receives will at best be fragmentary; few, if any, will be free from some degree of error, and on many of the most important questions he may have no information at all.

There are two courses of action that the commander cannot adopt. Although the information available to him is fragmentary and at least partly mistaken, it would be folly for him to dismiss all the data before deciding on his plan of attack. Nor can he postpone action and wait for the day when all the necessary information will be at hand, if only because that day will never come. He must decide now upon his plan of action for the immediate future. Having no choice, he coordinates the evidence before him, attempts to discount manifest errors, estimates the probabilities with regard to the information which he lacks, and on that basis plans the campaign against the enemy. Obviously, his own temperament and insight will profoundly affect his judgment on the objective facts before him, and will often spell the difference between victory and defeat.

Mankind may be compared to the commander-in-chief, in its long struggle to comprehend and master a world which it did not create. Each scientific discipline may be represented by a scout going out into the unknown and bringing back a report on one or another aspect of reality. These presentations are of the highest value, yet they are inevitably compounded of truths, half-truths, downright errors, and large areas of no information at all. From all these reports, each human being must construct a credible view of the universe, which is the philosophy or religion by which he lives. Armed with his plan of campaign, man must go forth in the battle of life, a struggle he cannot postpone for the future, because he will not be living forever!

Like the commander-in-chief in the paradigm, religion must take into account the findings of science as they are available, and which it disregards at its peril. Yet it must go beyond science in constructing a worldview that will be satisfying and life-giving. The believer stakes his life on his vision of God and the good in the world.

The reason for the tensions that have existed in past centuries between religion and science is now clear. At any given moment in human experience, the prevailing conception of the universe as taught by religion will be based upon the scientific conclusions achieved earlier. If, in the interim, science has pressed forward to new frontiers of discovery, it will necessarily come into collision with the accepted religious teaching of the time. Superficially, it will seem that science is attacking religion, but actually it is the presuppositions which religion accepted from earlier periods that science is seeking to replace. An enlightened religious approach will therefore find it both a challenge and an opportunity to reconsider its fundamentals and to bring them into harmony with what is true and life-giving in the new advance of science. Religion and science are both partners in man's unending quest for understanding as the key to the good life.

In conclusion, religion, if it is vital, will always be dependent in substantial measure upon science, just as science in turn derives its basic faith and insights from the same fundamental presuppositions that underlie religion. Science and religion, properly comprehended, are neither antagonists nor identical activities, but complementary enterprises. The human spirit needs both, in order to see life whole and find it good.

Chapter 4

Can Religion or Science Serve?

THERE IS, of course, one familiar and easily accessible body of ethical doctrine available to modern man. It may be found in the area of religion—the corpus of ideas and feelings, attitudes and actions inculcated by what is rather imprecisely subsumed under the rubric of the Judeo-Christian tradition. This tradition has dominated Western civilization for nearly two millennia, maintaining that its Scriptures are the word of God, so that its ethical code is divinely revealed and hence is obligatory upon man.

Here honesty demands that my own standpoint be made clear. I believe in the possibility and the reality of God's communication with mankind. What is more, I am convinced that belief in the doctrine of revelation, properly understood, is intellectually more credible than its denial. A believing Christian would find revelation in the belief of Jesus and accord a position of primacy to the Sermon on the Mount. A faithful Muslim would point to the Suras of the Qoran instead and see Mohammed as the "messenger of Allah." For all their differences, both would be united in the belief that God reveals His will to His creatures.

For the Jew, an event of transcendental importance took place on Mount Sinai, a prime act of communication between God and man, the Decalogue being the product of that meeting.

The nature of the encounter between God and man is beyond human power to explain, and so the Revelation on Sinai has been interpreted literally, philosophically, and mystically. However it be conceived of, or even if we avoid any attempt at interpretation, Sinai transformed a group of cowardly and quarrelsome slaves into an eternal people whose role it is to serve as a kingdom of priests and a holy nation, a people that has continued to bulk large in the consciousness of the human race for two thousand years and more.

The Revelation on Sinai was not the only meeting of God and man, only the most central event in a process which began long before, with the patriarchs, and continued long afterwards, with the prophets and sages of Israel. Nor is there any ground for denying the possibility that however changed in form and expression, the Divine-human encounter is operative even in the present. To be sure, it is a difficult and perilous task to decide who is a true prophet and who is a false one, but, as the ancient texts clearly demonstrate, it was no easier to decide this question of life and death even in biblical times.

It is important to point out that revelation is a two-way communication, with both God and man playing active roles, an insight religious fundamentalism has yet to learn. Man is not a passive receptacle but an active participant in the process of conversation with the Divine. In other words, the human component enters into every deposit of revelation, be it the laws of the Torah, the admonitions of the prophets, or the teachings of the sages. Revelation is thus the clearest instance of the Divine-human symbiosis, or, in Buber's language, the I-Thou encounter.

Jewish tradition clearly avers that this partnership of God and man is also present in the two other cosmic events: man is God's co-partner in the act of Creation at the beginning of time, and man's actions play a decisive role in the act of Redemption by the Messiah at the End-Time.

Obviously this belief in revelation is an act of faith, not susceptible of logical demonstration or mathematical proof, like a geometric theorem, or scientific verification in the laboratory. This act of faith in God's revelation to Israel I find highly persuasive on the basis of some considerations that may be cited briefly. The first is the Jewish people itself. During a discussion with Voltaire, Frederick the Great of Prussia challenged the French philosopher to cite one authentic miracle. Voltaire's answer was, "Sire, the Jews." It is not merely that the ancient Hebrews were a small, weak, divided people, clinging precariously to the eastern shores of the Mediterranean, surrounded by powerful foes. It is not the longevity of the Jews, which makes their religion the oldest living faith on the planet that is significant, but their vitality, reflected in the fecundity of talent and genius that has continued to shape civilization to the present day.

Unlike the ancient Greeks, together with whom they laid the foundations of Western civilization, the Hebrews were not particularly distinguished for art, science, or philosophy. Yet in the first chapter of Genesis, the Torah first projected the view of the world as a universe, a cosmos governed by one Divine will, thus laying the foundation for the doctrine of the uniformity of nature, which is basic to the entire scientific enterprise.

As Martin Buber pointed out, the ancient Greeks had no conception of "the whole earth" and "the end of days," both of which are basic elements of biblical thought. For the Greeks, even for Plato, the noblest and wisest among them, the world is forever divided into Greeks and barbarians, so that the ideal Republic of the future needs to be guarded by a permanent warrior class. The events of human history are a series of discrete incidents, generally part of a cyclical process of repetition, lacking any direction, and, by that token, any goal or purpose.

On the other hand, the biblical account of the creation of Adam served as the seedbed for the conviction that all humanity is one and all men are brothers. The theme is repeated in the life of Noah, whose three sons, after the Flood, are the ancestors of all nations.

It was the biblical legislators, historians, and prophets who saw the entire human race as a unity, and history as an unfolding process acted out by man and directed by God toward an age of justice and peace. The eighth-century prophet Isaiah looked at his world from the unlikely vantage point of a tiny, weak kingdom in western Asia, about to be gobbled up by the Assyrian Empire. Yet he saw the succession of events in history as part of a Divine purpose using forces of evil to destroy evil and usher in the good. The process would culminate in universal justice and peace among the nations, under the aegis of the moral law.

A few decades earlier, a wandering shepherd and farmhand named Amos, with no access to modes of communication even remotely resembling our own, surveyed the lives and actions of all the nations within his purview, not hesitating to condemn his own. Incidentally, he revealed an incredible grasp of world affairs. To Amos's impartial gaze, all of the nations were found wanting by the standard of justice and compassion, and he therefore announced their punishment in the name of the one just and powerful God.

The profundity of insight into the nature of the world and human society revealed in the words of the Torah and the prophets I find inexplicable in purely naturalistic terms. Considerations such as these offer support, though admittedly not proof, for a belief in Divine revelation.

Whatever attitude is adopted toward revelation, it is indisputable that the faith in the Divine origin of the moral law provided a powerful sanction for adherence to its precepts. This faith was all but universal for Christians and Jews until modern times. The basic attitudes of the Judeo-Christian tradition on sex, love, and the family, the virtues of truth and responsibility, justice, and mercy, fair play and the sense of honor, are still officially normative in Western society, but they are in rapid dissolution around us. Astronomers tell us that there are stars millions of light-years away which may have long since disintegrated, yet their rays still continue to travel toward the earth, until they finally become extinct. Modern man has continued to walk by the light of the faith of earlier generations, but for many of our contemporaries, the original star has been dissolved and the last faint rays of the light are reaching us, with total darkness ahead.

If modern men and women were prepared to accept a dogmatic basis for religion and a Divine sanction for an ethical code, our quest would be over. A revived belief in Divine retribution, a conviction that if not here then in the hereafter, *ith din v'ith dayyan*, "there is a judge and there is judgment," would serve to restore allegiance to the moral law. However, the likelihood of such a universal conversion is minimal.

Democracy may be defined as that system of society in which the lower classes are at liberty to imitate the vices of their betters. Be it vice or virtue, skepticism is no longer the exclusive possession of the elite and the affluent; it has permeated the ranks of the poor and the uneducated. Even when skepticism does not exist, the secular spirit has penetrated every area of society and every level of thought, so that the simple faith of our grandfathers is possible today for fewer and fewer of their descendants.

Moreover, even those who believe in God today are not necessarily prepared to accept the specific provisions of any given law code as Divinely revealed. Many religious believers would insist on the right and the duty to interpret past traditions and would invoke history to justify development and change in the field of ethics as everywhere else. The wholesale disregard by Catholics of church teachings on divorce, birth control, and even abortion is a striking case in point. Nor is this attitude limited to Catholicism. For vast numbers of modern men and women, if not for the majority, a dogmatic basis for ethics is no longer tenable. The commandments "Thou shalt" and "Thou shalt not" can no longer suffice as a basis for ethical conduct, because either apodictic statement at once evokes the skeptical question, "Why?"

What about the widespread revival of religion today? On every hand, religious triumphalism is visible; with millions of born-again Christians and thousands of *ba'alei teshuvah*, "returnees," in Judaism who have "found" religion. We shall have occasion to analyze this phenomenon in greater detail below. What is directly germane to our present theme, their moral concerns are almost entirely limited to sexual behavior. For most Americans, the term "immoral" connotes infractions of the traditional sex codes that are officially maintained in the West, and little more. An officeholder guilty of massive depredations on the public treasury is triumphantly reelected to office again and again, at times from a prison cell. But a sexual offense is unforgivable.

By and large, for the born-again Christian and the Jewish returnees, the goal of their religion is their personal salvation, a "navel religion" centered upon themselves, their concerns being success in this world and bliss in the next. Compassion for the weak and the underprivileged, the building of a just society, the safeguarding of tolerance and freedom, and the establishment of world peace—these ideals are dismissed as "secular" and outside the scope of "real religion."

In sum, the unbelief of many, if not most, modern men and women, as well as the absence of ethical sensitivity on the part of many of the believers, offers scant hope that established religion can play a significant role in achieving a viable basis for morals in our generation. An ethical code adequate to our needs is not likely to find sufficient sanction and support in traditional religion, if only because religion itself is in need of sanction and support. George Orwell pointed to the heart of the contemporary crisis and to the difficulty of overcoming it when he wrote: "The real problem of our time is to restore the sense of absolute right and wrong, when the belief it used to rest on—that is the belief in personal immortality—has been destroyed. This demands faith, which is a different thing from credulity." His formulation needs to be somewhat broadened—it is belief in Divine retribution, either in this world or the next, which served as the theological underpinning of the social order. Whether we applaud the fact or deplore it, established religion *per se* cannot supply a basic consensus for an ethical code for the twentieth-century man.

Is there another, more consensual basis available for an ethical system in the modern age? The obvious answer that immediately comes to mind is science, and this on several apparently compelling grounds. In the first instance, the extraordinary discoveries of science have revolutionized our understanding of the world in all its aspects and of the nature of man. Obviously the "ought" called for by ethics must depend on the "what is" disclosed by science. Second, the progress of technology has transformed the condition of man's existence more radically during the twentieth century than in the millennium preceding. Clearly the world that man has created—and now threatens to destroy—must affect the standards of his behavior. Finally, science appears to be free from one of the basic weaknesses of religion—the divisiveness and strife among the believers. Since the values of science are universally recognized and appropriated by every social, political, and economic system, capitalist and Communist, authoritarian or democratic, science would seem to offer the consensus upon which a universal system of ethics can be erected. Hence in many quarters the call has gone out to devise a "scientific ethic," above prejudice, superstition, and hatred.

Nevertheless, I venture to suggest that science cannot supply the content of a moral code or even a rationale for one. The reason is inherent in the very nature of the scientific enterprise. To be effective and trustworthy, science must be free from value judgments, whether ethical or aesthetic. The scientific investigator must divest himself of any predilections or prejudices he may have. If he fails to do so, his colleagues—often indistinguishable from his competitors and opponents—will quickly lay bare his Achilles' heel.

There is only one commandment in the Scripture of science, "Thou shalt not lie." Science must seek to tell the truth as it finds it without fear or favor. It has both the duty and the right to explore every aspect of reality—whether in the external universe or within man—and to attempt to establish the facts as they are. This is the only scientific imperative.

In a stimulating lecture entitled "The Ethical Basis of Science," delivered under the auspices of the Technion in Haifa, Israel, Professor H. Bentley Glass suggests three ethical values that are essential to science: freedom of expression, willingness to acknowledge the truth, including one's own error, and a sense of community, which is possible only if communication is open with all other scientific researchers. Now, these three principles may be *presupposed* by science; they cannot be created by it. Moreover, they may constitute *necessary conditions* for the ideal functioning of the scientific enterprise, but they are not *sufficient* to serve as a rationale for a free and just society. From the purview of science, it is unnecessary to include such ideals as human equality, personal freedom, social justice, and compassion for the weak, yet these qualities are basic for a worthwhile ethical system.

Moreover, in our own day, we have seen societies that have substantially suppressed even the values that have been proposed as constituting the ethical basis of science and yet they have succeeded in cultivating scientific research and making technological progress with at least a fair measure of success. Such totalitarian regimes as Nazi Germany and Communist Russia are cases in point. They lack the basic values postulated by Professor Glass. Nevertheless, they have proved redoubtable competitors with democratic states in various fields of research and development.

Praiseworthy as is the attempt to endow science with an ethical dimension, the fact remains that it cannot create ethical values, it can only utilize them. Once science has given us the truest description of reality of which it is capable, its authentic task is done. It is not within the power of science to determine what ought to be done with that information. The scientist who engages in atomic fission is participating in a legitimate scientific enterprise. Whether society will use it to build an atomic bomb or to fight cancer is not, strictly speaking, the domain of science at all.

An obvious distinction that has frequently been drawn declares that science, *qua* science, is concerned with the real world as it is, ethics with man and society as they should be. Science deals with facts, ethics with values. In a word, science is morally neutral and must remain so if it is to be true to its functions.

Now this limitation applies to science, not to scientists. Obviously, scientists, being human beings of intelligence and sensitivity, have their attitudes and their points of view on all of these issues of values and goals. We may go further. Possessing greater intellectual capacity than the generality of men, scientists have a correspondingly greater responsibility to have their views made known and made effective. But when they do so, they function as citizens, not as scientists. Decision-making in the realm of public policy is not the province of science. By that token science cannot serve as the progenitor of ethics.

How does technology relate to the issue? Technology, the application of science to practical goals, occupies a middle ground between science and ethics. If science is the pursuit of truth, and ethics the quest for the good, technology may be described as the search for the useful. Ideally, technology attempts to utilize the truths of science for the advancement of the good of society; but this holds true only in theory, not in practice. Since society is not a monolithic unity, complex questions arise as to whose good is being sought—that of the Aryan race or of the Russian proletariat or of the white European worker or of the mammoth American corporation or of the South African black or of the one sex that males, with characteristic modesty, used to call the weaker.

In rare instances, but these are of the greatest importance, the issue of whose benefit is being sought may involve the human species itself. Shall technology advance the interests of one superpower as against another by the threat of obliterating mankind through ever more awesome weapons? Or shall technology refuse to make itself the handmaiden of the armaments industry or the slave of one group—political, economic, or ethnic—by making its goal the preservation of the entire human race?

The decision as to which particular project in applied science or technological exploration should be undertaken is a moral decision; the major responsibility falls upon society and its foci of power. But the technologist, who has the option of participating or refusing to participate, is also morally involved. Hence, the agonized soul-searching of many workers on nuclear or conventional weapons is entirely comprehensible.

The relationship of technology *vis-à-vis* science and ethics may be put slightly differently. The *method* of technology is derived from science, but its *goal*, the benefit of society, however broadly or narrowly that term is defined, *is derived from an already existing ethical system* that it did not originate and to which technology gives its allegiance.

The autonomy of science as against ethics is basic, but the dichotomy between them is not absolute. In several significant respects, science makes highly important, indeed indispensable, contributions to the search for ethical value. To the extent that it describes the world in which man lives, it helps to define the limits within which we can make ethical demands upon man. It is to science, and science alone, free and untrammeled, that we must look for an accurate picture of the natural resources of the planet which man inhabits, its mineral riches and its supply of air, water, and space which man must husband carefully if he is not to perish. It thus supplies the raw materials for ecological ethics.

Equally important is the role of the life sciences, both biological and psychological, that help us to understand the nature of man, his capacities and his limitations. A viable ethical system must be governed, of necessity, by the limitations set by the natural universe, as well as by the attributes with which man is endowed. In indicating what cannot be expected of man or of his natural environment, the contribution of science is invaluable; when it is ignored the consequence is disaster.

Science makes a third, highly important contribution to ethics. By its very nature, science is a dynamic enterprise, constantly engaged in extending the borders of its knowledge and in modifying previously accepted positions. It therefore stimulates an openness to new ideas, a willingness to surrender outmoded notions, and a sense of humility before the unknown. These qualities are badly needed to jolt man out of the comfortable, fixed, and immovable positions to which he grows accustomed with time. The momentum of scientific progress is virtually the only remedy for the inertia of intellectual sloth.

Nor is this all. If, as science conclusively demonstrates, man's picture of the universe and his relationship to it is in constant flux, it follows that the system of values that man erects upon the substructure of reality must also partake of this dynamic quality. This is not to suggest that every new scientific discovery requires a complete transformation of man's worldview. Yet it is undeniable that major discoveries, such as those of Copernicus, Darwin, and Freud, imperiously demand, and ultimately bring about, far-reaching revolutions in man's worldview, his religious faith, and his ethical system, as we have seen.

In sum, science supplies the indispensable prerequisites for an ethical system. But the system of values both for the individual and for society cannot be found in science *per se*. Science can help tell us how to get where we want to go, but it cannot tell us where we ought to go.

It seems clear, therefore, that in this age of dissolving traditions, we cannot find a basis for an acceptable ethical system in any specific religious creed, if only because of the varieties of belief and unbelief rampant in the modern world. Because of its own essential nature, science can utilize but cannot generate an ethical system.

Chapter 5

Natural Law for the Modern World

IF NEITHER traditional religion nor modern science, for whatever reason, can supply a foundation for morality, are we doomed to wander forever without map or compass in a savage and unknown land? Are we compelled to adopt a relativistic theory of human behavior?

One extreme foundation was proposed by Ernest Hemingway: "What is right is what you feel good after; what is wrong is what you feel bad after." Even this sardonic definition may be given a measure of validity if we follow it up by asking, "How soon after? Five minutes after? Five days, five months, or five years after?"

Hemingway's remark is, of course, a wry reference to the idea of "conscience as a guide." But conscience cannot be the source of ethical principles. Undoubtedly, it has served for untold centuries as an influence for ethical conduct and, even more, as a stimulus to repentance for immoral behavior. But conscience *per se* is not a creative force in the shaping of ethical ideals. It is an inner-directed authority, enforcing the standards prevalent in the society from which they have been absorbed. Whether the norms are practiced or merely preached in a given group, and whether they are worthy or unworthy, the consciences of its members are not likely to rise above that level. A cannibal who has gorged himself on human flesh may feel acute discomfort afterwards, but it is more likely to be a pain in the stomach than a pang of conscience. This fact led H. L. Mencken to define conscience as "the inner voice that warns us somebody may be looking." A religious believer would find this definition entirely satisfactory if the noun were spelled with a capital S—Somebody!

Whether the ideals are practiced or only preached in a given society, when the voice of a prophet challenges the conduct of his contemporaries, he speaks in the name of standards to which they ostensibly subscribe.

A far more intellectually respectable approach to the problem of a source for moral standards is that of situational ethics, of which Fletcher is perhaps the best-known exponent. In essence, this school of thought denies the validity of general and abiding moral principles that are applicable to each and every problem as it arises. On the contrary, this school maintains that each situation must be evaluated and a decision reached in terms of the specific conditions prevailing then and there.

Without doubt, situational ethics has the great virtue of avoiding the application of simplistic and unbending principles to the complex problems confronting men and women. Situational ethics is far more conscious than absolutist ethics of the multiplicity of factors that enter into a moral decision, and it is far more sensitive to the weaknesses of human flesh that cannot be ignored in judgment.

The position of situational ethics is, of course, presented by its spokesmen with considerable subtlety and sophistication. It is undeniable that, as a corrective to absolutist ethics, situational ethics performs a very salutary function.

A detailed critique of situational ethics cannot be attempted here. In essence, however, it would seem that if we follow this route all our ethical problems are compounded. As each person is confronted by a moral problem, he becomes a battleground for opposing pressures, but there are no principles nor precedents to guide his decisions. Moreover, each man's neighbor is free to come to a different conclusion, since no two situations are completely identical. Finally, in the absence of objective standards, there would be no justification for rewarding one course of action and punishing another, or for establishing various degrees of one or the other—a condition approximating the state of affairs prevailing in our judicial system today. In other words, is our present confusion to be our permanent condition?

I believe that we have another resource available to us in the quest for a basis for ethics—the doctrine of "natural law." Though it has had a long and honorable history in Western civilization from ancient times through the medieval era and beyond, it has fallen on evil times in the modern age. At the outset, I am not suggesting that the natural law doctrine in its traditional forms can serve us today. We need to reexamine the history of natural law and the characteristics it has exhibited in the past, in order to create a new concept of natural law, broader and more dynamic than past formulations and, therefore, more serviceable in the present and future.

There are three principal periods in the history of the doctrine. It is significant that natural law arose during a period spiritually not unlike our own, during the breakdown of the fabric of classical civilization. Toward the close of the ancient world, the religious and mythical worldview of Greco-Roman civilization dissolved, no longer commanding the allegiance of most intelligent and sensitive men. Nevertheless, many of them felt the need for an ethical base for their personal lives and the governance of society. Largely under the aegis of Stoicism, an ethical code evolved which flowered into the doctrine of natural law.

The doctrine was much more fully elaborated in the Middle Ages, when scholastic philosophers, seeking to give a rational basis to the teachings of traditional ethics, spelled out its implications with great subtlety. From that day to this, natural law has been cultivated with great assiduity in Catholic theological circles, but in modern times its influence upon the body politic in general has been minimal. In part, the modern distaste for natural law is due to its linkage with a specific dogmatic system. In perhaps greater degree, its desuetude derives from the fact that natural law absorbed from its scholastic cultivators certain traits that made it seem irrelevant to the modern mind.

One important offshoot of natural law should be noted. Western civilization encountered another era akin to our own during the sixteenth, seventeenth, and eighteenth centuries. With the breakdown of the feudal system and the erosion of the medieval worldview came the emergence of national states, each of which asserted its total sovereignty *vis-à-vis* all others. Some doctrine was needed to govern their mutual relationships, and so international law came into being, representing a secular adaptation of doctrines largely derived from natural law.

The Industrial Revolution and the rise of the middle class led to the demand for individual human rights, which also required a theoretical foundation. The new economic order needed to break the rigid patterns of feudal society and to grant equality to all men without regard for their lineage, religion, or economic position. The new mercantile and industrial entrepreneurs demanded freedom from external restraints on the development of burgeoning capitalism. Thus, there arose the ideals embodied in the slogans of the French Revolution—Liberty, Equality, Fraternity. Though these ideals were never completely translated into reality, and the banners of the French Republic and Napoleon did not usher in the Messianic Age for humanity, they did mark a great step forward in human liberation.

Today it has become fashionable in some quarters to denigrate the "Age of Reason" and to extol the Middle Ages, on a highly selective basis, to be sure. But this is not the first time that men have ignored the wisdom embodied in the rabbinic injunction, "Cast no stone into the well from which you have been drinking." (B. Baba Kamma 92b:Bemid-bar Rabbah ch.22) To retreat from the eighteenth century means to open the door to the rebirth of tyranny over the body and soul of man.

To revert to our theme, natural law, in secularized form, was now pressed into service once more, producing the classical political documents of the eighteenth century, the American Declaration of Independence and the French Declaration of the Rights of Man. They mark the apogee of the secularized natural law doctrine in modern times. However, this secularization was far from complete. There was no acceptance of a *specific* creedal formulation in the Declaration of Independence to be sure, but reliance upon a "Creator" was expressed in the American document. It declared "that all men are *created* equal, that they are endowed *by their Creator* with certain unalienable Rights, that among these are Life, Liberty and the pursuit of Happiness," and it expressed a "firm reliance on the protection of divine Providence."

During the nineteenth and the twentieth centuries, the influence of natural law reached its nadir. In the modern age, it has been generally regarded as a quaint survival of Greco-Roman thought and of medieval scholasticism, and dismissed as totally irrelevant to modern man and his condition. During the last few centuries, the natural law doctrine has remained almost exclusively the province of the Catholic Church and, latterly, of some theoreticians in "neoconservative" circles who are seeking to stem the flow of change in society. This attempt has seemed entirely comprehensible, in view of the tendency of the church to glorify medievalism and the desire of neoconservatives to offer a sophisticated justification for perpetuating privilege and inequality in contemporary society. Robert M. Hutchins once noted that natural lawyers have been more active in defining a "just war" than in furthering disarmament or a new conception of sovereignty.

This conservative characteristic is not, however, necessarily inherent in natural law. I would suggest that the reason why natural law has tended to be "static" in its application lies in its cultural origins, in the two periods in which it arose and in which it reached its highest development. The Greco-Roman civilization that fathered natural law saw life as unchanging and human history as cyclical and repetitive. The Middle Ages, in which natural law reached its fullest development, were also marked by a static conception of life.

To be sure, the Jewish and Christian religions looked forward to a Divine intervention in human affairs that would take place at "the end of days," but this was taken to mean "beyond history" and "in the world-to-come." On the other hand, in this temporal world, here and now, medieval thought had little conception of change and growth. The feudal system, with its permanent stratification of classes, gave expression to this static view in the social and political order.

Natural law necessarily took on the coloration of these two periods, which saw its gestation and its maturity. From these eras it derived its bias in favor of the static, the unchanging, the immovable.

But if we rethink its postulates, natural law can serve as a consensual basis for an ethical system for our time. To achieve this purpose, one important step must be taken. In order to safeguard its vital essence and free it from the accidental entanglements wrought by history, we need to recognize that the assumed sources of natural law have been too narrowly construed. Actually, they are not limited to the Greco-Roman world! As will be demonstrated in the following chapters, there is another culture sphere, that of the Hebraic tradition, that supplies precisely the element of dynamism which the static Greco-Roman worldview did not possess.

Classical treatments of natural law have generally defined it as a body of unchanging principles that can be deduced from nature and from reason, both of which were regarded as unambiguous and unchanging. Particularly in modern times, the validity of both these claims has been challenged. Critics have not been slow to point out that the teaching of "nature" is far from clear. Which aspect of the natural world is normative for man, the gentleness of the lamb or the ferocity of the lion?

It is clear that here an important modification both in substance and in terminology is required. Actually it is not "nature" but "human nature" with which ethics must reckon and the needs of which it must serve. Clearly the rapid expansion of scientific knowledge and the accumulation of new insights into human nature through biology, psychology, sociology, and other sciences require a dynamic concept of natural law.

The motive that led advocates of natural law to make nature a ground principle was their desire to give their teaching an absolute and binding character; they therefore seized upon nature as one of the pillars of natural law. Both in ancient and in medieval times, a static conception of natural law was thoroughly congenial to the structure of society.

Today it is a truism that flux and change are the basic characteristics of human life. In our day, the legal philosopher Hans Kelsen has contrasted the immobility of natural law doctrine with the dynamic character of modern positivism, and therefore he has argued against the usefulness of natural law today. However, the static approach of natural law is not an inseparable feature. We may grant that the basic characteristics of human nature are constant, but that does not mean that they are unchanged through all the vicissitudes of time and circumstances. Thus the twentieth-century thinker Rudolf Stammler has been led to evolve a theory of "natural law with variable content."[1] Actually there were earlier adumbrations of a more flexible approach. Thomas Aquinas, in his *Summa Theologica* (II, 2, 57), had conceded that some secondary principles of natural law might be modified as human nature changed, though the only modifications he contemplated were for the worse!

Obviously, changes in the body of facts will affect the body of values. A textbook in biology or physics published in 1900 will differ markedly from one published in 1980, but the essential goal and methodology of the science in question remain constant. We may illustrate the constant and the variable in natural law by an important and obvious example.

The Sixth Commandment in the Decalogue, rendered variously, "You shall not kill"[2] or "You shall not murder," expresses what is perhaps the most fundamental and enduring imperative in natural law. Nevertheless, for the ancient Hebrews this prohibition was felt to be entirely compatible with the practice of blood-vengeance. If a man was unintentionally slain, any relative of the victim could hunt down and kill the accidental killer with impunity (Num., chap. 35).

In the three millennia and more since Sinai, the mass murder of human beings in war was not looked upon in any society as violating the prohibition of murder. Even today pacifism is the faith of a small minority who see in war a colossal violation of the principle. The day will come when their ranks will grow, and ultimately nations will recognize that the commandment is applicable to them as well.

A similar process is under way with regard to capital punishment. The execution by the state of convicted criminals is still held, by large segments of the population, to be permissible. However, sentiment against the practice continues to rise. The day will come when executions ordered by juries and judges will be recognized as judicial murder. The principle "You shall not kill" remains unchanged; the understanding and the application of the commandment vary with increased knowledge of the facts and a growing sensitivity to ethical values.

John Cogley defined natural law as "simply the belief that there is a moral or ethical order which a human being can discover and which he must take account of, if he is to attune himself to his necessary ends as a human being."[3] Basically, the postulates of natural law deal with *human nature*, with *law* and with *reason*, and with their interrelationships. Unfortunately, advocates of natural law in the past have treated human nature as *unchangeable, uniform,* and *totally known.* It is these extreme formulations of the basic assumptions underlying natural law, not the assumptions themselves, that have served to congeal the doctrine and make it seem irrelevant in a world constantly in flux.

Essentially, natural law declares that only that law is legitimate and has a claim upon men's loyalty which is *in harmony with human nature.*

Second, it believes that human nature is *constant* through time, not necessarily unchanging, but with sufficient continuity to make possible generalizations regarding its basic traits, its needs and desires, its limitations and potentialities. Third, it regards human nature as being *universal* in space, modified, to be sure, by environmental factors, but still sufficiently stable to permit a generalized theory applicable to all men. Finally, it regards human nature not as known but as *knowable* through the canons of scientific investigation and rational thought.

The caveats we have just noted have too often been ignored by advocates of natural law, who have treated human nature as *unchange-able, uniform,* and *totally known.* More than a little of the difficulty stems from these distortions. Inherently, however, there is nothing in natural law that negates the exploration of the dimensions of human nature as an ongoing and probably unending enterprise.

Since human nature is constant, universal, and knowable, law represents the effort by society to safeguard the requirements and proper needs of its members through the theory and practice of justice and not merely by the establishment of a structure of legal procedures. Legality is not distinct from justice, but neither is it identical with it. It bifurcates into legal procedure and equity. Ideally viewed, the law begins in the effort to codify the dictates of justice.

However, for several reasons, a legal system never becomes coterminous with justice. First, the law develops a life of its own and elaborates a complex of practices which ultimately become codified in the statute books. By that time, however, society has often moved on to new insights, or it has been modified by new conditions requiring new and often radical applications of the time-honored principles. Hence a cultural lag between positive law and the new frontiers of justice is a universal feature of every social system.

Second, justice is not identical with law, because justice includes aspects of human relationships that are beyond the power of the law to govern. The law makes it punishable to injure one's fellow; justice requires that we help him. Beating one's father is a legal crime enforceable with sanctions; no system of law can compel a man to love or reverence his parents. There thus emerges the paradox that law, which arises in order to make justice operative in society, falls perpetually behind it. These areas of behavior beyond the jurisdiction of the courts the Talmud calls "matters handed over to the heart" and describes them by such terms as "unpunishable but forbidden" and "unpunishable by human law but guilty by the law of God."[4]

In a rational and just society, the goal will always be to close the gap and bring legal practice as close to equity as possible. Believing in the existence and knowability of human nature and in the reality and rationality of justice, natural law regards a theory of justice as the necessary foundation for any legal system worthy of the name.

Finally, natural law believes in man's reason as an ever present instrument for evaluation both of human nature and of the law, in the light of legitimate human needs and aspirations. Moreover, the concept of justice continues to grow with the expanding boundaries of human experience from the jungle to outer space.

These three assumptions on human nature, justice, and reason are all that are required by the doctrine of natural law. One may hazard the guess that had natural lawyers restricted themselves to these three elements, the doctrine would not have aroused the widespread suspicion with which it is viewed in many quarters today. It is no service to the cause to underestimate the substantial roadblocks in the way of the rehabilitation of natural law in the modern age or to minimize their validity. Many who stand outside the dominant tradition of natural law but are sympathetic to its potential value would agree with Hutchins in his observation that natural law appears to be "a body of doctrine that is either so vague as to be useless or so biased as to be 'menacing.' "

Similarly, the philosopher Brand Blanchard has spelled out the unhappy alternatives that confront modern advocates of natural law: "The natural law which we are to take as our guide remains deplorably misty. If natural law is to be usable, we must be able to tell what is natural."[5]

He then adds two more objections: "The advocates of natural law fix some absolute rules which often turn out to be incredible." As examples, he quotes John Henry Newman as saying that it would be better for millions of men to die in extreme agony than for a single man to commit the slightest venial sin. He also cites George F. Grant as maintaining that it would be wrong to convict an innocent man even if it were the price of averting a world war. These hypothetical examples are not merely incredible—they are nonsense. Newman has ignored the obvious consideration that the agony of a million of God's creatures is a greater evil than a venial sin. Grant has ignored the phenomenon of martyrdom through the ages, the sacrifice of one's life for a cause or for one's fellowmen, universally regarded as the highest form of ethical conduct.

Finally, Blanchard argues, "It is not true that if we abandon the Law of Nature as our test, we have nothing left to fall back upon. We can still fall back on the majority view of modern moralists, namely that 'we should so act as to produce the greatest good.' "

This last argument is the crux of the argument. Blanchard proposes that instead of natural law as the norm we use the standard of "producing the greatest good," yet he fails to recognize that the next question, "What is the greatest good for man?" catapults us at once into a discussion of human nature—its needs, its fears, and its hopes. In a word, natural law has been driven out of the door only to enter by the window.

Far weightier is the objection to natural law repeated by virtually all its critics, the argument from the history of the doctrine. It is undeniable that the theory of natural law has been subjected to not a few misinterpretations, unwarranted conclusions, and downright errors, both intellectual and moral, and the end is not yet in sight. On the one hand, the history of a doctrine, including the uses to which it has been put, is not the determining factor as to its inherent validity. On the other hand, its *curriculum vitae* cannot be ignored, if only because a knowledge of its history can help alert us to congenital weaknesses inherent in the concept.

William Lee Miller pointed out—and with substantial justice—that in natural law,

> those aspects that can be linked to the given physical nature of man are made to predominate over those aspects that arise from the possibilities of developing human culture. . . . The natural law emphasis would appear to incline toward an undue bias toward the former—toward the static and fixed guide lines rooted primarily in elemental facts. Thus, it would appear to have an undue conservative bias.[6]

Specifically, it has been asked, Has the natural law tradition helped in emancipating women? It is doubtful whether the record of history would bear out the contrary view that it is easy to show that natural law can be and *often has been in fact* an instrument of social reform. The most that can be said for the history of natural law in modern times is that it has at times provided a rationale for some social reforms that were initiated and fought for under other auspices, by men and movements far removed from its presuppositions.

The conservative bias in natural law is undeniable, its tendency to see human nature as essentially given rather than growing, as fixed rather than flexible. However, there are two interrelated questions that should be asked. First, is this bias inherent in the doctrine of natural law itself? Second, can it be remedied?

It has been pointed out that natural law took on the coloration of two periods, that of Greco-Roman civilization, which saw its gestation, and the Middle Ages, which marked its greatest development. From them it derived its bias in favor of the static, the unchanging, the immovable. The august authority of Aquinas virtually dominated the work of all his successors. The later practitioners of natural law did little more than elaborate on the work of their predecessors. The spirit remained largely the same.

The modern world, however, is marked by its dynamism and by its perpetual flux. Growth and change have always been realities of life—but today they are consciously recognized and even welcomed. Moreover, the vastly enlarged horizons of understanding opened up to modern man by the physical and life sciences make it possible to do far more justice to the nature of man and his environment than was possible in the past.

A cynical observer might therefore argue that natural law needs only to be saved from its friends in order to win over its enemies! A fairer and more sympathetic view would be that natural lawyers today need to remember that the Greco-Roman philosophers and the medieval theologians are not the only sources of natural law. As many seventeenth- and eighteenth-century thinkers knew, there is another tradition in natural law, too long overlooked and neglected. It is the highly important Judaic component, embodied in the Hebrew Bible, the Apocrypha, and rabbinic literature, and of comparable antiquity. Its major insights will be presented below. The Judaic strand in natural law is particularly significant, because, unlike its Greco-Roman counterpart, it is fueled by a dynamic sense of history moving toward a great consummation. It possesses an insatiable thirst for righteousness and a passionate hatred of injustice and cruelty, attributes not generally present in Greek and Roman culture.

There is enduring value in the innate conservative bias of natural law, in the emphasis it places upon the permanent, unchanging elements of human nature. Given the polarity of human nature, this tendency in natural law performs another important function—it serves as a brake upon extreme innovation and change that destroy existing structures but are unable to replace them with better ones. But if natural law is to be a vital resource in the modern age and not merely a vestigial remains from a vanished past, it will need a generous infusion of the modern consciousness of development. On every issue before it, natural law theory must be aware of the dialectic of continuity and change which constitutes the phenomenon of progress.

On the negative side, too, natural law theory will need to reckon with the deep propensity in the human soul for self-seeking and self-deception, to which our age has become painfully sensitive. It cannot ignore the insights of traditional religion regarding the innate weakness of man, whether expressed in the Christian doctrine of original sin or in the less extreme Jewish concept of the two *yetzera*, the good and the evil impulses.

Nor can natural law overlook the universal phenomenon of rationalization, the seemingly boundless capacity of men to disguise their instinctual drives and submerged desires and to project them in rational and moral terms. What modern psychiatry has amply documented was intuitively felt by the prophet: "The heart is deceitful above all, and desperately sick, who can know it?" (Jer. 17:9).

These insights will necessarily complicate the task of delineating the attributes of human nature which is basic to the natural law enterprise. But they do not negate the conception of human nature as constant, universal, and knowable. Nor do they refute the conviction that human reason and the human conscience—itself an outgrowth of reason—remain the only available standards for creating and evaluating the norm of justice as the foundation of law.

The essential difficulty with the concept of natural law lies in a misunderstanding of its basic affirmation. This error has given rise to questionable interpretations or doubtful applications of principles that are in themselves sound. Thus, it is an axiom of natural law that the proper norms of social conduct and legal injunction are derived from "nature." The full meaning of this affirmation becomes clear, however, only if we understand what it negates. Without denying the affinities of man for other living creatures or his relationship to the universe as a whole—quite the contrary—it is human nature, not animal or physical nature, which is the proper norm for natural law. "Social Darwinism" is not a consequence of natural law, but a violation; the jungle is not the natural habitat of man.

It therefore follows that the investigation of human nature cannot be limited to those physical aspects which man has in common with the lower animals. Unlike many of them, man is a social as well as a biological being. Hence, such manifestations of human nature as friendship, love, reason, and culture are not artificial grafts upon human nature but are inherent elements in it. When a given society makes it impossible for many of its members to exercise these attributes freely, it is violating the canons of natural law. The instinct for self-preservation and the sexual drive men and women share with all living creatures; it is love that is specifically human. Where love is debased or denied, the principles of natural law are being flouted.

There are, undoubtedly, great difficulties involved in the objective description and analysis of these specifically human traits, particularly since they are not susceptible to quantitative techniques. But these problems of the investigator do not invalidate either the reality of these attributes or their "natural" character. The "morally relevant nature of men" cannot be delineated unless we reckon with the entire complex of human nature. Within its dimensions we must include the physical, intellectual, aesthetic, and spiritual aspects, without which human nature is not human.

It is beyond our goal and our ability to spell out the entire code of conduct for the individual and society that would emerge from a natural law deriving from a comprehensive study of human nature, from the use of reason to evaluate human needs, desires, strengths, and weaknesses, and from adherence to the standard of true justice. That is a task facing our entire generation. But natural law offers a viable basis for an ethical system to which all people can give their allegiance, whatever their race, creed, sex, or ethnic background.

Natural law, which originated with the Greeks, is, to be sure, not tied to any specific theology like that of Judaism or Christianity. However, as the classic phrases in the American Declaration of Independence clearly imply, the assumptions of natural law rest upon some affirmations regarding the nature of the universe, its origin and purpose, and the nature of man, his rights and duties, his powers and limitations.

In treating reason, justice, and kindness rather than irrationality, greed, and cruelty as the basic traits of human nature, we are adopting a series of axioms that by definition are not capable of "proof." We are, quite legitimately, bringing value judgments to bear upon the observable phenomena of human behavior. These value judgments, whether we are aware of the fact or not, have their sources in a worldview fashioned by a theistic metaphysics. In a sense not intended by Anaxagoras, it is true that man fashions God in his own image. More accurately, man's nature bears witness to the character of his Creator, who cannot be inferior to His creatures. John Stuart Mill declared these words of the psalmist to be the most powerful argument for the existence of God:

> Shall He who implants the ear not hear,
>   He who forms the eye not see?
> Shall He who instructs nations not correct them,
>   He who instructs men in understanding?

> (Ps. 94:9–10)

This faith in God is, of course, not being logically demonstrated. But the Hebrew psalmist, like the English philosopher, finds it in conformity with reason. Based upon this theistic view of the world, Judaic thought elaborates a body of ethical teaching that is a unique blend of realistic understanding and idealistic aspiration. This tradition is an indispensable contribution to natural law in our time, a resource of incomparable simplicity, profundity, and power.

Part III

The Judaic Contribution

Chapter 6

Jewish Sources of Natural Law

THE EXISTENCE of a Judaic component in natural law is not a modern discovery. In the seventeenth and eighteenth centuries, several Christian scholars, such as Hugo Grotius, recognized that a fundamental source of natural law is to be found in the biblical tradition. The Cambridge Hebraist John Selden was convinced that a doctrine of natural law is explicitly set forth in the talmudic concept of the Noahide Laws, which rest upon biblical foundations. He devoted a work to the theme, *De Jure Naturale et Gentium Juxta Disciplinam Ebraeorum* (1655). The distinguished legal scholar Max M. Laserson, of Columbia University, was working on the subject at the time of his lamented passing two decades ago. The Noahide Laws have been treated by other scholars, though not generally for their potential contribution to the ethical foundations of contemporary society.

With the global collapse of morality in our day, the need for a sound basis for ethics grows increasingly clear and increasingly desperate. In this important task, Judaic sources have a significant contribution to make toward the revitalizatin of natural law.

In seeking ethical principles that will be binding upon all men and societies, it would be difficult to improve upon the Ten Commandments given on Sinai. Time-bound as every utterance must be, their brief, all-encompassing formulation bears the stamp of universality. The Decalogue, or Ten Words (Exod. 20, Deut. 5), may be viewed as an unsophisticated adumbration of natural law. Its apodictic commands are all regarded as self-evident and requiring no justification beyond themselves. The last six commandments are exclusively concerned with man's relations with his fellows: his obligation to honor his father and mother and the prohibition of murder, adultery, stealing, bearing false witness, and covetousness.

The first four words have no less significant implications. As the medieval poet and thinker Judah Halevi pointed out in another connection, the First Word proclaims: "I am the Lord your God, who brought you out of the land of Egypt, out of the house of bondage," not "who created heaven and earth." God introduces Himself as the great Liberator in the first recorded revolution in history, thus taking His place on the side of the oppressed, against the tyrant and exploiter. The Second Word prohibits the making of images of the Godhead and thus effectively opposes defining and limiting the cosmic source of the universe. The cryptic Third Word apparently forbids associating the Name of God with anything false or unworthy. The Fourth Word establishes the Sabbath rest for all living beings, master and servant, humans and animals, thus establishing the right of all living creatures to be free from endless, unremitting toil.

What is almost as notable about the Decalogue as its inclusions are its omissions. In ancient documents such as the Egyptian "Prostestations of Guiltlessness," in *The Book of the Dead*, ethical standards are invoked, but they are a minority as against ritual observance. The Decalogue, on the contrary, is almost completely ethical in emphasis; the countless prescriptions of Hebrew ritual law are totally absent. Even in the case of the Sabbath rest, it is the cosmic theme of God as Creator that is stressed in Exodus, and the ethical theme of all creatures' right to rest that is emphasized in Deuteronomy.

Another major formulation of biblical ethics is to be found in the Holiness Code in Leviticus (Lev. 19–22). It contains the Golden Rule, "You shall love your neighbor as yourself," which follows upon the prohibition of taking vengeance or nursing a grudge (Lev. 19:18). The broadest possible application of the Golden Rule is clearly indicated by the explicit reference to the alien as well: "You shall love him [i.e., the stranger] as yourself, for you were slaves in the land of Egypt" (Lev. 19:34).

Both the Decalogue and the Holiness Code offer no detailed theological doctrine. They do not presuppose faith in one God who is the ruler of a universe rooted in righteousness.

The prophet Micah formulates a threefold categorical imperative, addressed by God to *'adam*, the Hebrew term for "human being," not to an Israelite alone, or even to males only, a fact not noted until the rise of feminism: "He has told you, O *'adam*, what is good and what the Lord your God demands of you, to do justice, to love mercy, and to walk humbly with your God" (Mic. 7:6).

Today, all competent scholars recognize that the hoary charge of "Jewish legalism" was a weapon in religious polemics that has survived in secular guise, not an objective analysis of the true character of the tradition. In the Judaic consciousness, body and soul, the spirit and the letter, are not antithetic, but complementary aspects of life, organically related to each other. It is not our purpose to offer a conspectus of all the provisions of biblical ethics, the details of which are spelled out in the various law codes and individual enactments embedded in the Bible, and elaborated in the Talmud. Our concern is to highlight the broadly human, universal aspect of Judaic ethical doctrine.

Because this source is generally unfamiliar, one other passage should be recalled. The biblical code of ethical conduct is not limited to forbidding gross offenses; it also is concerned with the subtle sins of respectable people. This recognition emerges clearly from the great Code of A Man of Honor spoken by the suffering Job (Job, chap. 31), in which he sets forth the norms of conduct by which he has lived. Job lists fourteen infractions from which he himself has been free. In accordance with biblical usage, they are not organized thematically. They include: (1) lusting for a maiden (vv. 1–2); (2) cheating in business (vv. 5–6); (3) taking the property of others (vv. 7–8); (4) engaging in adultery (vv. 9–12); (5) acting unfairly toward slaves in the courts (vv. 13–15); (6) showing callousness toward the poor (vv. 16–18); (7) manifesting lack of pity for the homeless wayfarer (vv. 19–20); (8) perverting the just claims of the widow and the orphan (vv. 21–23); (9) loving gold and trusting in one's wealth (vv. 24–25); (10) worshipping the sun and the moon (vv. 26–28); (11) finding joy in the calamity of one's foes (vv. 29–31); (12) failing to practice hospitality (v. 32); (13) concealing one's sins because of the fear of mob opinion (vv. 33–34); and (14) expropriating the land of others within the letter of the law (vv. 38–40).

Only one, the worship of heavenly bodies, is "theological"; but its implications are clear. Giving one's ultimate loyalty and allegiance to any creation or artifact is idolatry; it undermines the foundations of a moral society. All the other actions Job lists are infractions of right relations with one's fellowmen.

Hebraic thought rarely formulates abstract principles. Nevertheless, the first explicit doctrine of natural law is set forth in the apocryphal Book of Jubilees, which was written before the beginning of the Christian era. It attributes to Noah, who was not a Hebrew, a code of conduct binding upon all men.

In the twenty-eighth jubilee, Noah began to enjoin upon his sons' sons the ordinances and commandments and all the judgments that he knew and he exhorted his sons to observe righteousness and to cover the shame of their flesh and to bless their Creator and honor father and mother and love their neighbor and guard their souls from fornication and uncleanness and all iniquity.

(Jub. 7:22)

The Talmud explicitly declares that all men, by virtue of their humanity, are obligated to observe fundamental principles of conduct, which it calls the "Seven Laws of the Sons of Noah." Six of these basic Noahide Laws are negative—the prohibition of idolatry, murder, incest, theft, blasphemy, and cruelty to animals—and one is positive—the establishment of law and order in society (*B. Sanhedrin* 56a–60a; *Tosefta Avodah Zarah* 8:4–8). The last-named injunction, curiously enough, does not appear as a specific commandment in the legal corpus of Judaism—it is obviously axiomatic, universal in character.

In seeking a biblical basis for these principles of conduct, the rabbis of the Talmud, by their special methods of exegesis, relate them to the verses setting forth God's injunction to Adam in the Garden of Eden (Gen. 2:16–17). Thus their binding character on all human beings, who are descended from both Adam and Noah, is doubly underscored. Individual rabbis suggested that various other prohibitions be added to the list, but these Seven Noahide Laws remain basic.

The New Testament seems to refer to the Noahide Laws in the Book of Acts (15:20 and 29), while natural law is explicitly cited by Paul in the Epistle to the Romans.

For when the Gentiles, which have not the law, do by nature the things contained in the law, these, having not the law, are a law unto themselves; which show the work of the law written in their hearts, their conscience also bearing witness, and their thought the meanwhile accusing, or else excusing one another.

(Rom. 2:15–15)

The rabbinic doctrine of the Noahide Laws makes ethical conduct, rather than creedal adherence, obligatory upon all men. It is, therefore, a code of law rather than a system of belief which it enjoins. Yet though the Noahide Laws have only minimal theological content, they are by no means lacking a metaphysical foundation. The Seven Laws include the prohibition of idolatry and of blasphemy and, therefore, imply the recognition of a Divine Creator and Governor of the world.

Among medieval thinkers, the doctrine of the Noahide Laws merged imperceptibly with that of natural law, as in the work of Baḥya ibn Paqudah, the most popular Jewish moral philosopher of the Middle Ages (11th cent., Spain). Before him, the tenth-century philosopher

Saadia, influenced by the concept of natural religion *(fitra)* maintained by the Arab Kalam philosophers, virtually identified the truth of Divine revelation with those achievable by human reason. Leo Strauss has shown that Judah Halevi equates the law of reason, which underlies all codes, with the law of nature. On the Christian side, John Selden, who identified the Noahide Laws with natural law, represented the effort of the natural law school theorists in the period of the Enlightenment to establish points of contact with the Hebraic tradition. However, as has already been noted, in the last few centuries, the Greco-Roman sources of natural law have continued to be cited, while the Judaic element has generally been ignored.

This doctrine of the Noahide Laws is extremely interesting from several points of view. It represents in essence a theory of universal religion which is the heritage of all men. Characteristically Jewish is its emphasis upon right action rather than right belief as the mark of the good life. Its spirit is epitomized in the great rabbinic utterance: "I call Heaven and earth to witness that, whether one be Gentile or Jew, man or woman, slave or free man, the Divine spirit rests on each in accordance with his deeds" *(Yalkut Shimeoni* on Judg., sec. 42). In its all-encompassing sweep, this passage recalls the famous words of Paul: "There is neither Jew nor Greek, neither bond nor free, there is neither male nor female, for you are all one in Christ Jesus" (Gal. 3:28). Significantly, the equal worth of all men in the rabbinic formulation does not derive from common doctrinal belief, nor does it depend upon it; it requires only loyalty to a code of ethical conduct.

In another direction as well, the Noahide Laws have a significant contribution to make to natural law. It is a fact generally overlooked or ignored that however great the contributions of religion to civilization, freedom of religion is not among them. The ideal of religious liberty is essentially a gift we owe to the secularists. Nevertheless, religion has a great stake in the ideal of freedom of thought, in connection with which it has played an ambivalent role, both for good and for ill. A detailed discussion of the contribution of Judaism to the theory of religious freedom, which is fundamental to a pluralistic society, is presented later in this book. By requiring no creedal affirmation, the Noahide Laws prepare the ground for freedom of conscience.

The ideals of religious liberty and religious tolerance are among the most precious blessings of the modern age. Nevertheless, even our irreligious age is marked by some of the bloodiest episodes in history, which have religion either as their reason or their excuse. The unceasing slaughter of Protestants and Catholics in Northern Ireland, the conflicts in Pakistan, Kashmir, and India and the persecutions within each country itself, the civil war in Lebanon—all demonstrate that religious tolerance must never be taken for granted. Like all forms of liberty, it needs to be won anew in every generation, cherished with passion, and defended with vigor.

The recent onslaughts on the integrity of the First Amendment to the American Constitution, coupled with the upsurge of religious intolerance including acts of terrorism in the United States and the Western democracies, may seem pale by the side of religious bloodbaths elsewhere. But the danger is real and present wherever the ideal of religious liberty rests on secular foundations alone and is not incorporated into the body of belief and practice taught by the religious tradition.

The Judaic insights cursorily presented here as significant contributions to an evolving body of natural law, undoubtedly rest upon the substratum of religious faith. The basic postulates, transcending any specific historical creed, may be briefly set forth as follows:

1. The recognition of a law-abiding universe, not merely in the physical realm, which science has continued to reveal, but also in the social order, which is governed by the law of retribution or moral consequence, embedded in the very structure of the world.

2. The faith that this universe is hospitable to man's aspirations and ideals.

3. The conviction that all men and women have a common origin, the handiwork of a Power beyond themselves, and are linked to a common destiny for good or ill, being brothers to one another.

4. The understanding that man is an animal, but more than an animal, for he is blessed with the attribute of free will that makes him rightly responsible for his actions. Hence he is deserving of reward for his positive deeds and punishment for his sins of commission, omission, and permission, the offenses he perpetrated, the right actions he left undone, and his acquiescence or silence in the face of the evils of society that he left unchecked and unopposed.

The Noahide Laws offer a basis in natural law that can enable human beings who differ in their worldviews and ritual practices to remain peaceful fellow-travelers on the same planet, conscious that they face a common destiny.

But life on this planet is not limited to human beings. The vast number of species in both the animal and the plant kingdoms are also our life's companions. According to Genesis, mankind is given "dominion" over all other living creatures. What does dominion mean, and what obligations does it entail? On few subjects are ignorance and misinformation more rampant than on the attitude of the Judaic tradition toward man's environment and his fellow creatures. These insights will be presented below.

Undoubtedly, there will be conscientious and sensitive men and women who are honestly unable to subscribe even to so broadly based a system of belief as outlined above. But I believe that for the overwhelming majority of men and women, whether they give their allegiance to a specific religious tradition or to none, and whether they are scientists, technologists, or laymen, such a basis for ethical standards would be acceptable.

Morality, which includes both ideas and action, must rest upon a foundation firmer than convention or predilection or the police power of the state. It must avoid the weaknesses of relativism without succumbing to the temptations of dogmatic absolutism. Only then can it help to extricate mankind from the chaos and conflict that threaten its survival. It is to natural law, properly understood and interpreted, that we must look for a basis for the moral system our age so desperately needs.

We have noted some of the Judaic sources that can contribute to this enterprise. The most important source is yet to be discussed. Paradoxically, it has come under greater attack in modern times than any other portion of the Bible—the Creation narrative at the beginning of Genesis.

Chapter 7

The Truths of Genesis

"AMERICANS AND ENGLISHMEN," George Bernard Shaw once said, "are two nations separated by a common language." One is often tempted to make a similar statement with regard to Jews and Christians, who share a common Scripture, in whole or in part, in the Hebrew Bible. Perhaps the most striking instance of this divergence is the role that the Paradise narrative in Genesis plays in both religions.

For traditional Christianity, the tale of Adam and Eve in the Garden is of transcendental significance; indeed, the entire Christian drama of salvation would be inconceivable without it. Basing himself primarily upon the narrative of Adam and Eve in Genesis, Paul enunciated the Christian drama of salvation: Adam and Eve, disobeying the Divine will and eating of the forbidden fruit of the Tree of Knowledge, were guilty of the primal sin. The Fall of Adam placed an ineradicable stain upon all his descendants, who are doomed to perdition. God, however, in His infinite love, sent His son to redeem mankind from the consequences of the Fall by his suffering. Only faith in the Savior and his sacrifice can save mankind from perdition.

This doctrine of innate evil in man was maintained by various sectarian groups in Judaism at the beginning of the Christian era, as is clear from the Book of Baruch and the Dead Sea Scrolls. The innovation of Christianity lay in the role of Jesus as Savior. For traditional Christianity, the significance of Genesis is thus primarily theological.

Far less importance is attached to the Genesis narrative by normative Judaism. For classical Judaism, the narrative reveals the strength of human weakness, the propensity to sin characteristic of men and women. The transgression of Adam and Eve in disobeying God's will is

68

the first tragic illustration of this human trait, but Judaism finds no evidence in the text of Scripture that the sin in the Garden of Eden placed an eternal stain upon human nature. It finds in Scripture a straightforward account of the punishment meted out upon all three sinners: the serpent, Eve, and Adam:

> The Lord God said to the serpent, "Because you have done this, cursed are you above all cattle, and above all wild animals; upon your belly you shall go, and dust you shall eat all the days of your life. I will put enmity between you and the woman, and between your seed and her seed; he shall bruise your head, and you shall bruise his heel."
> To the woman He said, "I will greatly multiply your pain in childbearing; in pain you shall bring forth children, yet your desire shall be for your husband, and he shall rule over you."
> And to Adam he said, "Because you have listened to the voice of your wife, and have eaten of the tree of which I commanded you, 'You shall not eat of it,' cursed is the ground because of you; in toil you shall eat of it all the days of your life; thorns and thistles it shall bring forth to you; and you shall eat the plants of the field. In the sweat of your face you shall eat bread till you return to the ground, for out of it you were taken; you are dust, and to dust you shall return."
>
> (Gen. 3:14–19)

> Then the Lord God said, "Behold, the man has become like one of us, knowing good and evil; and now, lest he put forth his hand and take also of the tree of life, and eat, and live for ever"—therefore the Lord God sent him forth from the garden of Eden, to till the ground from which he was taken.
>
> (Gen. 3:22–23)

In sum, the snake is made to crawl upon its belly, woman must suffer pain in childbirth, and man must eke out his difficult existence by backbreaking toil. Most important of all, by being driven out of the Garden of Eden, humanity loses access to the Tree of Life and thus is stripped of immortality, becoming subject to death.

In sum, the theological importance for normative Judaism of the Paradise narrative is comparatively slight and the divergence from the Christian view considerable. For Christianity, man sins because he is a sinner; for Judaism, man becomes a sinner when he sins.

There have been scholars and thinkers in our day who, basing themselves on differences such as these, have contended that the popular concept of the "Judeo-Christian tradition" has no validity at all because the two religions have virtually nothing in common. That this position overstates the facts considerably, to put it mildly, is clear on many grounds. One has only to contrast the content and timbre of Judaism and Christianity on the one hand, and the indigenous religions of India, China, and Japan on the other, to recognize how many points of similarity and contact the two religions of the West share with each other.

Probably the most striking illustration of the congruity of outlook is afforded by the majestic opening chapter of Genesis, the narrative of creation. Both traditions are at one in recognizing in this chapter a major statement on the nature of man and his role in society. By the same token, the opening chapter of Genesis, both in its literal form and as interpreted by later tradition, constitutes the single most important contribution of the Hebrew ethos to a theory of natural law.

That the Bible is not a textbook in science is generally recognized, except in fundamentalist circles, today a numerically significant exception. Genesis is not intended to teach twentieth-century man astronomy, geology, and biology, let alone astrophysics or biogenetics. But while Genesis is not contemporary science for us, its importance for the history of science should not be overlooked. Actually, the Creation narrative in Genesis rests upon a profound scientific insight. It is true that the ancient Hebrews, unlike the Greeks, evinced no outstanding talent for scientific thought. Yet incredibly, it was Genesis rather than the Greek philosophers and scientists who arrived at the concept of a uni-verse created by one Will and hence governed by laws of nature universally applicable.

Generally high tribute has been paid to the Creation story for its literary qualities. The Latin writer Longinus, in his treatise *On the Sublime,* cited the first chapter of Genesis as a supreme example of sublimity in literature, a judgment that has been echoed through the centuries.

Nevertheless, neither the literary greatness of the Creation narrative nor its profound scientific insight is as significant as its basic affirmations. More precisely, the literary power of Genesis is the instrument for the transmission of its truths. To be sure, the Creation narrative seeks to buttress its insights by utilizing the scientific knowledge of its own day, but the conclusions are impervious to the shifting sands of scientific theory. Their religious and ethical validity does not depend upon the doctrine of a special creation in six days, which was entirely plausible to the ancients, nor are they impugned by the modern view of evolution, going on for aeons, which commends itself to us today and which will undoubtedly undergo modification in the future. In fact, if all the rest of the Bible were to be lost, it would be possible to reconstruct the fundamentals of religion and ethics from the opening chapter of Genesis.

The religious truths in Genesis are explicit in the biblical text itself. The basic religious affirmations of Genesis may be set down in six propositions, basic truths, axioms, or acts of faith, call them what we may:

1. *The world has a plan and a purpose known only to God.* "In the beginning God created heaven and earth" (v. 1). The world is the handiwork of one God who created the world in accordance with His will. The universe is not an accidental concatenation of atoms or sub-atomic particles, the result of a fortuitous "big bang" in outer space. Whatever the process involved, the world is the product of a Divine Intelligence which we call God, working out a plan and purpose. The world is cosmos, not chaos.

Regarding that purpose, men can only speculate, but the order and rationality of nature, from the microcosm of the atom to the macrocosm of outer-space systems, testify to the existence of a plan. The medieval philosopher Maimonides declared that the purpose of God's plan was beyond men's power to fathom. Supreme Court Justice Oliver Wendell Homes used a military metaphor: "We are soldiers in a great campaign, even if we are not privy to the battle-plan."

This inability to discover the Divine purpose is the root of the metaphysical *Angst* of the biblical thinker Ecclesiastes. He was deeply distressed at man's inability to fathom the purpose of creation, but he did not waver in his conviction that such a purpose existed.

"He has made everything beautiful in its proper time, and also put the love of the world into man's heart, yet so that he cannot find out what God has done from beginning to end" (Eccles. 3:11; see also 7:14; 8:7, 17; 11:5).

Most religious spirits have found contentment and serenity in the conviction that a beneficent Will is at work in the world, though hidden from men. But whether these limitations on man's knowledge are congenial or not, the sense of a cosmic plan and purpose remains the foundation for a religious worldview.

2. *All life is holy, integral to the Divine order of creation.* "So God created the great sea monsters and every living creature that moves, with which the waters swarm, according to their kinds, and every winged bird according to its kind. And God saw that it was good. And God blessed them, saying, 'Be fruitful and multiply and fill the waters in the seas, and let birds multiply on the earth' " (vv. 21–22). The process of creation underscores the unity and holiness of all life, for the Creator blessed the so-called lower orders of creation in words identical with the benediction pronounced upon the human race in verse 28, cited below.

One of the ethical consequences of this insight into our unity with the animal world is the horror at inflicting unnecessary pain upon them. At the one end of the spectrum is the prevention of cruelty to animals, for which the rabbis coined the poignant phrase, "the pain of living creatures." At the other end of the spectrum is the doctrine of vegetarianism, the avoidance of the use of animals for food. Though espoused by a small minority, vegetarianism has excellent biblical warrant in its favor. In verse 29, God permits only the eating of fruits and vegetables. Not until Noah emerges from the Ark after the Flood are he and his descendants allowed to eat meat, with the proviso that blood is not to be ingested (Gen. 9:8–9). The pouring out of the blood after the slaughter of an animal for food is enjoined by biblical law (Lev. 17:13–14), since blood is the seat of life. The act constitutes a symbolic sacrifice, a recognition that all life is sacred.

3. *Men and women are equal in God's plan.* "God created the human being *[ha'adam]* in His image, in the image of God He created him, male and female did He create them" (v. 29). For generations men read the words, but remained blind to their clear intent. Not the male alone, but the female as well, is fashioned in the Divine image. The Hebrew *'adam* does not mean "male," but "human being." The terms for "male" are *'ish* and *gebher*.

Every human being is endowed with the gifts of the spirit that make him, in the words of the Eighth Psalm, "little lower than God." If both sexes are equally sacred, they are—or should be—equal in status.

4. *Every human being is fashioned "in the Divine image."* There is no richer metaphor in literature than "the image of God." Its interpretations through the centuries have been legion. Earlier thinkers referred it to the immortality of the soul or to man's power to rule over animal creation. It has been equated with the striving for justice or with the quest for truth. Some have related it to the presence in man of a conscience, a monitor of his actions. Others have called attention to man's faculty of consciousness, his awareness of self. Man, it has been pointed out, is the only creature that can laugh and cry, that possesses a sense of time and a knowledge of his mortality.

That the phrase is a metaphor is clear from the earliest—and the greatest—commentary ever written on the opening chapter of Genesis. The anonymous genius who wrote the Eighth Psalm was seeing the beauty and majesty of the heavens and was overcome by the paradox of man's nature—physically insignificant, but spiritually God-like. Recalling the words of Genesis, he wrote:

> What is man that You are mindful of him,
>   and the son of man that You care for him?
> You have made him little less than God,
>   and have crowned him with glory and honor.
> You have given him dominion over the works of Your hands;

You have put all things under his feet,
All sheep and oxen
   and also the beasts of the field,
the birds of the air, and the fish of the sea,
   whatever passes along the paths of the sea,
O Lord our Lord,
   how majestic is Your name in all the earth!

(Ps. 8:4–10)

The relation of an image to the original suggests the basic intent of the metaphor. Man is endowed on a small scale with the attributes which God possesses in their plenitude. For us they are preeminently the power of reason, the freedom to choose, and the capacity to create. But however the phrase is interpreted, the "image of God" is the plus in man, over and beyond all other living creatures with whom he is otherwise linked in countless ways. The Divine image is the patent of human dignity and infinite value.

The marvels of space exploration have, thus far at least, not succeeded in discovering another being to challenge the uniqueness of man in the cosmos.

5. *Man is the responsible ruler of the created world.* "God blessed them, and God said to them, 'Be fruitful and multiply, and fill the earth and subdue it; and have dominion over the fish of the sea and over the birds of the air and over every living thing that moves upon the earth' " (v. 21). Man's special position in the cosmos endows him with special responsibilities, both to his own species and to all living creatures. He has an obligation to preserve the life with which he has been endowed and so to order his society that it promotes the life and well-being of its members. His dominion over the earth and its inhabitants is not a license to destroy, but a responsibility to conserve the earth and its inhabitants, that which God has created.

To read into this passage permission for man to ride roughshod over other living creatures or to despoil the earth of its treasures, or to pollute air and water, is to pervert the glory of creation that is clearly indicated in the closing verse, 31.

The meaning of man's mastery of creation is spelled out in the second chapter of Genesis. Man is placed in the Garden of Eden with the explicit mandate *l'ovdah unleshomrah,* which the New English Bible renders properly, "to till it and to care for it." Possessing a superior endowment, man is empowered to be not a ruthless tyrant, but a responsible ruler of the world of nature.

6. *The world is good.* "God saw everything that He had made, and behold, it was very good" (v. 31). Here the basic judgment on creation—

"God saw that it was good"—which is repeated on each day of creation (vv. 3, 10, 12, 18, 21, and 25) reaches its triumphant climax. The Hebrew phrase *tobh me'od,* "very good," is also read by the ancient rabbis as *tobh mot,* "even death is good." It is an affirmation that in spite of all the tragedies and frustrations in human experience, the world is good, and life is a blessing.

Later generations, confronted by massive difficulties, were not always able to sustain so optimistic a view of life and the world. The Talmud (*B. Erubin* 13b) informs us that for two and a half years a controversy on the value of life persisted between two schools of rabbis. The School of Shammai maintained, "Better for man not to have been created than to have been created." The contrary view was upheld by the School of Hillel, who declared, "Better for man to have been created than not to have been created." The darker view of Shammai prevailed, but with a characteristic ethical addition: "The decision was 'Better for man not to have been created, but now that he has been, let him carefully examine his actions."

The biblical and the rabbinic views are not irreconcilable. It is man who has perverted creation. The world is good; man often is not. His duty is to guard against the evils of cruelty, greed, and indolence. Thus he can help redeem the world and restore it to its pristine goodness and beauty.

A close reading of the biblical text thus makes it clear that we have here a classic presentation of the basic affirmations of religion. However, the Hebrew ethos was not satisfied to stop at this level of interpretation. Rabbinic Judaism found, in the opening chapter of Genesis, a series of ethical postulates, which, as will be demonstrated below, constitute a charter of man's rights and responsibilities, in effect, an all-inclusive ethical code.

A passage in the Mishnah which deals with the cross-examination of witnesses in capital cases introduces a homily designed to impress them with the transcendental importance of telling the truth. The text of this injunction, at once naive and profound, deserves to be quoted in full.

(1) Mankind was created through Adam alone to teach that whoever destroys a single human life is regarded as though he destroyed an entire world, and he who saves a single human life is as though he saved an entire world.

(2) The human race began with a single individual for the sake of peace among all men, so that no man might say, "My ancestor is greater than yours."

(3) The beginning of the human race with Adam also makes it impossible for heretics to say, "There are many heavenly powers."

(4) Moreover, the creation of humanity through one ancestor proclaims the greatness of the Holy One, blessed be He. For a human mint-master strikes off many coins from a single mold and they are all identical. But the King of Kings, the Holy One, blessed be He, stamps each man in the mold of Adam, and yet no one is identical with his fellow.

(5) Finally, the creation of Adam teaches that each human being is obliged to declare, "For my sake was the world created."

(M. Sanhedrin 4:5)

An ancient supplemental rabbinic work, the Tosefta (*Sanhedrin* 8:3), which is contemporaneous with the Mishnah, adds another significant inference from the creation of Adam.

(6) Mankind has a single ancestor so that no sinner may say, "I am a sinner by inheritance, being a descendant of sinners," and no saint may say, "I am a saint by virtue of my descent from saints."

A brief comment on section 3 of this Mishnah is in order. In the period of the Mishnah, polytheism, the belief in a plurality of gods, was all but universal. Less widespread, but important nevertheless, was the doctrine of dualism—that there were two cosmic powers in the world, one good and one evil. This view was espoused by Zoroastrianism, Manichaeism, and all the varieties of Gnosticism. It had considerable attraction for some mystical circles in Judaism and Christianity as well.

This basically theological section aside, the passage sets forth all the fundamentals of man's role in the world, his rights and his obligations derived from his God-given nature. Indeed, it would be possible to extrapolate from these few lines the entire ethical system of Judaism.

It should be noted that the structure of the passage is the key to the understanding of its contents. Section 1, which proclaims the dignity of every human being, is the basis for section 4, which establishes man's right to freedom—basically the right to be different from others. Section 2, which enunciates the equality of all people, is the foundation for section 5, which sets forth the right of every human being to share in the blessings of the world that God created and pronounced good. *In sum, the inherent dignity of all men is the source of their inalienable right to liberty, and their innate equality is the basis for their claim to justice.*

Some important observations on the Mishnah's teaching on freedom and on justice need to be spelled out. The differences among men are God-given and hence not superficial or unimportant. They are not the artificial invention of priests or tyrants or the products of the corruption by civilization of the original innocence of the human race, as some eighteenth-century thinkers believed. Nor are these distinctions among men an unfortunate aspect of human nature with which society must struggle and which it would be better to eliminate. The ancient sages saw more truly into human nature when they recognized the physical and spiritual differences among men as God-given, innate, integral features of personality. In other words, human differences are not merely legitimate, but, when properly utilized and expressed, they are valuable resources for the enrichment of human life and culture.

The right to justice inheres in all men, whatever their ethnic origin or racial character. The right and the duty to enjoy God's world and its blessings are inalienable, having been conferred upon them by God and not by the state or a social contract. Hence, these rights, which should be enforced and protected by a just government, cannot be abrogated by human fiat.

The final section, added from the Tosefta, underscores man's moral freedom and responsibility. It declares that men cannot take refuge in their heredity, either to arrogate superior virtues to themselves or to excuse major vices. Determinism, whether theological or scientific, cannot overturn the indispensable principle that human beings are accountable for their actions. Only this axiom makes possible a viable society, resting on individual responsibility, without which the world returns to chaos. The medievals sought to blame their shortcomings on the stars; moderns seek to attribute them to their genes. Both are mistaken.

Thus the first chapter of Genesis, standing majestically at the opening of the Book of Books, sets forth the fundamentals of belief and the essentials of conduct for humanity. Within this brief campass, we have the Alpha and Omega of a moral code so desperately needed today.

Part IV

Challenges to Faith or Morals

Chapter 8

A Cruel God or None: The Challenge of the Holocaust

IT HAS BEEN a major thesis of this volume that neither science nor religion, though indispensable enterprises of the human spirit, can supply the rationale for a moral system in our day. Instead, it has been suggested that natural law can provide the basis for a viable ethical system when it is properly comprehended and interpreted and enriched by the insights and attitudes of the Judaic ethos. If natural law is to avoid the pitfalls that have brought it into disrepute in the modern age, it must rest upon two pillars: the Greco-Roman on the one hand, the Judaic on the other.

Among the advantages of natural law in a secular age is its freedom from entanglements with specific creeds and dogmas, concerning which many differ and others disbelieve. Nevertheless, it has been indicated that natural law is not free from basic assumptions, just as Euclidean geometry, for all its rigorous logic, begins with axioms and postulates. Natural law does rest upon a faith in the rationality of the universe and the constants of human nature, both deriving from a Supreme Being who is Creator and Ruler of man and the world.

This faith was never easy to maintain; today, in the cruelest of centuries, millions of men and women find it totally impossible to believe in a rational world and a just and puissant God. As we have noted, natural law has had its passionate advocates and equally convinced opponents in the past, but never more so than in the present. Before proceeding to explore the specific contributions to natural law that may be derived from the Hebraic tradition, it therefore behooves us to deal with three challenges to the basic faith underlying natural law.

Though the objections vary in importance and in the number of their adherents, each one poses a threat to the philosophical foundations upon which a viable moral code for our day must rest.

We shall first concern ourselves with the challenge to faith posed by the most massive and abominable event in the long, dark history of human cruelty, the Holocaust. The agonizing dilemma which Augustine put in simple terms has been burned into the heart and flesh of tens of millions of human beings brutally done to death and many millions more who survived: "If God can remove evil and does not, He is not good; if He cannot, He is not powerful." In a world where Hitler held sway for half a decade, and his poisonous legacy has survived for half a century, untold numbers of men and women have discarded the faith by which they had lived, and now echo Macbeth's view of life as "a tale told by an idiot, full of sound and fury, signifying nothing." But ethical nihilism can lead only to catastrophe. By exploring the implications of the Holocaust, we may discover, not a solution, but an approach to the Holocaust which can enable men and women to face it and rise above it.

In the following chapter we shall analyze a familiar phenomenon of our day, the rise of fundamentalism, which ostensibly came into being in order to buttress ethical living, but actually has debased it. The fundamentalism, both Christian and Jewish, which has made its greatest progress in the United States is surely not to be identified with the Muslim fundamentalism in Iran, Lebanon, or Saudi Arabia. Nevertheless it has sanctioned, where it did not spearhead, the decay of ethics in our day.

Finally, we shall address ourselves to a threat to the ethical enterprise from an unexpected quarter, the teaching of the Danish theologian Søren Kierkegaard. Though he lived in the nineteenth century, he became highly influential in the twentieth, when the flight from reason and the distrust of man's capacity to solve his problems by his intelligence and activity have impelled many men and women to discard social action in favor of "putting their faith in God."

Kierkegaard maintained that religious faith in God is independent of ethics, and that at its highest, faith is free to disregard the imperatives of ethics. Taking the patriarch Abraham, whom he called the "knight of faith," as his model, Kierkegaard found an apparently unimpeachable source for his theory of the teleological suspension of the ethical. Our analysis will demonstrate, I believe, that his view rests upon a misreading of the biblical text and is neither biblically nor philosophically tenable.

We now turn to what is unquestionably the greatest stumbling block to religion, the problem of evil, traditionally expressed as "the suffering of the righteous and the prosperity of the wicked." Throughout the ages sensitive and suffering human beings found the testimony of tradition being challenged by the evidence of experience.

The dialectic between faith and doubt finds poignant expression in the literature of Sumer, Babylonia, and Egypt, centuries before the Bible. However, it is the Bible, the most magnificent testament of faith in God, that contains the most powerful confrontations with God. The lawgiver, historian, sage, and psalmist, all the biblical "men of faith," do not hesitate to demand that their God abide by the standard of righteousness they derive from Him. Abraham, who would stake his entire existence on obedience to the Divine command, asked, "Shall not the Judge of all the earth do justice?" (Gen. 18:25). Jeremiah, who sacrificed his personal well-being on the altar of his prophetic calling, bitterly cried out:

> You will emerge victorious, O Lord, if I challenge You,
> But I shall present my charge against You.
> Why does the way of the wicked prosper and the
> treacherous are at ease?
>
> (Jer. 12:1)

The righteous Job, who had been stripped of family, wealth, health, and honor, affirms his innocence, and castigates his Maker with equal passion:

> If it be a matter of power, He is strongest.
> But if of justice, who will arraign Him? . . .
> I am blameless, I am beside myself, I loathe my life.
> It is all one, I say—
> The blameless and the wicked, He destroys alike—
> The land is given over to the hand of the evildoer,
> Who is able to bribe the judges.
> If not He, who then is guilty?
>
> (Job 9:19, 21–22, 24)

In a low key, but all the more devastating on that account, is the judgment of the biblical thinker, Koheleth.

For the fate of men and the fate of beasts is the same.
As the one dies, so does the other, there is one spirit in both.
Man's distinction over the beast is nothing, for everything is vanity.
All go to the same place, all come from the dust and return to the
dust.

Who knows whether the spirit of man rises up or that the spirit of
the beast goes down to the earth? . . .
Again I saw all the acts of oppression that are done under the sun.
Here are the tears of the oppressed, with none to comfort them, and
power is in the hands of their oppressors, with none to avenge
them.
So I praise the dead who already have died, more than the creatures
who are still alive.
And more fortunate than both is he who has not yet been born,
Who has never seen the evil deeds that are being done under the
sun.

(Eccles. 3:19–21, 4:1–3)

It is a tragic fact of life that all men are born for trouble and no nation
goes through life unscathed. Nevertheless, no other religious or ethnic
group has been exposed to oppression and cruelty on so large a scale
and for so long a time as the Jewish people. Its history reveals two major
and opposing responses to mass cruelty and persecution which emerge
in every period of major crisis.

For some, the suffering is seen as a mark of Divine favor, God calling
them to repentance and deeper piety. This type of human behavior is
clearly evident following all the great catastrophes of Jewish history.
After the destruction of the Second Temple (70 c.e.), the expulsion of the
Jews from Spain and Portugal (1492–97), the debacle of the pseudo-
Messianic movement of Shabbetai Zevi, and the Chmielnicki massacres
(1648–49)—after each calamity there was an upsurge of piety, mysticism, and asceticism. The results are written large in Jewish literature,
religion, and history. The same law—the rise of pietism after catastrophe—is operative in our age as well.

For many others, however, tragedy induced varying degrees of rebellion and defection rather than submission and renewed loyalty. Alienation, disbelief, formal conversion, at times self-hatred and hatred of
one's background were some of the negative reactions to major disaster.

It is the melancholy distinction of our age to have been witness—and
participant—to the greatest horror of all time, a horror that the most
vicious of psychopathic criminals could not have conceived. For this
descent into hell, a new term, "genocide," had to be invented. Jews
were far from being the only victims; Nazism brought in its wake the
destruction of twenty million men, women, and children, belonging to a
dozen nationalities and religions. But in the case of the Jewish people,
there was a horribly unique element—the clearly articulated goal of the
"final solution"—the total elimination of Jews from the face of the earth.
The dimensions of the destruction that Hitler achieved were staggering.
Six out of every seven Jews alive in Europe at the beginning of the Nazi

movement were dead at its collapse. Six million men, women, and children had been cruelly done to death with fiendish scientific efficiency.

For many victims of the Holocaust and for the survivors who experienced Nazi bestiality at first hand, it seemed clear that the Holocaust represented a totally new dimension of evil, a demonic force without parallel in the past. Many thinkers of opposing schools, both those who seek to uphold faith in the God of traditional religion, as well as those who declare that the faith can no longer be sustained, are in agreement on the unique character of the Holocaust. They insist that the Nazi campaign of mass murder cannot be categorized as merely another instance of man's propensity for evil, differing only in degree, but not in kind, from the wars and massacres that have disfigured human history through the ages. On the contrary, we are told, the technological processes of destruction utilized by Hitler, from his sophisticated techniques of propaganda to the efficiency of the gas chambers and the ovens in the crematoria, set the Nazi Holocaust totally apart from any other event in history.

Here is where the consensus ends. Beyond this point, a variety of responses to the Holocaust have been proposed. Many "traditional" spokesmen for religion offer a "defense" of God that is nothing less than blasphemous. They maintain that the Holocaust presents no theological problem at all, since it is a clear illustration of the working of the principle of Divine retribution. The massive sins of our age, its immorality and impiety, its neglect of the Torah and disregard of the *mitzvot*, have brought on condign punishment in the form of the Nazi butchery. What is called for, therefore, is repentance, a sincere plea for God's forgiveness, a return to the ways of the fathers, evidenced by fervent observance of all the minutiae of the ritual.

Though maintained by some highly influential religious leaders, this defense of God must be pronounced a major offense to Him. The thousands upon thousands of shootings, burnings, and poisonings by the Nazi beasts—what sins could conceivably have been committed of equal magnitude? Moreover, the death of hundreds of thousands of children recalls the unforgettable conclusion in the Book of Jonah when God rebukes the prophet and reminds him: "You pity the plant, for which you did not labor, nor did you make it grow, which came into being in a night, and perished in a night. And should I not pity Nineveh, that great city, in which there are more than a hundred and twenty thousand persons who do not know their right hand from their left, and also much cattle?" (Jon. 4:9–11).

Even in "religious" circles this "answer" has convinced only a few, and tends to be repeated only in the most fundamentalist circles.

A less obnoxious response falls back upon a theological doctrine to be found in some earlier eras both in Christianity and in Judaism, known as *Deus absconditus*, "the concealed God," in Christian thought, and as *hester panim*, "the hiding of God's face," in Jewish mysticism. For reasons unknown, the argument runs, God hid Himself from the world during the bloody years of Nazi activity, leaving these savages free to work their will. Actually, this doctrine is of very little help, for it lets the original question still stand: Why did God permit this monstrous evil to be inflicted upon so many millions of His innocent children? This approach shields God from evil, but it isolates Him from the world.

A third response, couched in varying forms, makes no effort to answer the problem, and adopts a stance of faith in the face of the unknown. With consummate artistry and deep sincerity, Elie Wiesel has continued to confront his God, asking the question "Why?" but never articulating a response. The contemporary philosopher Emil Fackenheim is the author of the famous call to Jews to fight and live on: "We must not give Hitler a posthumous victory." But eloquent as these words are, they are a slogan, not a program, and surely not a solution.

Finally, another response is heard, one possessing tremendous emotional impact. Beginning with the contention that Nazism represents a radical dimension of evil, a demonic force, proponents of this view insist that Nazism and the Holocaust are not to be explained by cause and effect, and are therefore not susceptible to analysis and prevention. The Holocaust has laid bare the dark viciousness of the human soul, always present but now unleashed. Before this ultimate darkness, we can only stand in fear and trembling; we are helpless.

Because of the deep emotions involved, it is easy to understand why such an approach would resonate among those who suffered in their own persons or in those of their loved ones or were close witnesses of the Nazi horror in action. From where they stand, to try to offer an analysis of the causes of Nazism and to study its operation means to "trivialize" the Holocaust. To recall the tens of millions of non-Jewish victims of Nazism means to "universalize" it and rob it of its poignancy and depth. To call attention to earlier efforts to exterminate a people, such as the Turkish massacre of the Armenians in World War I and Haman's decree of extermination of all Jews throughout the Persian empire, described in the Book of Esther—such efforts are stigmatized as attempts, well-meaning or otherwise, to demean the victims of Nazism by diminishing their tragedy.

One possible consequence of the demonic theory of Nazism is expressed with incomparable power by the American-Jewish theologian Richard Rubenstein, whose *cri de coeur* must find an echo in every sensitive heart. He is driven by the monstrosity of Nazism not only to reject with justified scorn the blasphemy inherent in the "explanation"

offered by some "traditionalists" that the Holocaust is God's just punishment for an evil generation. He goes much further and insists that
there is only one possible alternative. Modern man must conclude that
"the belief in God as the Lord of history must be rejected." Rubenstein
believes passionately that "Jewish paganism is the most viable religious
option available to contemporary Jews." He urges Christians as well as
Jews to adopt "non-theistic forms of religion often based on ancient
pagan or Asian models." He himself opts for the "ancient earth gods
and the realities to which they point," because they alone offer men the
opportunity to "celebrate" what he, following in the footsteps of Sartre,
Camus, and Genet, regards as the human condition "entirely enclosed
within the fatalities of an absurd earthly existence." In brief, modern
man has only two choices—either a cruel God or none. For Rubenstein
there is no God and Israel is His witness.

The response to reactions such as this, even those less extreme in
formulation, must, it seems to me, be expressed on two levels simultaneously—they are psychologically comprehensible but rationally untenable.

One can understand this reaction without accepting its conclusions. It
would be unfeeling to demand that those who sit in dust and ashes
mourning their loved ones embark upon an objective analysis of Nazism, its causes and effects. When a young mother finds her infant child
strangled in its crib, it would be both callous and stupid to offer to
console her by calling attention to the statistics indicating that only a tiny
percentage of babies die because of crib-deaths. For her, the entire
universe has been blacked out, and life has lost all meaning, until she
begins to pass beyond the early, acute phases of grief. But it would be a
grave disservice to all mothers, including the young mourner, if physi-
cians did not undertake to study the etiology of crib-death and seek to
discover techniques for alleviating and conquering it.

Ours is a law-abiding universe. Even the Nazi movement had its
causes, social, economic, political, psychological, religious, some reaching back over centuries, others of more recent origin. To seek to unravel
the complex of evil and analyze its sources is not only an intellectual
imperative, it is a moral and practical obligation of the highest importance, so that we may take the necessary steps to prevent a repetition of
this horror.

I would suggest that such a rational approach to the Nazi horror is, in
fact, far superior to the newly packaged religions that "celebrate" the
"absurdity" of human existence. As is so often the case, it is necessary to
rescue the religious tradition from the hands of its official defenders.

Though one hesitates to do so, it must be pointed out that a peculiar form of moral blindness inheres in the "demonic" theory of the Holocaust, the assumption of the radical character of its evil. At which point does a sin become monstrous; at six million victims or at five million, or three or one? Is it not true that the suffering and death of a single child is an infinite calamity before the throne of mercy? Are the conventional theologians, therefore, wrong in regarding the Nazi Holocaust as morally on a par with the mass deaths perpetrated by the builders of the Egyptian pyramids, the palaces of Babylon, or the roads and bridges of the Roman Empire? Do Dachau and Auschwitz and Bergen-Belsen differ in quality from the massacres of the Crusades and of Chmielnicki, the tortures of the Inquisition, the pogroms of Czarist Russia? What about the conscious and systematic starvation of millions in the early years of Soviet Russia and Communist China, or the thousands of deaths in Biafra and in Bangladesh? Is a statistical yardstick to be employed in determining the dimensions of human suffering and the challenge it poses to faith in God?

If, on the other hand, the problem does not arise for the first time with twentieth-century Nazism, we have a moral and intellectual duty to examine the insights at which men arrived in earlier periods of agony and wrath.

I suggest that there are five biblical ideas which modern men, like their predecessors, may draw upon in constructing a view of human life and destiny capable of sustaining them in the face of the evils of existence, including even the monstrosity of Nazism. These fundamental insights, set down here in bare outline, need to be felt as well as understood in order to come alive.

1. *The glory of life and the goodness of God.* This basic principle of Jewish theology has become familiar to many moderns in the presentations of Hasidism offered by Martin Buber in the previous generation and by Elie Wiesel in ours. Unfortunately, these brilliant reinterpretations of Hasidism are highly personal. Thus, Elie Wiesel declares, "Man owes it to himself to reject despair. . . . There is no alternative. *One must impose a meaning on what perhaps has none and draw ecstasy from nameless, faceless pain*" (emphasis added).

However comprehensible such an approach may be, it would not have been shared by the great examplars of traditional religion, whether they were rationalists or mystics, philosophers or saints. Neither they nor their disciples would have agreed that they were imposing a meaning on life *where there was none.* The biblical skeptic Koheleth has sometimes been described as reflecting an existentialist outlook, but this is an error. He denied that his more traditionally minded contemporaries, the priest, the prophet, and the Wisdom teacher, "knew" the "answer" to the meaning of existence, but he did not maintain that there was no meaning to life. "Everything He has made proper in its due time, and He has also placed a love of the world in men's hearts, except that they may not discover the work God has done from beginning to end" (Eccles. 3:11).

The medieval philosopher Maimonides similarly maintained that the purpose of creation was veiled from man, but he did not deny that it existed. The triumphant affirmation of life in the face of all evil goes back to the opening chapter of Genesis: "God saw all that He had made and behold, it was very good." As we have noted above, the rabbis used a wordplay on the Hebrew phrase *tobh me'od*, "very good," pronounced as *tobh mot*, to emphasize that even death is part of the life process and therefore good.

The psalmists were no Pollyannas; when they praised God, it was because they had descended to the depths.

> O Lord, You brought me up from Sheol,
> You preserved me from going down to the Pit.
> Sing praises to the Lord, O you his saints,
> and give thanks to His holy name
> For His anger is but for a moment,
> and His favor for a lifetime.
> Weeping may tarry for the night,
> but joy comes with the morning.
>
> (Ps. 30:4–6)

The most familiar of the psalms, the Twenty-third, has been woefully misunderstood. It is not the faith of a child who has experienced no suffering, but the strong faith of one who has walked in the valley of the shadow of death and taught himself to fear no evil.

> Though I walk through the valley of darkness,
> I fear no evil, for You are with me;
> Your rod and Your staff, they comfort me.
> You have prepared a table before me in the presence of my enemies;
> You anoint my head with oil, my cup overflows.
> Surely goodness and mercy shall follow me all the days of my life;
> and I shall dwell in the house of the Lord forever.
>
> (Ps. 23:4–6)

Out of the crucible of suffering, the poet has forged his faith.

> Though the wicked sprout like grass,
> And all the workers of iniquity flourish,
> They are doomed to destruction forever.
>
> (Ps. 92:8)

The evil in the world challenges the glory of life; it cannot blot it out.

2. *Man's right and duty to confront evil in the world.* Biblical faith does not interpret man's cruelty, which reaches its apex in the Holocaust, as a "punitive visitation" by God that must be borne in submission. Far from accepting evil in the world, Jewish religious thought challenges God and demands His adherence to the moral law. Many of the most moving tales in Hasidic lore picture Rabbi Levi Yizhak of Berditchev confronting God in the name of his suffering, poverty-stricken brothers and demanding justice for them.

Here, too, the roots are centuries older than Hasidism. The Book of Job is a deeply moving protest against the injustice visited upon God's creatures. The final judgment of the book is not that Job is wrong or blasphemous in challenging his Maker. On the contrary, it is the conventional defenders of God who stand in need of forgiveness: "For you have not spoken the truth about Me, as has My servant Job" (42:7). In a striking ironic utterance, God declares that it is Job who must plead that his antagonists be forgiven.

The Hebrew prophets were not only God's spokesmen to men but men's champions challenging God. Not quietism but valiant action is the dominant theme of the Hebrew Bible. The Puritans demonstrated that they were in truth Old Testament Christians when they declared, "Rebellion to tyrants is obedience to God."

3. *The core of mystery in evil.* To be sure, biblical and postbiblical thinkers offer many positive answers to the problem of evil, of greater or lesser plausibility. We are reminded of a truth easily forgotten, that evil is not always triumphant—that, on the contrary, wickedness often does bring disaster in its wake. The psalmists underscore the need for men's patience and faith, because the process of retribution is slower at times than we would wish, often extending over generations. Experience teaches, too, that suffering may turn out to be a blessing in disguise.

Yet no matter how valid these insights may be, the presence of the Book of Job, the profoundest work in the Bible, has always prevented the acceptance of these conventional, man-made answers as final and complete explanations. Job prevents men from forgetting that a core of mystery in evil remains. In the words of Rabbi Yannai in the *Ethics of the Fathers*, "We do not know the reason either for the suffering of the righteous or the prosperity of the wicked"—or for the death of a child or the devastation of an earthquake. The disastrous Lisbon earthquake of 1755 led to Voltaire's brilliant novella *Candide*, which satirized Leibniz's philosophical optimism then fashionable. But Voltaire's masterpiece did not reckon with the profound insight of biblical religion that, after all the legitimate explanations are advanced, an irreducible element of mystery still inheres in the world. Voltaire urged his readers, "Let us cultivate our own gardens." While the "tough-minded" in every age are willing to follow the sage Ben-Sira's advice, given nineteen centuries earlier, to "have no concern with mysteries," the "tender-minded," as William James called them, continue to confront the perennial issues of existence in which the mystery of evil is central.

But the Book of Job goes beyond the position of *ignoramus*, "We do not know." Granted that a total answer to the problem of evil is denied us, yet a basic response is available in the "Speeches of the Lord" (chaps. 38–41), expressed, not explicitly, but by implication. The poet presents a triumphant affirmation of the glory of the natural order often transcending human standards of beauty. He thus suggests persuasively that the moral order also has pattern and meaning, even when it is veiled from men, for both aspects of reality are the creation of the One God, who is both Lord of nature and God of history. These Speeches of the Lord Out of the Whirlwind do not demand mere submission to God on the ground that man's understanding of the natural world is limited. With power and passion, they call for recognition of the reality of a pattern in the moral sphere as well. As against bitter atheism or sad agnosticism, Job offers a reasonable and hopeful faith in the structure of the world and human experience. Within this larger framework supplied by Job, more specific insights are to be found in the biblical books of Genesis, Deuteronomy, and Isaiah.

4. *Man's freedom.* Basic to the biblical view of man is the conviction, stated three times in the Book of Deuteronomy and implicit everywhere else, that man is morally free: "Behold, I place before you this day life and the good, death and evil" (Deut. 30:15). Every individual, every generation, every nation, every society is endowed with this fateful and perilous privilege of freedom in the moral sphere. It has been the great achievement of modern science, of biology, psychology, economics, sociology, and other disciplines, to reveal the pressures and limitations to which man is subjected by virtue of his biological constitution, his sexual drives, his economic needs, his cultural background. But as all human experience demonstrates, no man is wholly *determined* by these factors—even the degree to which he is *conditioned* by them differs with each individual.

That man is morally free is reaffirmed by the talmudic statement "Everything is in the hands of God except the fear of God" (*Berakhot* 33b). The basis for this conviction lies in the biblical doctrine in Genesis that man is created "in the image of God." As we have seen above, this profound metaphor, the implications of which are far-reaching, declares that man partakes, on a small and imperfect scale, of the preeminent attributes of God. The "image" has been identified variously with the gift of immortality, the capacity for love, the love of righteousness, the power of creation. Above all, it has been interpreted as the power of reason. Now, what is reason in the intellectual sphere is freedom of will in the moral arena, and this, in turn, is the basis for responsibility in the social arena. For without freedom there is no possibility of holding anyone responsible for his actions, and the fabric of society must dissolve into anarchy.

Since man, unlike any other creature known to us, has been endowed with the fateful power of freedom of choice, he can, and all too often does, choose evil, including the monstrous evil of Nazism. The freedom of man is not only indispensable to religion—without it no society can long endure. The major ills afflicting human life—war, poverty, and, in large measure, disease—are not the will of God but the act of man, the bitter fruits of the freedom he has abused. Consequently, not God, but man, can stamp them out by the exercise of intelligence and the moral will.

But even if the reality of man's freedom—and man's responsibility—is granted, an excruciating question remains. Why is it possible for some men to sin—and cause others to suffer? The agonizing cry, "Why do the wicked prosper and the righteous suffer?" will continue to reverberate as long as men live. Here, too, we have no total answer, but some light may be found in an insight of the unknown prophet of the Babylonian Exile, whose words are embedded in the Book of Isaiah. Basic to his worldview, but permeating biblical and rabbinic thought as a whole, is the concept of the interdependence of mankind.

5. *The interdependence of mankind* is no pleasant Sunday School platitude, but a realistic assessment of the human condition. The rabbis were once asked to cite the greatest verse in the Bible. As might be expected, one, Rabbi Akiba, quoted the Golden Rule in Leviticus (19:18), "You shall love your neighbor as yourself." The other, Ben-Azzai, more surprisingly, cited the prosaic opening verse of the genealogies in Genesis (5:1), "This is the book of the generations of Adam; in the day that God created Adam it was in the image of God that He created him" *(Sifra, Kedoshim)*. The verse embodies two fundamental truths about man—the dignity of each human being created in the Divine image, and the unity of all men derived from a single ancestor. The biblical lawgiver, prophet, and sage all emphasize the thought that the entire human race is a unit, both "horizontally," through space, and "vertically," through time. All the members of a single generation in space have a common destiny they cannot escape, and the various links in a family through time are also indissolubly joined together, both for good ("the merit of the fathers") and for ill ("the sins of the fathers upon the children").

There is one overriding difficulty involved in applying the idea of the interdependence of mankind to Nazism or even to lesser evils. Put in the simplest of terms, the question will be asked, Why is the punishment for evildoing not visited upon the evildoers? Why did the Nazis do evil and innocent men, women, and children suffer? Perhaps a simplistic parable may shed some light upon this agonizing question. Let us assume that a youngster who loves ice cream gorges himself with one cone after another until he develops a stomach ache. If the organs of the body could speak, the stomach might complain and say, "It was not I who sinned by overeating, but the palate that was guilty. Why should I pay the price for the palate's sin by suffering the pain?" The self-evident answer is that the stomach and the palate are not independent entities put parts of a larger organic whole. Each human being, particularly in an age when individualism has run riot, likes to think of himself as a discrete entity, an independent soul, sharply demarcated from all his fellows. The fact is, however, that by a thousand invisible threads, each human being is associated, for weal or woe, with the entire human race. He is organically linked in time with all the generations of his ancestors before him and his descendants after him. He is inescapably joined in space with all men and women who are his contemporaries. The wicked sin and the innocent suffer—that is a consequence of the interdependence of mankind.

The concept of the interdependence of the human race was not permitted to remain a pious abstraction. It became an indispensable weapon for survival in the critical period of the Babylonian Exile. After the burning of the First Temple and the destruction of the Jewish state, the exiled Jews not only sat weeping by the rivers of Babylon, but agonized over their tragic lot. Some lost heart and, deciding that "God is dead," were assimilated to the triumphal paganism all about them. Others, of sterner stuff, vigorously challenged the justice of God that made them lowly and oppressed aliens while the heathen conquerors ruled the world. In response to this situation, Deutero-Isaiah enunciated the doctrine that this uprooted and degraded people was the "Servant of the Lord." The prophet believed that Israel was suffering contumely and misery at the hands of the nations, not because of its sins, but because of its role in the world as the teacher and witness to God's law of justice, freedom, and peace. When the nations finally outgrew their moral immaturity and achieved insight and understanding, they would accept the Divine law of righteousness. On that day, they would cease to despise and attack Israel, and, on the contrary, would accord it a place of dignity and honor within the family of mankind.

It should be noted that, contrary to widespread opinion, the prophet is not enunciating the concept of vicarious atonement, which is a theological doctrine, but the reality of vicarious suffering, which is a fact of life, a datum of human experience that every mother, and indeed, every parent, knows at first hand. When one loves another human being, one is bound to suffer with and for the loved one.

Even when conscious love is absent—even when there is indifference or hatred—the fate of all men is inexorably intertwined, for we are all brothers in a merciless, as well as in a merciful, sense. As a graphic parable of the rabbis puts it, we are in the same boat and one man cannot bore a hole in it with the excuse that it is only under his own seat that he is making the hole.

That man's baleful actions take place on a more colossal scale today than in the past does not render the prophetic insight irrelevant. For each soul is of infinite worth and all human suffering is on an infinite scale, so that six thousand crucified by Alexander Jannaeus in the second century B.C.E. is qualitatively no less grievous than six million exterminated by Hitler, and no more heinous than three men nailed to a cross by the Romans.

When we become aware of the perilous nature of human freedom and of each man's interdependence and involvement with his fellows, and when we recognize the reality of vicarious suffering, we are no longer compelled to regard suffering as meaningless, life a horror, and the world an absurdity. It becomes possible, even in the most brutal of centuries, to believe that there is meaning and plan in the universe, even if it is far less neat and pleasant than we would wish.

To be sure, the horrors spawned by twentieth-century technological man are far more extensive than those of his medieval forebears or his ancient ancestors, but equally enlarged are his capacities for good. Perhaps the most important moral advance in the modern age is man's refusal to accept most forms of suffering as ineluctable elements of the human condition. Modern man denies that war is ineradicable, that poverty will always be with us, that racial injustice and social oppression are eternal. Perhaps the citadel of death cannot be razed, but disease can be controlled and minimized. As against the major sins of which modern man is guilty, we must set the major virtue of his refusal to acquiesce in evil as inevitable.

In the past, only the prophets of Israel had the vision and the faith to believe that war would cease, that poverty could be destroyed and oppression be uprooted. No matter how lacking our age may be in moral greatness, it has one distinction—for perhaps the first time in history, the conquest of poverty, the uprooting of oppression, and the elimination of war are regarded as entirely realizable goals. Since these objectives seem remote in the present, we blame the "enemy" on the other side for the evils of the day. The chaos and conflict, even the hostility and violence of our age, point, not to the absurdity of the human condition, but to its potential for good.

The faith that derives from the Bible recognizes that the Messianic Age of justice, freedom, and peace will not be ushered in without pain and destruction. The battle of Armaggedon remains the prelude to a new heaven and a new earth. The rabbis spoke of "the birth pangs of the Messiah." Some of them went so far as to say, "Let the Messiah come and I not be there to see him!" (*B. Sanhedrin* 98b). Nevertheless, the Messianic hope is basic, not only to religion, but to human life itself.

Undoubtedly, many men today, their spirits crushed by the world they see, will be unable to muster this confidence in the meaning of life. They will prefer one or another of the unfaiths that shock and fascinate so many of our contemporaries. But many others, who are neither enslaved by nostalgia for the past nor overwhelmed by the evils of the present, do not feel compelled to choose between a cruel God and none. The world is not a fool's paradise; it need not be a living hell. The human race has the capacity to build a home for its body and spirit upon this earth that will fulfill the purpose of a God, who "created it not for chaos but for habitation" (Isa. 45:13).

Chapter 9

The Revival of Religion and the Decay of Ethics

IN THE PRECEDING CHAPTER we have focused upon five fundamental biblical postulates that I believe are indispensable for an ethical philosophy of life for modern men and women. Unencumbered by the trappings of the specific religious traditions, they are accessible to devotees of all formal creeds and of none. Nonetheless, these ideas are undeniably religious—that is to say, they rest upon a faith in a Supreme Being whose power and goodness we can recognize as manifest in nature and in history, even when His ways are beyond our comprehension.

Paradoxical as it may seem, this nexus between religious belief and ethical conduct, or to use the traditional phrase, between faith and morals, is under attack from several quarters in the religious camp. The widespread loss of faith posed by the horrors of the Holocaust has already been treated. The striking phenomenon of the return to religion by born-again Christians and by Jewish *ba'alei teshuvah*, "penitents" or "returnees," will be discussed in this chapter. Another and more recondite challenge to the centrality of ethics in religion, first articulated by the Danish theologian Søren Kierkegaard and widely accepted in many circles, will be discussed in the next chapter.

One of the most remarkable phenomena of American life, not without its analogues in Western Europe, is the revival of interest in religion among large numbers of men and women, including the youth. Much of this concern is intellectual in character, expressing itself in the proliferation of courses on religion in colleges and universities and in the frequent presence of religious themes in literature and the arts and in the pages of our newspapers and journals.

Another aspect of the return to religion is practical. It is evident in the power that organized religion and its spokesmen wield in the political sphere, affecting all branches of government and all aspects of society.

The most striking and ultimately the most important aspect of the return to religion is personal. It has effected a marked change in life-style from the secular ambience still prevalent in society. The new way of life expresses itself in a new and passionate piety in prayer, in Bible study, and in the punctilious observance of religious ritual. Hundreds of thousands, and perhaps millions, of men and women have been introduced to the Bible and other great religious classics that had become sealed volumes for most of our contemporaries. The churches and synagogues of all denominations, particularly those of a marked fundamentalist cast, have enjoyed a great influx of worshippers and supporters. This far-flung movement would seem to guarantee the survival of religion for the foreseeable future and disprove the prophecies of its imminent demise. It is safe to say that most observers would regard these developments as basically positive.

If there are grounds for restrained enthusiasm in the face of this phenomenon, they are to be found in the simplistic content of the new-found faith, in the narrowness of vision which it imposes upon its adherents, and, perhaps most important of all, in the separation it has introduced between religion and ethics.

In the past, it was virtually axiomatic in Western society that an organic link exists between religion and ethics. In fact those who find the tenets of religion intellectually unconvincing often defend it on the ground that it is essential in order to preserve the moral fabric of society. This is basically the position of Kant in his *Critique of Practical Reason,* and indeed the standpoint of the Friends in Job. It is therefore a striking paradox in our day that the revival of religion in Christianity and in Judaism has been accompanied by a sharp decline in genuine ethical concern.

Given the distinct religious traditions of Christianity and Judaism, it is no wonder that the revival of religion takes on different forms in Christianity and in Judaism, exemplified respectively by the born-again Christians and the Jewish *ba'alei teshuvah.* It has not been sufficiently noted that while the divergences between the two groups are real, being rooted in varying historical circumstances and expressed in special life-styles, the two movements are essentially parallel in nature. They both arise in the same postmodern society, to which they react in largely similar terms, and they both exhibit similar psychological traits and ideological attitudes.

In Judaism one monstrous event has played a fundamental role—the unspeakable horror of the Holocaust, which brutally exterminated six million Jews, men, women, and children, and left scars on virtually all Jews who survived. The inexplicable annihilation of six out of every seven Jews living in Europe before the rise of Nazism destroyed the faith of many Jews in a righteous God and drove some of them out of the Jewish fold completely. For others, however, the suffering visited upon the Jews was seen as a Divine punishment for having strayed from the faith of their fathers. For them, the Holocaust became the starting point of a process of repentance for insufficient religiosity. The "new life" of the returnees expresses itself negatively by the rejection of the ideals and convictions as well as the culture and customs of the modern world, and positively by a meticulous observance of the manifold rituals of traditional Judaism.

In their life-style, the returnees seek to recapitulate the life-style of the East European Jewish *shtetl*, or village, in the eighteenth and nineteenth centuries. They are to be seen in the major American cities and even in the smaller towns, easily recognizable by their long coats, black hats, beards, and sideburns.

In addition to the direct survivors of the Holocaust and their families, there are thousands of American Jews who have been drawn to these circles because they seek a safe harbor from the stormy sea of modernism, with its fears, doubts, and uncertainties. Many of them are young, and all of them welcome the reinforcement provided by a self-assured, dogmatic worldview, in order to break with the drug-, alcohol-, and sex-centered culture in which they have been immured. For them, as for their Christian counterparts, religion and irreligion are simple affairs: "Where there is no faith, there are no answers; where there is faith, there are no questions."

Obviously, the Holocaust experience and its aftermath has had little impact on the life and thought of Christian religious groups, both mainline and cultic. Perhaps, as the Eckardts, Littell, Flannery, and Ruether have been urging, it should have. The fact is, however, that the Holocaust is a searing reality only for Jews and for a relatively small number of sensitive non-Jews.

The impact of the Holocaust and the special life-style of the Jewish returnees aside, the similarities between Christian and Jewish fundamentalists are striking. Both groups reflect the sense of helplessness felt by the average individual, as he sees himself crushed by the Behemoth of power, represented by all the levels of government bureaucracy, the wealth of massive corporations, and the ubiquitous impact of the press, the radio, and television. They are overwhelmed by the new, potentially dangerous technology and feel outraged by the unfamiliar "permissive" patterns of behavior of the younger generation today. That modern behavior patterns are immoral emerges directly from the fundamentalist reading of the Scriptures. For both Christian and Jewish fundamentalism, the biblical text is the cornerstone.

The foundations of Hebrew philology and biblical exegesis were laid by Jewish scholars in the early Middle Ages, and carried forward by Christian scholars from the Renaissance to the present. Today, Protestant, Catholic, and Jewish scholars are united in the historical-critical study of the Bible and the use of the comparative method, which has given us a vastly enlarged understanding of the Bible, its background, and its meaning. However, both Christian and Jewish fundamentalists are at one in maintaining the literal character of revelation, and the inerrancy of Scripture, its seamless uniformity and its universal applicability—often with an assist by the particular interpreter. Moreover, the received text has been transmitted perfect and error-free.

There is a difference, however. For Jewish fundamentalism, it is not the literal meaning of the biblical text which is normative, but the rabbinic exegesis embodied in the Talmud and the Midrash. Since the concern of the talmudic sages was basically not the original meaning of the Bible, but its practical relevance to the radically changed conditions prevalent in the Greco-Roman world of their day, the rabbinic interpretation often differs widely from the "plain meaning" of the text. For Christian fundamentalism, the literal meaning of each verse may be applied to any circumstance, anywhere and always.

For both groups, scientific biblical scholarship is an enemy of true religion, a temptation to sin, and a dangerous heresy to be fought and, if possible, suppressed by every available means.

Here a divergence in method also makes itself felt. Christian fundamentalists have adopted the strategy of confrontation; Jewish fundamentalists prefer the tactic of insulation. Thus, the former find that they cannot ignore the challenge to the literal reading of Genesis posed by evolution. Undeterred by the Scopes trial, fundamentalists have carried on an all-out battle against the teaching of the theory of evolution in the public schools, demanding the introduction of "scientific creationism" as an "alternative" to scientific theory. In many states they have achieved a substantial measure of success. Many textbooks have all but eliminated the term "evolution" and the very mention of Darwin's name, since many publishers are eager to please and thereby to profit.

Jewish fundamentalists also reject evolution as contradicting the Book of Genesis, but they rarely subject it to a frontal attack. Instead they prefer to insulate their adherents from any contact with ideas like historical change or psychoanalysis and try to prevent any contact by their disciples with persons advocating such notions. They oppose their devotees' seeking a higher secular education, except for vocational purposes. Mathematics, physics, chemistry, and above all technology are relatively "safe," but social, historical, and humanistic studies are rightly regarded as most inimical to fundamentalist dogma and therefore forbidden. In the field of Judaica, virtually every discipline is ruled out as inimical to the faith. Hebrew language and literature, Jewish history, modern Jewish theology and philosophy, even undue absorption in the study of the biblical text—all are proscribed as evidence of defection from Torah-true Judaism.

In some modern Orthodox Jewish circles, natural science is taught, with the result that the piety of these groups is highly suspect. But in those institutions, the effort is made, as a distinguished spokesman put it, to make sure that the "science of the students is not influenced by their religion and their religion is not affected by their science." To be sure, the tactic does not always work out as expected and defections are not uncommon; some are not capable of the "compartmentalized mind." Some go over to the modernist enemy, but others remain within the group, repent their sins, and develop various degrees of intellectual schizophrenia.

Having arisen out of a profound aversion to the modern spirit, fundamentalism finds "humanism," "modernism," and "secularism" all equally pernicious. Since all three terms are equally vague in meaning, they lend themselves admirably to denunciation. Yet in a deeper sense, fundamentalists cannot escape their environment. They, too, are "children of modernity," though alienated children to be sure. Many of their peers have been overcome by a sense of despair and have sunk into cynicism; others have embarked upon the mindless pursuit of pleasure and physical sensation, while still others exhibit unlimited and uninhibited aggression and violence in society. Even more than their "unbelieving" contemporaries, the fundamentalists, living in a world of terrifying change, have lost hope of being able to deal rationally and effectively with their problems by their own intelligence and activity. But unlike the majority of their generation, the "penitents" have consciously adopted a way of life that protects them against the perils of "decadence"—and the term includes virtually all of modern life and thought.

But not quite everything.

In one crucially important regard, the fundamentalists and their opponents are at one—in embracing the philosophy of "making it" as the goal of existence, with economic success as the highest good. In addition, fundamentalism offers a bonus—eternal life or salvation in the world-to-come, to be won by taking refuge in a salvific Christ who needs only to be believed in or in an unchanging Torah that needs only to be obeyed.

Once the decision has been made, the Jewish returnees find communities of like-minded believers available and eager to receive them. The nucleus of these communities are often a segment of Holocaust survivors. They fall under the spell of one or another charismatic rabbi (pronounced Rebbe), a phenomenon for which a precedent already exists in the century-old Hasidic communities of Lubavitch, Satmar, Belz, and other less well-known centers. Other, non-Hasidic penitents are students in a yeshiva or talmudical academy, either in Israel or in the United States. Each master offers the authoritative exposition of God's truth—eternal, unchanging, infallible, and fully available only to his own adherents.

The ideological factor is one side of the coin; the other is psychological. Modern men and women may lament the sense of alienation, loneliness, and anomie that seems to be their destiny, but they often feel themselves powerless to effect a change. These communities of believers offer a remedy. In a society increasingly technological and nonhuman, anonymous and impersonal, cold and uncaring, each sect brings to its devotees the psychological support of a closely knit community marked by a warm sense of fellowship, brotherly love, and mutual responsibility.

Unfortunately, these attractive qualities *vis-à-vis* members of the group are generally accompanied by hostility and contempt and at times even by outright violence toward those outside the circle of true believers. This antagonism is displayed not only toward modernist groups like Conservative, Reform, Reconstructionist, and secular Jews, but also toward those who share the same body of beliefs and practices, but look to another father-figure as their leader.

Careful and not unsympathetic observers in the general community have pointed out that Christian fundamentalists manifest precisely the same attributes—a tendency to fragmentation and bitter partisanship, the result of an unshakable conviction that one's particular group and it alone has the Saving Truth, and that all others, whether they be "secularists," humanists, or non-Christians, on the one hand, or followers of different and competing fundamentalist preachers on the other, are either deluded or deceitful.

Christian fundamentalists are often linked to television preachers like Jerry Falwell or Oral Roberts on an individual basis, so that the sense of community is much less marked among them than among Jewish fundamentalists, for whom the community is the central fact of life. But for both Christian and Jewish fundamentalists, their faith, which is a bulwark from within, serves as a barrier from without.

Hence a concern for those outside the charmed circle tends to become muted or to disappear completely in favor of a *Binnenmoral*, an "inner-group morality." This attitude is neither hypocritical nor dishonest; it is the logical consequence of the fundamentalist siege mentality that dictates the principle that "he who is not with us is against us." Thus there emerges the paradoxical result that the revival of religion has been accompanied by a decay in ethical consciousness.

In Christianity, the tendency to downgrade ethical conduct in favor of religiosity may find proof-texts in the New Testament. The classic theological argument regarding the efficacy of faith as against works as the requisite for salvation had been decided long ago in favor of faith, the Epistle of James notwithstanding. Fundamentalism builds upon this foundation—since all men are sinners, the precise degree of sinfulness of the individual is unimportant. Since it is only faith in the power of Christ that saves, the level of ethical conduct is secondary at best. Nor is the material well-being of men and women the first consideration; what matters is their spiritual condition.

Hence, in an age of massive social and economic problems, most Christian fundamentalists have eliminated social concerns from their agenda. Decades ago, S. Gresham Machen, who has been described as the founder and intellectual leader of American fundamentalism, publicly denounced laws that sought to prohibit child labor.

Jerry Falwell, the founder and leader of the Moral Majority, has urged the elimination of unemployment insurance: "When the bums get hungry, they'll look for jobs." A well-known political figure identified with these groups proposed taxing unemployment benefits so as to make unemployment "less attractive" for the millions of American families without work.

No doubt the hostility to social welfare programs among fundamentalists also derives from their belief in the myth of "the good old days"; actually they were far from good when they were not old. The rugged individualism of eighteenth- and nineteenth-century America has the aura of a simpler and more manageable age. But in very substantial degree, the dismantling of the social welfare system undertaken by the Reagan administration with the blessing of fundamentalist preachers and their followers reflects the atrophy of the ethical conscience and the growth of self-centeredness, the *hubris* of the successful and their scorn for those less adept at "making it." Poverty, illness, squalor, these are regarded as the just punishment for the failures in society, who by definition are sinners.

Many of the adherents of fundamentalism are themselves older people, but they and their leaders remain silent in the face of the chipping away at the Social Security system. Mass poverty and need, reflected in the millions of American families living below the poverty level, leave them unmoved.

There is a striking paradox in the fact that Christian fundamentalists, who believe in the Prince of Peace, and Jewish fundamentalists, who cite the rabbinic dictum that God's greatest gift to the world is peace, are noticeably absent from the various peace and antinuclear movements. As Harvey Cox points out, "In our day while the fundamentalists attack all that is wrong with the modern soul, they almost never mention the advent of nuclear weapons with their capacity to end human life on the globe. Ironically, the conservative critics do not dwell on this awful nuclear uniqueness. They leave it mainly to the radicals."

Only two elements of traditional morality remain alive in fundamentalism. The first expresses itself primarily in a call for private charity for the "truly needy" and for the particular church making the appeal. That many of those who loudly call for "reliance upon the private sector" are not conspicuous on lists of donors is purely an accident. It suggests, however, that their slogan is a technique for accelerating the destruction of child-care centers for working mothers and reducing assistance for college students of lower-class or minority origins, curtailing medical care for the poor and the aged, and cutting Social Security payments down, if not out.

The second element of social morality in fundamentalism is almost exclusively limited to the area of sexual behavior. Fundamentalism, both Christian and Jewish, is dedicated to a code of rigid sexual mores, marked by a pronounced hostility to "permissiveness" as the root of all evil. Birth control, divorce, homosexuality, abortion, and extramarital relations, for all their complexities and the vast differences among them, are all lumped together and excoriated as the works of the Devil. It is ironic that the Jewish tradition is much more sympathetic to several of these modern practices, such as divorce, birth control, and even abortion, than contemporary Catholic and fundamentalist Protestant doctrines. But this fact is carefully suppressed by the spokesmen for Jewish fundamentalism, who ignore the evidence or misinterpret it, in order to make it agree with their current attitudes, and denounce all who derive different conclusions from the sources in the tradition. Only loose sexual morals seem to arouse the concern and the wrath of fundamentalist religious leaders. One is tempted to repeat the wise comment of a Hasidic teacher: "Why do you worry about my soul and your body? Worry instead about my body and your soul!"

In contemporary Judaism, the decay of the moral sense takes yet another form. In the Jewish tradition, faith in God is expressed by the meticulous observance of the *mitzvot*, which include both ethical and ritual commandments. However, since ethics is universal, being common to all men, ritual is seen as more specifically "Jewish" in character. Hence, scrupulous observance of each ritual prescription, rather than adherence to the ethical injunctions, is the touchstone of piety.

The "returnee" is unconcerned with broad social problems which are human in origin and hence transient and ultimately unimportant. The major emphasis on moral conduct inculcated in biblical and rabbinic literature is ignored. The ethical imperatives are not expunged, but they tend to be applied largely, if not exclusively, only to the members of one's own circle. Isolated passages are dredged up from the Talmud to give the appearance of halakhic legitimacy to behavior toward "outsiders," whether Jew or Gentile, that is distant at best and at worst downright hostile. For all the adulation, bordering upon idolatry, that Jewish fundamentalists lavish upon the rabbis of the Talmud, their modern disciples are light-years away from the talmudic sages who dared to put into the mouth of God the prayer, "Would that men forgot Me but kept My law!" (P. Hagigah 1:7).

This analysis of the mainsprings of Christian and Jewish fundamentalism may seem unduly critical. The potential for good in the mass return to religious piety and observance and consequently a new openness to spiritual values has been noted, but may not have been sufficiently stressed. Perhaps with time, intolerance may be transmuted into fervor and narrowness of vision transformed into depth of insight. One hopes that the increased familiarity with the sacred texts will inspire fundamentalist believers to dedicate themselves to the advancement of the biblical goal, the establishment of the Kingdom of God on earth. At present, however, that does not seem to be the case; the upsurge of religious zeal has not produced a deeper ethical sensitivity on the domestic or the international scene.

In conclusion, the Jewish and Christian forms of fundamentalism, for all their differences, represent the same response, at once truculent and fearful, to the challenges of the modern age. Our society, which no longer feels the need to disguise its aggressiveness and materialism—let alone control and subdue these vices—finds in the various fundamentalist versions of religion an imprimatur for its anti-intellectualism and its indifference to human needs. Fundamentalism is a faithful expression of the goals that seem to dominate our age. That may well prove to be its epitaph.

Chapter 10

The Faith of Abraham:
A Case Study

AS WE HAVE SEEN, the revival of religion in its various fundamentalist versions has, among other consequences, brought in its wake a tragic decay in moral concern and a virtual elimination of ethics from the content of religion as it is currently being preached. The loosening of the once-thought-indissoluble bond between religion and morality in our day has been largely an unsophisticated and even unconscious process operating on an *ad hoc* basis.

However, the insistence that the heart of religion lies in faith in God rather than in one's relation to his fellowmen has a long history and respectable antecedents. We may recall A. N. Whitehead's definition of religion as "what a man does with his solitariness."

Obviously, this description has great value in focusing on the I-Thou encounter between man and his Maker as the essence of the religious experience, an aspect on which the great founders and prophets of religion would heartily concur. But Whitehead's definition, by implication at least, effectively removes ethics from the heart of religion. For ethics cannot be acted out in "solitariness." This exclusion Moses, Elijah, Isaiah, and Jeremiah would emphatically deny.

Nevertheless, the effort to eliminate or attentuate the place of ethics in religion continues to be made on many levels. Thus, a profound and deeply moving attempt to cut the nexus between religious faith and moral conduct, made over a century ago by the Danish theologian Soren Kierkegaard (1813–1855), has won favor with many theologians and philosophers. Kierkegaard's deep religiosity, his passionate sincerity, and his profundity of thought have made him highly influential. His insistence that it is impossible to attain objectivity in truth, his opposition to all logically structured systems of philosophic or theological thought, and his insistence that what matters is how one lives one's convictions and not merely what one believes his convictions to be—all these aspects of his thought have proved highly congenial to our age, which is marked by a powerful anti-rational temper. Undoubtedly, Kierkegaard is a seminal figure for most of the various existential schools now in vogue.

One of Kierkegaard's best-known concepts that has found considerable support in theological circles is his doctrine of the teleological suspension of the ethical. In brief, he maintains that true faith in God may be called upon to set aside the normal canons of morality in order to obey a higher call, that of the Divine will. In his book *Fear and Trembling*, Kierkegaard finds a biblical basis for his idea in the account of the sacrifice of Isaac as narrated in Genesis, chapter 22. He calls the Patriarch Abraham a "knight of faith" because he disregards the accepted canons of ethics and humanity in the face of the command of religion, and is ready to sacrifice his beloved son at God's behest, though the act is clearly immoral.

This striking idea has appealed strongly to many theologians, particularly in Protestantism, but it has won favor with some Jewish thinkers as well. Thus, it has been accepted by Emil Fackenheim,[1] as well as by his critic, David Ellenson.[2] It has been defended by Jacob I. Halevi,[3] though Marvin Fox has argued that the teleological suspension of the ethical contravenes the authentic spirit of Jewish tradition.[4]

Halevi, who sets a very high valuation upon Kierkegaard's thought, declares that the teleological suspension of the ethical has been generally misunderstood by Kierkegaard's critics. By "ethical" Kierkegaard means the universal, that which is comprehensible to all men. By "religious" he means the private or particular, which cannot be made intelligible to others. Moreover, we must love the ethical in order to suspend it for the sake of the religious, that is to say, in obedience to the voice of God.[5] Halevi maintains that Kierkegaard is in harmony with rabbinic thought, indeed, that "his superb interpretation of Abraham had already been accomplished centuries before him by the Rabbis."[6] To prove this point, Halevi cites the Midrash that when Abraham received the call to leave his father's home, he received permission to suspend the command of *kibbud 'av*, "honoring one's father."[7] Halevi goes so far as to declare that the Kierkegaardian suspension of the ethical is "the core" of the rabbinic worldview.

In a footnote, Halevi tries to meet the objection that the teleological suspension of the ethical can be used to justify persecution, even a holocaust.[8] His attempt cannot be pronounced successful. Perhaps

Hitler's murderous hatred for the Jews excludes him from being a bona fide example of the suspension of the ethical, which requires that one "love" his victims. But, surely, Torquemada and his associates in the Inquisition would qualify, for when they burned heretics at the stake they were actuated by a deep love for them—they wished them to suffer a few minutes of torment in the *auto-da-fé* on earth in order to be spared eternal hellfire in the beyond. In essence, Halevi agrees with Kierkegaard that the *Akedah*, "the binding of Isaac," was a violation of the principles of ethical conduct. Abraham set them aside because of a higher imperative: his faith in God.

On the other hand, Fox maintains that the biblical account, read literally, is out of keeping with Jewish teaching; the narrative must therefore be interpreted in the light of rabbinic exegesis. The rabbis sought to demonstrate that both God's command and Abraham's willingness to obey were rational and moral. In support of his position, Fox draws upon rabbinic legend and homily. Thus, he cites several talmudic and midrashic passages that explain God's command to Abraham to sacrifice his son as a deserved punishment upon the patriarch. For earlier, when Abraham and Sarah were celebrating Isaac's weaning with a feast, Abraham neglected to offer thanks to God for the blessing of a son. Another Midrash explains the *Akedah* as Isaac's triumphant rejoinder to the taunts of his older half-brother, Ishmael, who had undergone the rite of circumcision at the age of thirteen and argued that he had thus shown a greater devotion to God than had Isaac, whose circumcision had taken place as an infant with considerably less risk.[9] Fox concludes that rabbinic thought provides "a perfectly understandable reason why God asks and Abraham is ready to offer up such a sacrifice." He concludes, however, that "as it stands, the story is absurd."[10] Thus, in effect, he accepts the Kierkegaardian thesis which he set out to disprove.

That the Midrash can be cited on both sides of the issue to support or to rebut Kierkegaard is not at all astonishing. Rabbinic Judaism was not monolithic, and a latitude of view was especially evident in the field of Aggadah, as every student of rabbinics knows.

The legends to which we have referred and others of a similar tenor are frequently very moving.[11] Indeed, they are entirely comprehensible in terms of the mind-set of the rabbis and their motivation. They were concerned with building morale for a persecuted and physically powerless people who were frequently called upon to undergo torture and martyrdom.[12] The Binding of Isaac became the Sacrifice of Isaac, the paradigm of Jewish martyrdom in the Middle Ages, during the Crusades, and after. In some versions, Isaac is actually sacrificed, an experience that untold thousands of his descendants underwent during two millennia of persecution and hatred. From the tale of their ancestor's selfless and heroic devotion to God, Jewish men, women, and children drew strength in their affliction, often suffering torture and death "for the sanctification of God's Name."

However, it is no disrespect to the sages to suggest that a modern mind, even that of a believer, may be unable to see in these legends a "perfectly understandable" justification for the sacrifice of a child's life. That the biblical account of the *Akedah* needs to be accounted for *on its own terms* is all but ignored. After all, the Bible was read and treasured for centuries before the emergence of the rabbinic interpretations now embedded in the Midrash. Moreover, Kierkegaard can hardly be faulted for not being familiar with rabbinic exegesis.

Actually, there is a more fundamental objection to the Kierkegaardian thesis. It is based upon an anachronistic reading of the Genesis narrative, on a failure to take into account the full biblical record and the historical background of the period. As a result, Kierkegaard's concept, for all of its undeniable pathos, must be regarded as a distortion of biblical faith itself.

When the *Akedah* narrative is read in the larger context of the Book of Genesis, it offers no support for the doctrine of the teleological suspension of the ethical. Just four chapters earlier, when God reveals to Abraham his decision to destroy the sinful cities of Sodom and Gomorrah, Abraham does not hesitate to dispute the decision. He proceeds to bargain persistently with God for the lives of the inhabitants of the sinful cities. Here there is no hint of "submission" by the "knight of faith" to the imcomprehensible will of God. Abraham feels that God's decision is in disregard of the ethical law, and he expresses his unshakable conviction that God cannot ignore the principle of righteousness, "Shall not the Judge of all the earth act justly?" (Gen. 18:21).

One more observation is in order. In the case of the planned destruction of Sodom and Gomorrah, God would not be violating the canons of morality and fairness. He would simply be applying the measure of justice rather than of mercy to sinners who richly deserved to be punished. Nevertheless, Abraham speaks out against the Divine decision in the name of the ethical principle of mercy which even God must obey. How, then, can Abraham himself have submitted to an active violation of the ethical law? In view of Abraham's ringing affirmation of the binding character of the moral law, how is his uncomplaining acceptance of God's command to sacrifice his son to be understood?

There is at least one explanation that is frequently advanced. It is often maintained that the *Akedah* narrative is intended to teach that God is opposed to child sacrifice and that, instead, He is to be worshipped by ethical conduct.[13] This interpretation cannot be sustained. This is not to suggest that the Bible favors, or even condones, the practice of child sacrifice. Quite the contrary. But it is irrelevant to the biblical narrative of the *Akedah,* and there is not a hint of it in the context. Isaac's life is spared because father and son have withstood the test successfully without the necessity of the lad's death. Because Abraham has demonstrated his willingness to obey God's command without flinching, his reward is clearly announced:

> By Myself I have sworn, says the Lord, because you have done this, and have not withheld your son, your only son, I will indeed bless you, and I will multiply your descendants as the stars of heaven, and as the sand which is on the seashore. And your descendants shall possess the gate of their enemies.
>
> (Gen. 22:16–17)

Both the prohibition of child sacrifice and the glorification of martyrdom are important themes in Jewish religious experience, but they cannot be legitimately invoked for the understanding of the biblical narrative.

Why, then, did Abraham not raise the moral issue, as he had with Sodom and Gomorrah? When the *Akedah* is viewed in the context of biblical faith and against the background of Oriental religion as a whole, there is no "suspension of the ethical" involved. The sacrifice of a child was an all-but-universal practice in ancient Semitic religion and beyond. To be sure, offering up one's child was an infinitely more painful gift to one's God than sacrificing the firstborn of one's cattle or tithing one's crops. Yet it took place time and time again among Semites and Indo-Europeans. Literary documents and archaeology have revealed that child sacrifice was a staple of Semitic religion among the Arabs, the Phoenicians, the Canaanites, and the Carthaginians.[14]

The Bible, too, is well aware of the practice. Thus, we are informed that in a critical hour of battle with Israel, the ninth-century king of Moab, Mesha, sacrificed his son and won a victory over Israel (II Kings 3:25–27). A similar act is recorded of a Hebrew Judge (i.e., military chieftain) in an earlier period. In the eleventh century B.C.E. Jephthah sacrificed his daughter in literal fulfillment of a vow which he had taken (Judg. 11). The biblical historian does not spell out the fate of Jephthah's daughter, but leaves it to be inferred, so that his own negative attitude toward child sacrifice is clear.

It is obvious that the ancient Hebrews found the imitation of the Gentiles—especially their lower attributes—an irresistible temptation. Time and again the Torah forbade "consigning one's son or daughter to the fire," and the prophets castigated the practice (cf., e.g., Ezek. 16:21, 20:31, 23:37), but it persisted throughout the days of the First Temple (cf. II Kings 16:3, 21:6). The valley of Ben Hinnom in Jerusalem was the scene of these rites, in which both king and commoner participated (cf. II Kings 23:10, Jer. 32:35).[15] As late as the eighth century B.C.E., the prophet Micah quotes his contemporaries as asking in good faith:

> With what shall I come before the Lord,
> and bow myself before God on high?
> Shall I come before Him with burnt offerings,
> with calves a year old?
> Will the Lord be pleased with thousands of rams,
> with ten thousand rivers of oil?
> Shall I give my firstborn for my transgression,
> the fruit of my body for the sin of my soul?

It is in response to this question that Micah gives his great definition of true religion:

> He has told you, O man,[16] what is good;
> and what does the Lord require of you,
> only to do justice, love kindness, and walk humbly with your God.
>
> (Mic. 6:6–8)

After the destruction of the First Temple, child sacrifice disappeared in Israel, as the teachings of the Torah and the prophets bore fruit in the postexilic community. But in the patriarchal age, this horror of child sacrifice, an attitude in which Judaism was unique in the ancient world, still lay in the distant future. Abraham, living nearly a thousand years before Micah in a world permeated by pagan religion, did not see himself confronted by a moral crisis when he was commanded by God to sacrifice Isaac, and he proceeded to obey. His faith was being subjected to the most painful test possible, but he was not being asked to violate the moral law as he undestood it.

There is much in Kierkegaard's life and work that can deepen the true religious spirit. But there is no warrant, in the biblical account of the Trial of Abraham and the Binding of Isaac, for a doctrine of the teleological suspension of the ethical. Kierkegaard's interpretation of the text must be pronounced an anachronism made possible only by ignoring the testimony of history. It is a grafting of an alien concept upon the authentic biblical and Jewish understanding of God's will, which does not command or condone the violation of the moral law, either by God or by man. The entire Book of Job is testimony to the Hebraic insistence that God, no less than man, is answerable to the dictates of morality. Man's insight into the content of morality changes and, it is hoped, grows deeper with time. But, from the biblical period to the present, the maintenance of the ethical law and obedience to its precepts remain the categorical imperative of the Hebraic ethos.

The significance of the *Akedah* narrative, even on biblical ground, is clear and important. Abraham is truly a "knight of faith," and his entire career testifies to this exalted trait.

It is in obedience to God's call that he leaves his home and wanders into an unknown land, buoyed by the Divine promise that he would become a great nation (Gen. 12). He remains a wanderer in the land and a stranger among its inhabitants, compelled to defend himself and his kinsmen against attack, and tormented by the absence of a son through whom the Divine promise could be fulfilled. When he is assured that his own offspring will be his heir, "he trusted in the Lord, and it was counted as a merit for him." In the awesome "covenant among the pieces," the Divine promise is reaffirmed that after a period of exile and oppression in a foreign country, lasting four hundred years, his descendants will return and inherit the Promised Land.

The birth of Ishmael fulfills the promise of a son to Abraham, but it is clear that not through him will the covenant be established. Only at an advanced age are Abraham and Sarah blessed with the birth of Isaac, "your son, your only one whom you love" (see Gen. 12:1; 15:6, 13; 21:12; 22:2). Now comes the supreme test of Abraham's loyalty to God—his willingness to obey the Divine command to sacrifice this son as an offering.

The *Akedah* is the climactic act of faith in the life of the patriarch. In the words of the rabbis, "Abraham, our patriarch, underwent ten trials and emerged triumphantly from all in order to demonstrate how great was his love for God" (*M. Abot* 5:3). Abraham is being commanded to give up all that is most precious to him in the world, but he is not being asked to suspend his loyalty to the moral law. Were that the case, he would rise and protest. The abrogation of the ethical imperative God could not ask and Abraham could not grant.

Later generations saw in the Sacrifice of Isaac a prophecy of the future destiny of Abraham's descendants, who would be called upon through the ages to suffer martyrdom "for the sanctification of the Divine Name." This significance the biblical narrative continues to hold for us today, who have been the witnesses of the unspeakable horror of the

Holocaust. Time and again, the Jew has felt called upon to surrender his life for God's cause, but he has never been bidden to give up his faith in God's law of righteousness, nor to desist from the struggle to advance its cause. Recognizing the reality of this principle is indispensable for a functioning ethical code in society.

Part V

Judaic Values for the World Today

As we have noted earlier, the doctrine of natural law asserts that there are enduring principles of human conduct that are binding upon human beings because they are in conformity with reason and human nature. This contention, as well as the concrete conclusions drawn by practitioners of natural law, has been challenged, particularly in the modern world, on several grounds. First, natural law presumes a static view of human nature and society. This flies in the face of the realities of the modern age, which sees dizzying change as perhaps its most striking characteristic, and in which virtually nothing else is certain. Natural law, it has been further claimed, occupies itself with generalities that bear little relationship to the nitty-gritty problems of daily existence. Finally, it is argued, when natural law is applied to concrete life-situations, it invariably emerges on the side of reaction and oppression, defending the privileges of an elite, and manifesting a deep distrust for the masses of men and women.

It is undeniable that the history of natural law largely supports the indictment. However, it was pointed out above that these defects are not inherent in natural law itself, but are the result of the historical conditions under which it arose and developed, and the institutions and personalities who cultivate it.

The thesis of this volume is that in two respects Judaic tradition can make a signal contribution to natural law and by that token to the life and thought of our age. The first is the dynamism of the Hebrew vision of life and history, which is fundamental to the prophets of Israel. The second is the passionate concern for justice, freedom, and peace that characterized the biblical legislators, prophets, and sages, as well as their rabbinic successors. These two factors can revitalize natural law, and help it to serve as the basis for ethics in the modern world.

Nor is this contribution limited to general principles. No aspect of life was too insignificant or remote for the biblical and rabbinical legislators who spelled out the specific norms of conduct for their times. The same concern for the concrete and the relevant can help us grapple with four great issues of our time—the ecological imperative in a society bent on maximizing private gain at the expense of the public good, the ideal of freedom of conscience and thought challenged by those who regard themselves as the sole guardians of virtue and truth, the defense of a vital democracy confronted by implacable enemies on the right and on the left, and the establishment of a stable and enduring peace as the only alternative to the nuclear annihilation of the race.

Chapter 11

Ecology and the Judaic Tradition

THE ECOLOGICAL THREAT, indicated by the mounting evidence of the contamination of our environment, is perhaps the newest problem to affect the human race. Pollution, of course, is not new; technological progress has been with us for many decades. But only recently has pollution of air, water, and food been recognized as a major hazard.

In view of the importance of the issues involved, it should be of interest to explore the insights and attitudes on ecology in the biblical and post-biblical tradition. This is particularly true since Hebraic teachings on the subject are not merely unknown, they are often misunderstood even by those who should know better. Thus at a conference on the theology of survival held a few years ago, virtually all the scholars agreed that the traditional Christian attitude toward nature had actually "given sanction" to the exploitation and spoliation of our natural resources. Moreover, the source of this destructive attitude, they declared, is the Hebrew Bible, specifically, Genesis 1:28:

> God blessed them; and God said to them: "Be fruitful and multiply, and replenish the earth, and subdue it; and have dominion over the fish of the sea, and over the fowl of the air, and over every living thing that moves on the earth."

They solemnly pointed to this verse, and particularly to the phrase "and subdue it," as giving men the license to use and abuse the natural world and its resources as they see fit, without limitation or restriction.

The well-meaning theologians who passed these devastating judgments did not stop to notice that the same opening chapter of Genesis, in which man is given the right to "subdue" the earth and to "have dominion" over all living things does not even permit him to use animals for food. For the very next verse—Genesis 1:29—declares:". . .I have given you every plant yielding seed which is upon the face of all the earth, and every tree with seed in its fruits; you shall have them for food." This is surely a drastic limitation upon man's rights. Not until many centuries later, after the Flood, is man (in the person of Noah and his family) permitted to eat meat (Gen. 9:3–4). And even then, all men are forbidden to eat the blood of the creatures they have used for food, because the blood is the seat of life. Reverence for life dictates that the blood be poured out and not consumed. This ritual is a symbolic recognition that all life is sacred—all life, even the life of animals that men kill for the sake of sustenance.

Actually the paradigm of man's relationship to his environment is expressed in the task assigned to Adam in the Garden of Eden before the Fall: "He placed him in the Garden of Eden to till it and to guard it" (Gen. 2:15).

What is the meaning of the Hebrew phrase in the opening chapter of Genesis, "and subdue it"? The truth is that the passage in Genesis was never used to establish a principle of aggressive action by man *vis-à-vis* the environment. In fact, the Talmud relates the phrase to the first part of the verse, "Be fruitful and multiply." It then declares that since subduing enemies in war is primarily a male undertaking, the verb "subdue" must refer to a male obligation. Hence the duty to propagate the human race falls upon the male rather than upon the female (*B. Yebamot* 65b). It may be added, in view of the agitation revolving around planned parenthood, that the obligation to "be fruitful and multiply" is fulfilled in rabbinic law when two children are born to a family. The only point at issue is the sex of the children; while the School of Shammai requires that there be two sons, the School of Hillel requires one son and one daughter (*M. Yebamot* 6:6, *Yoreh Deah* 1:5).

This obligation, the first commandment in the Bible, underwent a complex development in postbiblical life and law.[1] Its application should obviously be different in the highly industrialized nations of the West and in the starving, vastly overpopulated countries of Asia and Africa. The Jewish community today constitutes a special case. It has undergone a forty percent *negative* "population growth" as the result of the Holocaust and is exposed to the inroads of assimilation and a minuscule birthrate in Europe and the Americas. In fact, it may be argued that modern Jews are too zealous in maintaining the rabbinic limitations on the commandment!

In any event, the Talmud relates the verb "and subdue it" to the propagation of the race. Medieval Jewish commentators saw in it a reference to the biological and ecological fact that man is the dominant species on this planet, able to exercise his will upon other creatures (with the possible exception of insects and some rodents) and to modify the environment as he chooses. Naḥmanides explained the passage as follows: "He gave them law and dominion on the earth to act according to their wish with the animals and creeping things and to build and uproot plants and to mine copper out of the hills and carry on other similar activities." The Italian commentator Obadiah Sforno gave the phrase a more restricted meaning: "And subdue it—that you protect yourself with your reason and prevent the animals from entering within your boundaries and you rule over them."[2]

The fundamental Jewish teaching on man's relationship to his environment is explicitly contained in two very broad and far-reaching ethical principles that are written large in biblical and postbiblical literature. The first principle governs man's treatment of the so-called lower animals; the second expresses man's proper attitude toward inanimate nature. Taken together, these basic principles, with their corollaries, have considerable relevance for directing and shaping man's proper attitudes and actions toward his fellow creatures and his environment on earth.

Judaic thought generally prefers to avoid abstractions. Nevertheless, the first principle relating to the treatment of "lower" animals carries a poignant name in rabbinic literature: *za'ar ba'alei ḥayim,* "the pain of living creatures." This concept, deeply rooted in the Bible, has been extensively elaborated upon in rabbinic law and ethics. Unique in its sympathy for what has been called "brute creation," the Fourth Commandment in the Decalogue enjoins rest for one's ox, donkey, and every creature on the Sabbath day (Exod. 20:11, Deut. 5:14; see also Exod. 23:12). Deuteronomy forbids the farmer to plow with an ox and a donkey yoked together, because the practice would obviously impose great hardship upon the weaker animal. Nor was the farmer permitted to muzzle an ox during the threshing period to prevent its eating any of the grain (Deut. 22:10, 25:4).

Equally significant was the desire of the Torah to spare the feelings of living creatures and simultaneously inculcate the spirit of mercy in man. Thus, it is forbidden to slaughter a cow or a ewe together with its offspring in the same day (Lev. 22:28). This twofold concern finds exquisite expression in the law in Deuteronomy:

> If you chance to come upon a bird's nest, in any tree or on the ground, with young ones or eggs, and the mother sitting upon the young or upon the eggs, you shall not take the mother with the young. You

shall let the mother go, but the young you may take to yourself, that it may go well with you, and that you may live long.

(Deut. 22:6–7)

The traditional laws of kosher slaughtering *(shehitah)* are designed to keep alive the sense of reverence for life by forbidding the eating of blood and by minimizing the pain of the animal when it is slaughtered.

In all societies, hunting has been highly regarded as a sport. Whatever the practice of the ancient Hebrews may have been, only two biblical figures are described as hunters and they were not Hebrews, Nimrod and Esau. Both were regarded very negatively in the postbiblical tradition and were taken to symbolize the anti-Jewish spirit.

Rabbinic law permitted hunting for practical purposes, such as food, commerce, or the removal of animal pests, but hunting for sport was strongly condemned in all periods as not being "the way of the children of Abraham, Isaac, and Jacob."[3] Albert Einstein cites a report, possibly apocryphal that Walther Rathenau said, "When a Jew says that he hunts for pleasure, he lies."

The contemporary concern with "endangered species" would seem to be adumbrated in a comment by the medieval legist and exegete Moses Nahmanides. We have already referred to the biblical prohibitions against slaughtering a cow and her calf on the same day and the taking of a bird with her young as emanating from the wish to spare the mother as much anguish as possible. In his commentary on the latter passage Nahmanides declares: "Scripture will not permit a destructive act that will bring about the extinction of a species, even though it has permitted the ritual slaughtering of that species for food. He who kills the mother and offspring on one day is considered as if he destroyed the species."[4]

Perhaps the most eloquent affirmation of preoccupation with the welfare of all living things—eloquent precisely because it is indirect and seemingly unintentional—occurs in the unforgettable climax of the Book of Jonah. The prophet Jonah feels himself aggrieved because his forecast that the sinful city of Nineveh will be destroyed has been averted—the people having repented. Jonah then finds a measure of comfort in a gourd, a large-leafed plant which the Lord has created especially to shield him against the sun. The next night God destroys the gourd and Jonah becomes very angry. A colloquy then ensues, which ends, be it noted, in characteristic Jewish fashion—with a question!

God said to Jonah, "Are you very angry for the gourd?" And Jonah said, "I am very angry, angry enough to die." And the Lord said, "You pity the gourd, for which you did not labor, nor did you make it grow, which came into being in a night, and perished in a night. And should I not have pity for Nineveh, that great city, in which there are more than a hundred and twenty thousand persons who do not know their right hand from their left, and also much cattle?"

(Jon. 4: 9–11)

Love and pity for innocent children are equated with mercy for animals.

The biblical ordinances regarding the treatment of animals laid down in the Torah are tolerably well known. In the Prophets, the eloquent climax in the Book of Jonah is deservedly famous. The biblical prophets, sages, and psalmists vie with one another in describing the harmony between man and nature as a fundamental element of life in the ideal future, which later generations described as the Messianic Age (Hos. 2: 20–24, Amos 9: 13–15, Isa. 11: 1–9, Joel 2: 21–26, Ps. 91, Job 5: 23).

A profound theological basis for ecology, including the right of animals in the world, is to be found in a biblical source that to my knowledge has hitherto never been invoked in this connection. The Book of Job is unique in its conception of the purpose of Creation, which is adumbrated in its climax in the Speeches of the Lord Out of the Whirlwind. After the debate of Job and his friends has ended and the brash young Elihu, though uninvited, has made his contribution to the heartrending problem of human suffering, the Lord, speaking out of the whirlwind, confronts Job in two speeches.[5] He offers no facile answer to the mystery of evil; instead He raises the discussion to an altogether higher level. With exultant joy, the Lord has the world that He has created pass in review before Job, and He challenges him to understand, let alone share in, the task of creation. In powerful lines, the wonders of inanimate nature are described. The creation of heaven and earth, stars and seas, morning and night, light and darkness is pictured. The snow and the hail, the flood and the lightning, the rain, the dew, the frost, and the clouds—all are revelations of God as Creator. But we do not have here a cold "scientific" catalogue of natural phenomena, such as is to be found in the Egyptian *Onomasticon* of Amenemope.[6] What is significant is not the explicit listing of the items, but the implication the poet draws from them—like the rain in the uninhabited desert, they were all called into being without man as their purpose and they remain beyond his power and control (Job 38: 1–38). This significant implication will be underscored more strongly as the speech proceeds.

The Lord now turns to the world of animate nature and glowingly describes seven creatures: the lion, the mountain goat, the wild ass, the buffalo, the ostrich, the wild horse, and the hawk. What they have in common, apart from being beautiful manifestations of God's creative power, is that they have not been created for man's use; they have their own independent reason for being, known only to their Creator.

This theme is powerfully reenforced in the second Speech of the Lord Out of the Whirlwind. He now pictures two massive creatures, Behemoth the hippopotamus, and Leviathan, the crocodile (40:15–24; 40:25–41:26). It is not merely that they are not under human control, like the animals already described; they are positively repulsive and even dangerous to man. Yet they too reveal the power of the Creator in a universe which is not anthropocentric but theocentric, with purposes known only to God, which man cannot fathom. The world is both a mystery and a miracle; what man cannot understand of the mystery he can sustain because of its beauty. Man is not the goal of creation and therefore, not the master of the cosmos.

The basic theme, that the universe is a mystery to man, is of course overtly expressed in the God speeches. There are, however, two other significant implications. In accordance with characteristic Semitic usage they need to be inferred by the reader.

The first is theological: since the universe was not created with man as its center, neither the Creator nor the cosmos can be judged from man's vantage-point. The second is ecological. Though the poet was not concerned with presenting a religio-ethical basis for ecology, he has in effect done so. Man takes his place among the other living creatures, who are likewise the handiwork of God. Therefore he has no inherent right to abuse or exploit the living creatures or the natural resources to be found in a world not of his making, nor intended for his exclusive use.

If we have read the meaning of the Speeches of the Lord aright, we now have a sound conceptual basis for one of the more beneficent aspects of twentieth-century civilization—the growing concern for the humane treatment of animals. This sensitivity expresses itself both practically and theoretically.[7]

On the practical side, a far-flung and highly varied network of organizations has arisen in Western Europe and America designed to protest the cruel treatment and undue suffering to which animals are often exposed in industry and even in scientific research. Many concrete proposals have been advanced for laws to protect animals against abuse and needless pain. The rising tide of protest against contemporary practices in these areas takes on many forms, some perhaps ill-considered and at times even bizarre and violent. On balance, however, the essentially positive character of the movement for animal rights is undeniable.[8]

Aside from a deepening involvement with concrete measures in this area, there has also been an increased interest in a philosophical basis for the rights of animals, with a growing literature on the subject as a branch of secular ethics.

The *Book of Job* offers a religious foundation for the inherent rights of animals as co-inhabitants of the earth, adumbrated two millennia earlier than the emergence of secular ethics in this area.[9]

By insisting on a God-centered world, to which man has only a conditional title, the *Book of Job* presents a basis in religion for opposing and ultimately eliminating the needless destruction of life and the pollution of the natural resources in the world.

As important as the biblical and postbiblical teaching on man's treatment of his fellow tenants on the planet is the attitude toward the natural environment inculcated by the Jewish tradition. It is referred to in talmudic and post-talmudic literature as *bal tashit*, "do not destroy." The phrase is borrowed from a striking passage in Deuteronomy which, strange as it may seem, deals with the laws of warfare.

> When you besiege a city for a long time, making war against it in order to take it, you shall not destroy *(tashit)* its trees by wielding an axe against them. You may eat from them, but must not cut them down, for are the trees in the field human beings, that they should be besieged by you? Only the trees which you know are not fruit-bearing you may destroy and cut down, in order to build siege-works against the city that makes war with you, until it falls.
>
> (Deut. 20:19–20)

This injunction ran counter to accepted procedures in ancient war practiced, for example, by the Assyrians, who were particularly known for their cruelty. In modern times, *Schrecklichkeit*, "frightfulness," was an accepted canon of German military tactics. It has continued as a prime method in war to this day. The "scorched-earth" policy was widely used in the Vietnam conflict, developing new technological efficiency in the use of poisonous chemicals. The term "defoliation" was a euphemism to cover up the horror of total destruction of the countryside by American forces and by the Communist enemy, who was not more merciful.

The biblical laws of warfare clearly forbade wanton destruction. But the rabbis went far beyond the law in Deuteromomy. With their genius for discerning a general principle in a specific law, they enunciated a universal doctrine under the rubric of *bal tashit*. They then proceeded to develop a comprehensive code on ecology by extending the biblical law in three directions:

1. The biblical passage forbade wielding an axe against a tree during a siege. The rabbis extended the prohibition to any other means of wanton

destruction in war, direct or indirect, including shifting the course of a stream so that the tree would dry up *(Sifrei, Shofetim,* sec. 203). They condemned the stopping of wells, a tactic King Hezekiah had adopted in wartime (II Chron. 32:2–4, *B. Pesahim* 56a). They forbade the killing of animals or giving them possibly polluted water to drink *(B. Hullin* 7b;*Tosafot B. Baba Kamma* 115 b, based on *B. Abodah Zarah* 30b).

2. Even more far-reaching was the extension of these prohibitions to apply not only to war tactics but to all situations, including the more usual conditions of peace. Under all circumstances, the wanton or thoughtless destruction of natural objects was prohibited. In addition, the pollution of the air by various enterprises, like a threshing floor operation, or the establishment of tanneries, furnaces, or cemeteries in proximity to cities was forbidden *(M. Baba Batra* 2:8–9, *B. Baba Kamma* 82b).

3. Going beyond ecological concerns was the extension of the doctrine "You shall not destroy" from objects of nature to human artifacts. The biblical passage deals with a tree, which is a product of nature. The rabbis of the Talmud applied the principle to all the artifacts of man: "Whoever breaks vessels, or tears garments, or destroys a building, or clogs up a fountain, or does away with food in a destructive manner, violates the prohibition of *bal tashit*" *(B. Kiddushin* 32a).

The general principle was clearly formulated: "It is forbidden to destroy or to injure *[hamekalkel]* anything capable of being useful to men *[lehanot bo bnei 'adam].*"[10]

There are, to be sure, variations among the post-talmudic authorities with regard to the exact legal status of the prohibition. Maimonides declares that only cutting down of a tree is biblically forbidden, and all the other extensions are only rabbinic in character.[11] Curiously, the *Shulhan Arukh* of Rabbi Joseph Karo omits the entire subject, including the explicit biblical prohibition. Various efforts to explain this fact have been made. However, there are other instances of similar omissions in this code. But the binding power of the commandment "You shall not destroy," with its extensions to conditions of peace and its application to human artifacts as well as to natural objects, was never in doubt. Over centuries the horror of vandalism became part of the psyche of the Jew.

The full dimensions of this profound ethical principle need to be appreciated. *Bal tashit* has nothing in common with the sanctity of private property. One is forbidden to destroy not only the property of others, but also one's own. This principle derives in part from the recognition that what we are wont to call "our" property is really not our own, but God's. It is this principle that is invoked to validate the two great laws of the *Sabbatical Year* and the *Jubilee Year.*

The Torah ordained that the farmer was permitted to plow, sow, and reap his harvest for six years. Each seventh year, however, was to be observed as "a Sabbath to the Lord." Neither the field nor the vineyard might be tended, and what grew was public property to be used equally by freemen and slaves, natives and strangers (Lev. 25:5–6).

The Sabbatical Year served served several purposes. The first was *ecological* in character. In the days before crop rotation or the availability of chemical nutrients for the soil, the practice of letting the land lie fallow enabled it to regain its fertility.

The second was *social* and *ethical*. Only the poor and the stranger had the right to eat the produce that grew by itself during the seventh year, just as they have the right to the gleanings, the forgotten sheaves and the after-growth in the corners of the field in other years. This was an important element in the far-flung system of social legislation for the underprivileged in ancient Israel.

Finally, even more fundamental than the agricultural and social functions, biblical law reaffirmed a *deep religious principle:* God was dramatically reasserting His ownership of the land, of which man is only a temporary custodian.

After seven Sabbatical Years had passed, the fiftieth year was ushered in as the Jubilee Year (Lev. 25:8–24). The law ordains that on the Jubilee all property that has been sold during the preceding half-century be returned to its original owner without compensation. This radical step is justified by the basic legal principle: "The land shall not be sold in perpetuity, for the land is Mine; for you are strangers and sojourners with Me" (Lev. 25:23). Psalm 24 gives this same principle poetic expression in cosmic terms: "The earth is the Lord's in all its fullness, the world and those who dwell therein."

The biblical laws of the Sabbatical and the Jubilee Years were long regarded as utopian legislation never put into practice. The Talmud itself declares that the Sabbatical Year ceased to function a decade before the destruction of the Northern Kingdom of Israel, which took place in 722 B.C.E. However, the agricultural and ritual provisions of the Sabbatical Year are observed even today by ultra-pious Jewish groups: they eat no produce grown in the soil by Jewish farmers in the Holy Land during the seventh year. Some also transfer any outstanding debts due them in the seventh year to the rabbinical court for collection, in accordance with a rabbinic ordinance by Hillel called the *prosbul*. By means of this legal fiction, the obligation may be collected by the creditor after the seventh year. Admittedly, these practices preserved today are external rites, but they point to an earlier period when these laws were basic to Israelite life. Moreover, in recent years, archaeological evidence has accumulated to indicate that the socio-economic aspects of the Sabbatical Year have analogues in ancient Mesopotamia, making it a reasonable assumption that the biblical regulations had a basis in reality.

Both the Sabbatical and the Jubilee Years have left their impress on modern society. In New York City's Rockefeller Plaza there is a short street running between Fifth and Sixth Avenues. Embedded in the pavement is a small metal tablet stating that this thoroughfare was the private property of Columbia University. Every year the street was closed off to traffic for one day, to reassert and thus maintain the university's title to the land—a modern variation of the same technique as that of the Sabbatical Year!

Basing itself explicitly on the biblical law, the Jewish National Fund, the Zionist land-purchasing agency in Israel, leases its property to individuals and groups, but does not sell it in perpetuity.

From this basic concept of God's ownership of the earth and all of its natural resources, if follows that any act of destruction is an offense against the property of God.

The principle of *bal tashit* contains still another religious insight. As we have seen, the Book of Job gives magnificent expression to the recognition that every natural object is an embodiment of the creative power of God and is therefore sacred. The law of *bal tashit* goes further. Whatever has been fashioned by *man*, the product of his energies and talents, is equally a manifestation of God's creative power one step removed, since man is himself the handiwork of God. Vandalism is, therefore, far more than a violation of private property or the destruction of potentially useful objects, it is rebellion against the cosmic order of the universe, which human beings are commanded to enjoy and forbidden to destroy, "For the earth is the Lord's in all its fullness, the world and all who inhabit it" (Ps. 24:1).

Chapter 12

Freedom of Conscience

RELIGIOUS PLURALISM is a major fact of life in the modern world and by the same token a challenge to organized religion and a problem for society. There is no country on the globe that is totally homogeneous religiously. The Arab states in the Middle East and Buddhist lands like Sri Lanka come closest to a religiously uniform population. Latin America is overwhelmingly Catholic, at least officially. But even here there are religious minorities. Muslim countries have achieved the enviable status of being *Judenrein*, except for tiny pockets of Jews still left in Syria and Lebanon. Yet they possess sizable Christian minorities, partly the products of earlier missionary activity and partly the consequence of modern economic and technological development. Latin America has significant numbers of Protestants everywhere, with smaller communities of Jews in the larger countries like Venezuela, Argentina, Brazil, and Uruguay. In the Western democracies, including the United States, the varieties of religious expression are almost limitless.

Pluralism is a fact. But is it a value? The oppression of Jews in Muslim lands has gone on for centuries, long before the birth of the State of Israel, but Jews are not the only victims. The discriminatory treatment of the Copts in Egypt and the persecution of the Bahai in Iran affect two groups that are virtually defenseless before the majority population. Christianity in the Arab world is rigorously consigned to a position of palpable inferiority. In Latin America, Protestants have often complained of the discrimination they encounter, mitigated somewhat by the felt presence of the Yanqui Republic in the North. As for the Jews, a tiny minority everywhere and always, sufferance has been the badge of their tribe for millennia.

123

Perhaps the most pervasive instance of persecution by the dominant state religion is the tragic position of Jews in Communist Russia. Soviet Jewry is denied the right to educate its youth in the culture and tradition of its fathers. Religious schools are forbidden, and Hebrew has the melancholy distinction of being the only language which may not be taught in the Soviet Union. Throughout Soviet Russia, less than a dozen rabbis and cantors function after a fashion in the handful of synagogues left open by the Communists. All means are utilized by the state to suppress underground religious and cultural activity. Jews who try to emigrate are dismissed from their positions and left stranded for years; if they protest too loudly, they are denounced as enemies of the state and sent to prison for long terms.

That a country that is officially atheist practices the harshest forms of religious persecution and denies intellectual freedom to its citizens is proof positive that intolerance is not the private preserve of traditional religion. The suppression of freedom is the logical consequence of absolutist thought, which feeds on the illusion that it possesses the absolute Truth. The degree of discrimination, persecution, and even extermination will depend on a variety of factors, but the essential attitude of antagonism underlies them all.

Does pluralism exist *de facto?* What about *de jure?* It is true that the idea of religious freedom and equality for all believers and nonbelievers is accepted as axiomatic among liberal religious groups, but two facts need to be kept in mind. First, religious liberals represent a small minority within the community of believers, whether they are a segment within the great denominations or constitute an independent sect. Second, the openness to religious pluralism among liberals derives from a lively sense of the tentative nature of all human efforts to comprehend the Divine. In all liberal religion, doubt is a basic ingredient of faith—a characteristic that may well be one of its major virtues. But for the vast majority of religious believers, doubt is an evil spirit to be exorcised by the perfect faith of the true believer, whether he be a Muslim in Saudi Arabia, a Catholic in Latin America, or an Orthodox Jew in Israel. It is highly laudable but not a particularly helpful trait of liberal religious groups to espouse a theory of religious tolerance; they are not likely to embark upon a program of religious persecution! What is needed is a theory of religious tolerance that traditional believers will find compatible with their system of faith and action. The American Jesuit John Courtney Murray, in his book *We Hold These Truths,* sought to find a basis for the democratic freedoms basic to American society that would be in harmony with Catholic theology.

There is available one tradition that has evolved a theory of religious tolerance without surrendering its conviction that it possesses the essential truth about God and man. The historical experience of the Jewish people as a minority group everywhere for nearly two millennia undoubtedly played an important role in the evolution of the Jewish theory of religious tolerance. Thus the Hebraic tradition has a significant contribution to make to a theory of pluralism *de jure* and mot merely *de facto*.

At the outset, it should be pointed out that while religion has made many great contributions to civilization, freedom of conscience is not one of them. It is basically a debt we owe to the secularists. It is in the modern age that religious liberty became a conscious human concern. The Sacred Scriptures of the Judeo-Christian tradition contain the most exalted ethical teaching known to humanity. Yet nowhere in their pages is religious liberty set forth either as a right of the individual or as an obligation of society toward its members. The great classical works in medieval Jewish philosophy from Saadia to Maimonides and Crescas, and the imposing theological treatises of the Church Fathers and the Christian scholastic theologians, do not offer any discussion or analysis of the concept. The sources of religious law, the Talmud and the rabbinic codes in Judaism and the great repositories of Catholic canon law, do not deal with this concept except indirectly in referring to heretics. I know no traditional ethical treatise, in which Judaism is particularly rich, which includes religious liberty as a virtue, and I would imagine that the same situation prevails in Catholic ethical literature.

To be sure, there were individual great-souled believers who had recognized the ideal of freedom of conscience before the modern era. History also knows of a few religiously motivated communities that had established religious freedom before the eighteenth century.

Perhaps the earliest instance of such a society is the Chazar kingdom in Central Russia, between the Volga and the Don rivers, which lasted from the sixth to the tenth century. The Tartar rulers and upper classes of Chazaria had adopted Judaism as their faith in the eighth century, and they accorded full religious liberty to Christians and Muslims as well.[1] The Dutch kingdom established by the Protestant William the Silent in the sixteenth century adopted the principle of toleration, though there were limitations on the doctrine in practice. The Puritan dissenter Roger Williams established the colony of Providence Plantations on Rhode Island, in the New World, making full freedom of conscience the basis of the commonwealth. The Catholic Lord Baltimore extended the right of worship to Protestants. But these were isolated and exceptional cases.

By and large, the principle of freedom of conscience became widely held and increasingly operative only with the Age of Reason. This revolutionary epoch shook both Jews and Judaism to their foundations through the impact of two related yet distinct forces, Emancipation and the Enlightenment. In the wake of the libertarian ideals of the new age, Emancipation broke down the walls of the ghetto throughout Western and Central Europe. With many hesitations and retreats, the Jews of Europe were finally admitted to political citizenship in the lands of their sojourning and granted most social, economic, and cultural opportunities. In the process of political Emancipation, the age-old structure of the Jewish community and its authority over its members were all but completely dissolved. Henceforth, the only bonds remaining were purely voluntary on the part of individual Jews.[2]

Even before Emancipation was complete, the Enlightenment had begun to undermine many of the presuppositions of traditional religion. Christianity had met major challenges before and was therefore able to fend off these attacks with a fair measure of success. Judaism, which for centuries had been isolated from the mainstream of Western culture, found itself almost helpless before the impact of the Enlightenment, particularly at the outset. The various schools of thought in contemporary Judaism represent different efforts at meeting the challenge of the modern world.

Yet, however unsettling the ideas of the Enlightenment proved to traditional religion, they had the positive influence of creating—I am tempted to say compelling—a spirit of mutual tolerance among the great faiths. Lessing's famous drama *Nathan der Weise* highlighted the new spirit. The drama, which had a Mohammedan Sultan and a Jewish Sage as its protagonists, contained the famous parable of the Three Rings. These rings, which were identical in appearance, had been fashioned by a father for his three sons, because he loved them all equally and could not bear to give his priceless ancestral heirloom to any one of them. The overt message of the parable was clear. The three rings symbolize the three monotheistic religions, Judaism, Christianity, and Islam, all of which are expressions of God's love for His creatures and of the reverence they owe Him in return. But scarcely beneath the surface was another implication—none of the three faiths can reasonably insist that it alone represents the true revelation of God and should therefore be granted a privileged position in a free society. According to a striking definition, liberty is the spirit that is never absolutely certain that it is right.

As we have noted, there were individual saints and sages who had found it possible to unite tolerance of religious diversity with a fervent attachment to their own vision of God. But for most men, freedom of religion was the fruit of the rise of secularism. With the weakening of religious attachment among large segments of the population came the conviction that "one religion is as good as another." This pronouncement is, in many cases, a euphemistic restatement of the unspoken sentiment that one religion is as bad as another. Yet whatever its motivations, secularism is to be credited with making freedom of religion not only a pragmatic principle in society, but also an ideal goal for modern men. In this sense, if we may adopt a phrase of Horace M. Kallen, secularism may be described as the will of God.[3]

RELIGIOUS LIBERTY IN A SECULAR WORLD

While we may be truly grateful for this gift of the spirit, it is important to recognize that the ideal of religious liberty on secular foundations suffers from several grave limitations. Its first obvious weakness is that, given its secular origin, the principle of religious liberty would work best where religious loyalty is weakest or nonexistent. If the soil from which freedom of conscience grows is religious indifference, which regards all religions as equally lacking in value, it is obvious that the principle will lose most if its effectiveness among those who regard religion as possessing high significance in human life. Above all, it will be unable to command the allegiance of those who look upon their own religious tradition as possessing a unique measure of truth beyond that of all others. Yet as the history of mankind demonstrates, it is in situations where religious loyalty is most fervent that the danger of hostility to those outside the group is correspondingly greater, so that the doctrine of freedom of conscience is most essential. Thus a secularly motivated doctrine of religious liberty can serve least where it is needed most.

Moreover, liberty of conscience in a purely secular framework can create, at best, only a truce and not a state of peace among the religious groups. This truce is dependent upon the presence of a secular policeman, be it the state or a society in which religious loyalties are weak. On the other hand, if the members of a given social order hold their religious commitments passionately, neither law-enforcement agencies, nor official opinion, nor even a Bill of Rights in a constitution is likely to sustain religious liberty for long. If U.S. Supreme Court Justice William O. Douglas is right in his now-famous dictum about America, "We are a religious people whose institutions pre-suppose a Supreme Being," freedom of religion will be in grave jeopardy when Americans take their pretensions to religiosity seriously, if the doctrine remains rooted only in a secular worldview.

This threat to religious liberty is not merely theoretical. The past few years have witnessed the rapid growth of religious commitment on many levels among the American people. As we have seen, there has been a massive increase in the number of "born-again" Christians, primarily in Evangelical Protestantism, but not limited to these denominations. In Judaism, a marked increase of *ba'alei teshuvah*, "re-pentant Jews returning to the tradition," has been noted primarily in Orthodoxy but also in the other interpretations of Judaism. In addition to these "mainline" churches, there has been a proliferation of cults, Oriental and pseudo-Oriental, as well as newly invented "spiritual" movements, with or without pseudoscientific terminology. They all promise relief from the modern ills of alienation, loneliness, frustration, and anomie, generally by demanding unquestioning obedience to some charismatic leader and the severing of all links with parents, general society, and secular culture. For them, a secular theory of religious liberty is suspect, if not meaningless, *ab initio*. The only hope that these and other religious groups will ever arrive at a *modus vivendi* in a pluralistic society lies in the articulation of a religious basis for religious liberty.

Finally, even if religious believers accept the practice of religious liberty, it will have no binding power upon their consciences unless they relate it to their religious worldview. They may extend freedom of religion to those who differ from them, but it will be, at worst, a grudging surrender to a *force majeure*, and, at best, a counsel of pru-dence, limited in scope and temporary in application.

Unless a nexus is established between the religious tradition to which the believer gives his allegiance and the doctrine of religious liberty, he will still be in mortal danger, even if he takes no step in that direction, of violating the Divine commandment, "You shall not hate your brother *in your heart*" (Lev. 19:17). Thus the integrity of the ethical code by which he lives will be gravely compromised.

In sum, a secular doctrine of religious liberty suffers from all the liabilities to which secular morality as a whole is subject.[4] A secular moral code can deal only with gross malfeasance and not with the subtler offenses of attitude and spirit—what the Talmud calls "matters entrusted to the heart." Nor can it supply the dynamic for an enduring allegiance to the ideal, even when it is within the power of a given group to impose its will on others.

These theoretic weaknesses inherent in a doctrine of religious liberty deriving from secularism are not merely theoretic. Many of the acute danger-points on the earth's surface today represent deep-seated con-flicts among groups who are passionate in their adherence to their religious beliefs. It is from their faith that they draw the seemingly endless energy for internecine conflict. It is in the name of their religion that they justify their unwillingness to lay down their weapons and seek a peaceful solution to their problems. We have only to call to mind the Catholic-Protestant civil war now going on for decades in Northern Ireland, the tragic bloodletting between Christian and Muslim Arabs in

Lebanon, and the wholesale violation of law and morality being perpetrated in Iran by adherents of the Ayatoullah Khomeini in the name of the Prophet of Islam.

The slightly older agony of Bangladesh and the continuing strife between Hindus and Moslems in India supply additional proof that where religious convictions are fervently maintained the concept of religious liberty is tragically difficult to inculcate. Here secularism is totally irrelevant, indeed meaningless.

If religious liberty is to be established as an ideal to which men will give their allegiance, each religious tradition must take seriously its obligation to live and function in a pluralistic society. The first basic step is to go back to its own sources in order to discover what it can contribute to a religiously oriented theory of religious liberty. This chapter seeks to explore the bases in Judaism for a doctrine of religious freedom.

THE RIGHT TO LIBERTY

At the outset, it should be noted that the concept of religious liberty possesses three distinct yet related aspects. Like so many ethical values, its roots lie in the instinct of self-preservation. In other words, *the first and oldest aspect of religious liberty is the right which a group claims for itself to practice its faith without interference from others.* The extension of this right to other individuals and groups is a great leap forward both in time and insight, which requires centuries to achieve and has all too often remained unattained to the present day. Indeed, even in our age, instances are not lacking of groups in virtually every denomination who define the right to religious liberty as the right to deny religious liberty to those who differ from them.[5]

In this respect, religious liberty is no different from any basic right, such as freedom of speech or assembly, which is first fought for and achieved by a group on its own behalf. Only later—and sometimes only half-heartedly—*is freedom of conscience extended to other groups who differ in belief and practice.* Finally, the third and most difficult stage in religious liberty emerges—and it is far from universal—*when a religious group, dedicated to its belief and tradition, is willing to grant freedom of thought and action to dissidents within its own ranks.*

The Jewish people has played a significant role in the emergence of religious liberty in its first aspect. With regard to the two other aspects, I believe that Judaism, nurtured by the Jewish historical experience, has some significant insights to offer all men.

We may preface our discussion of these three categories of religious liberty by pointing out that no other religious group has as great a stake in the present and future vitality of the doctrine as has the Jewish community. It is true that virtually every denomination finds itself a minority in one or another corner of the globe and, unfortunately, can point to infractions of its right to worship and propagate its faith. Protestants were long exercised over the situation in Spain and parts of Latin America. Catholics are troubled by the status of the church in Communist lands. Christians generally find themselves in difficult positions in parts of Africa and in Muslim autocracies in the Middle East.

Jews have had the sorry distinction of being a minority almost everywhere and always. In the thirty-six hundred years since Abraham the Jewish people have been masters of their own destiny as an independent nation in Palestine for a small fraction of their history. This status prevailed less than five hundred years during the days of the First Temple, for eighty years during the Second Temple, and now during the thirty-eight years of the State of Israel in our day. These six hundred years constitute no more than one-sixth of the recorded history of the Jews. Moreover, even during these periods of independence and autonomy, there were large Jewish communities outside Palestine, more populous by far than the Jewish population in the homeland. The survival of these Diaspora communities was directly dependent on the degree of religious liberty they enjoyed. Hence, the curtailment of religious liberty may pose a major problem for all denominations; it is an issue of life and death for the Jewish group.

There is, therefore, historic justice in the fact that the people for whom religious liberty is so fundamental were the first to take up arms in defense of this right. The earliest recorded war for religious liberty is the struggle of the Maccabees against the Syrian Greek King Antiochus Epiphanes, which broke out in 168 B.C.E. The Maccabean struggle was launched not for the sake of political liberty, territorial aggrandizement, national honor, or booty. It represented the armed resistance of a group in Palestinian Jewry who were resolved to protect their religious faith and way of life in a world where a determined effort was being made to impose the uniform pattern of Hellenistic culture and pagan religion on the entire Middle East.

Had the Maccabees not fought, or had they fought and lost, the Hebrew Scriptures would have been destroyed, Judaism would have been annihilated, Christianity would not have been born, and the ideals of the Judeo-Christian heritage, basic to Western civilization, would have perished. There was, therefore, ample justification for the practice of the early Christian Church, both in the East and West, which celebrated a festival on August 1 called the "Birthday of the Maccabees," testifying to the debt which Christianity, as well as Judaism, owes to these early, intrepid defenders of freedom of conscience.[6]

Thus the long struggle was launched for the first and oldest aspect of the concept of religious liberty. From that day to this, there have been communities which have conceived of religious liberty almost exclusively in terms of their right to observe their own beliefs and practices. For such a group, the degree of religious liberty in a given society is measured by the extent to which it, and it alone, is free to propagate its faith. Religious liberty is defined as "freedom for religion," and "religion" is equated with the convictions of the particular group.

This limited conception of religious liberty has a long and "respectable" history behind it. It is noteworthy that the only instances in history of forcible conversion to Judaism were carried out by descendants of the very same Maccabees who had fought for religious liberty for their own people. The Maccabean prince John Hyrcanus (135–104 B.C.E.) forced the Idumeans, hereditary enemies of the Jews, to accept Judaism. His son, Aristobulus, Judaized part of Galilee in the northern district of Palestine.[7] These steps were dictated less by religious zeal than by practical considerations, a universal characteristic of mass conversions to our own day. It was not the only time that politics was wrapped in the garb of religion, nearly always to the detriment of religion.

For centuries, the doctrine that "error has no rights," unmitigated either by intellectual subtlety or by practical considerations, continued to hold sway. Heresy, that is to say, dissident views within dominant religious organisms, could be suppressed either individually or collectively by peaceful persuasion or by physical force. For heresy was viewed as illegitimate and sinful and hence worthy of the heaviest penalties. With the rise of Protestantism, which emphasized "private judgment" and the reading of the Bible as the unmediated Word of God, a multiplicity of sects emerged. What was equally significant, their legitimacy was, at least in theory, not open to question by the state. Religious liberty now became a practical necessity for the body politic as well as a burning issue for minority sects. Basically, it is to these minority groups that the world owes a debt for broadening the concept of religious liberty.

LIMITED UNDERSTANDING OF RELIGIOUS LIBERTY

Yet, by and large, the ideal to which the various sects gave their loyalty continued to be religious liberty for themselves. When the Puritans left England and later emigrated from Holland to Massachusetts, they were actuated by a passionate desire for freedom of conscience, but in this limited sense only. Protestant dissenters, Catholics, Jews, and nonbelievers could expect scant hospitality in the Bay Colony, and when any appeared within its borders, they were given short shrift. Various disabilities for non-Protestants survived in some New England states as late as the nineteenth century. Religious liberty began as a practical policy designed to establish articles of peace between opposing sects. Only slowly and painfully did it emerge as an ideal to which men have given their loyalty quite distinct from ulterior considerations.

Freedom of religion in an open society must necessarily presuppose two elements which were less obvious in the stratified societies of earlier days. *It must include religious equality,* for there can be no true religious liberty if the formal freedom of worship is coupled with legal, psychological, social, or economic liabilities. That is the situation that prevails in Soviet Russia today. To be sure, a minority group cannot reasonably expect the same level of importance in society as the majority, but it has the right to demand that there be no restrictions or liabilities placed upon it by the state. In other words, full religious liberty means that the state will recognize the equality of all believers and nonbelievers, even though in society the relative strength of various groups will necessarily impose disadvantages upon the poorer and less numerous sects.

To cite a hypothetical case, a Protestant worshipping in a modest dissenter's chapel or a Jew offering his devotions in a simple prayer room could not reasonably object to the presence of a magnificent Catholic church in the community. But they would have legitimate grounds for objecting to a legal ordinance forbidding the building of a large Methodist church or an elaborate Jewish synagogue in the area. So would a Catholic finding himself restrained from erecting a church, a monastery, or a parochial school in a given community.

There is one additional element essential to full religious freedom: *religious liberty is not being truly safeguarded if it is purchased at the cost of religious vitality.* Frequently the position of the Jewish community on questions of church and state is misunderstood because it is attributed solely to the desire to avoid religious disabilities for itself and other minority groups, including the secularists. It is true that the position of minorities with regard to freedom of religion may parallel that of nonbelievers, who also oppose utilizing the power and resources of the state to buttress the claims of organized religion. But there is another and at least equally deep motivation for the Jewish position: a sincere concern for the preservation of religious vitality. This is possible only when religious convictions are free to be expressed. Here majority groups have as direct an interest as the minority.

A striking illustration is at hand in the controversy that arose when the U.S. Supreme Court outlawed as unconstitutional the prayer proposed by the Board of Regents of the State of New York for the public schools. Now that some of the smoke has cleared away, though by no means all the fire, it is clear that the Supreme Court was not "banishing God from American life." By the same token, it should be clear that Jews who, with few exceptions, wholeheartedly applauded the position of the Supreme Court (as did many other Americans) were not allying themselves with secularists and nonbelievers. They were defending what, according to their lights, represents the cause of the vitality of religion as well as its liberty. Religious practices that are imposed by psychological no less than by legal means do not strengthen but weaken the vitality of religion. In several European countries the state supports one or more churches, religious education is compulsory in the schools, and prayer is an obligatory exercise. These countries exhibit a low level of religious commitment among their adult population, far less than in the United States, where religious practice and belief are entirely voluntary and are not enforced by the state.

To be sure, the Regents' prayer was nonsectarian, but as anyone genuinely committed to religion knows, there are some religious practices that are more nonsectarian than others! A good case in point was afforded by the "nondenominational" Decalogue which, thirty-two hundred years after Moses on Sinai, was revealed to the school board of New Hyde Park, Long Island. From the most praiseworthy of motives, these guardians of the local public school system created a new text for the Ten Commandments which was neither Jewish nor Catholic nor Protestant, but one undoubtedly superior to them all. In their version the First Commandment read, "I am the Lord thy God who brought thee forth out of the house of bondage."[8] In one fell swoop, the entire historic experience of Israel, which lies at the basis of the biblical covenant and the Judeo-Christian tradition, was eliminated.

RELIGIOUS LIBERTY IN JUDAISM

We have dealt thus far with the first aspect of the ideal of religious liberty: the right which every religious group claims for itself to practice its faith freely, without restriction or interference from others. With regard to the two other aspects of the ideal of religious liberty—more theoretic in character—we believe the specific Jewish historic experience has significance for other religious groups and for the preservation of a free society itself.

As we have noted, there is, theoretically at least, no problem with regard to the doctrine of freedom of conscience for those who maintain that all religions are equally good—or bad. Some years ago, when

Communism was making substantial inroads among American college youth, I participated in a symposium on "Communism and Religion."[9] Among the panelists were a Methodist bishop, a Presbyterian minister, two rabbis, and Earl Browder, then a leading spokesman for Communism in the United States. As the various speakers for religion sought to develop their positions *vis-à-vis* Communism, Mr. Browder turned to us and declared, to the manifest delight of the youthful audience, "The Communists are the only ones who can establish peace and equality among all religions—because we do not believe in any of them!" The history of twentieth-century totalitarianism has demonstrated that religious intolerance can flourish under Communism and Fascism. Religious bigots can learn many a lesson in practicing their craft from the antireligious bigots of our age. The crude and brutal persecution of religion by atheistic regimes today makes the classic instances of religious intolerance of the past seem almost idyllic by comparison.

Nonetheless, it is true that the problem of evolving a theory of religious tolerance and practicing it is genuine and complex, particularly for those believers who are convinced that they are the repositories of the truth and that their fellowmen who differ from them are not so blessed. In this connection, the attitude of the Jewish tradition is particularly interesting. It arose within a community that believes profoundly that it possesses the authentic Revelation of God and that all other faiths contain, by that token, a greater or lesser admixture of error. Since such a standpoint is widespread among communicants of most creeds, it should be useful to examine the theory and practice of *religious liberty within Judaism*—the approach of the Jewish tradition toward dissidents within its own community. Even more significant for the world at large is the theory and practice in Judaism of *religious liberty toward non-Jews*—the attitude of the Jewish tradition toward (a) the rights of non-Jews seeking to maintain their own creeds, and (b) the legitimacy of such faiths from the purview of Judaism.

In order to comprehend the Jewish attitude toward religious differences within the community, it must be kept in mind that Judaism was always marked by a vast variety of religious experience, which is given articulate expression in the pages of the Hebrew Scriptures. The Hebrew Bible contains within its broad and hospitable limits the products of the varied and often contradictory activities of priest and lawgiver, historian, prophet and sage, psalmist and poet. It reflects the temperaments of the mystic and the rationalist, the simple believer and the profound seeker after ultimate truth. The reason inheres in the fact that the Hebrew Bible is not a collection of like-minded tracts, but is, in the words of a great modern exegete, "a national literature upon a religious foundation."[10]

This characteristic of the Bible set its stamp upon all succeeding epochs in the history of Judaism. It is not accidental that the most creative era in its history after the biblical era, the period of the Second Commonwealth, was the most "sect-ridden."[11] Even our fragmentary sources disclose the existence of the Pharisees, the Sadducees, the Essenes, and the Zealots, to use Josephus' classic tabulation of the "Four Philosophies." We know from the Talmud, which is a massive monument to controversy, that the Pharisees themselves, the dominant group in number and influence, were divided into various groups which held to strongly opposing positions, with hundreds of individual scholars differing from the majority on scores of issues. Although, unfortunately, too little is known about the Sadducees, the same variety of outlook may be assumed among them. With regard to the Essenes, the discovery of the Dead Sea Scrolls has indicated that the term Essenes is best used of an entire conspectus of sects who differed among themselves passionately. The Samaritans were also a significant group of dissidents, highly articulate in their divergence from a Jerusalem-centered Judaism. It was in this atmosphere that the early Jewish Christians first appeared, adding to the charged atmosphere of vitality and variety in Palestinian Judaism. There were also countless additional patterns of religious expression in the various Diaspora communities.

To be sure, all these groups in Judaism shared many fundamentals in their outlook, but there were important divergences, both within each sect and among them. The Talmud records that among the Pharisees the differences between the schools of Hillel and Shammai were deep-seated and broke into physical violence at one point.[12] Nonetheless, the Talmud declares, the Shammaites and the Hillelites did not hesitate to intermarry, and "He who observes according to the decision of Beth Hillel, like him who follows the school of Shammai, is regarded as fulfilling the Law" because "both these and others are the words of the Living God."[13] No such encomiums were pronounced on the Sadducees, who contradicted the fundamental principle of normative Judaism regarding the Divine origin and authority of the Oral Law. Those holding Sadducean views were stigmatized as "having no share in the world-to-come."[14] In this world, however, it is noteworthy that neither the Sadducees nor any others of these sects were ever officially excommunicated.

In the Middle Ages a variety of factors combined to contract this latitude of religious outlook in the Jewish community. First of all, the constantly worsening conditions of exile and alien status required, it was felt, a greater degree of group homogeneity. Secondly, most of the earlier dissident viewpoints disappeared. Thus, the standpoint of the super-nationalist Zealots was now totally meaningless, while that of the

Sadducees, who centered their religious life in the Temple at Jerusalem, was completely irrelevant to the life of an exiled people. Thirdly, the widespread emphasis on religious conformity imposed by the medieval world on its aberrant sects also proved a model and example. Father Joseph Lecler points out in his massive two-volume work, *Toleration and the Reformation*, that St. Thomas Aquinas was "relatively tolerant toward pagans and completely intolerant toward heretics." As Father John B. Sheerin notes, St. Thomas explicitly stated that "to accept the faith is a matter of free will, but to hold it, once it has been accepted is a matter of necessity."

No such precise and logical theory was ever elaborated in Judaism. The Jewish community lacked the power to compel uniformity of thought, even in the relatively rare instances when the leadership was tempted to embark upon such an enterprise. Nonetheless, some efforts *were* made to restrict religious liberty in the Middle Ages. The history of these undertakings is significant for the intrinsic nature of the Jewish tradition.

THE CONTRIBUTION OF MAIMONIDES

Somewhat paradoxically, the attempt to impose a measure of uniformity on religious belief was due to the emergence of medieval Jewish philosophy, which was nurtured in Aristotelianism, and to a lesser degree in Platonism. Maimonides, the greatest Jewish thinker of the Middle Ages, confidently proposed a set of Thirteen Principles which he hoped would serve as an official creed for Judaism. Though his statement attained wide popularity and was printed in the traditional prayerbook as an appendix, lesser men did not hesitate to quarrel with both the content and the number of articles of belief in his Creed, and it never became an official confession of faith.

An even more striking illustration of the enduring vitality of the right to religious diversity in Judaism may be cited. Uncompromisingly rationalistic as he was, Maimonides declared that to ascribe any physical form to God was tantamount to heresy and deprived one of a share in the world-to-come. Nowhere is the genius of Judaism better revealed than here. On the same printed page of the Maimonides Code where this statement is encountered, it is challenged by the remark of his critic and commentator, Rabbi Abraham ben David of Posquières, who writes: "Better and greater men [than Maimonides] have ascribed a physical form to God, basing themselves on their understanding of scriptural passages and even more so on some legends and utterances, which give wrong ideas."[15] The critic's standpoint is clear. Rabbi Abraham ben David agrees with Maimonides in denying a physical form to God, but he affirms the right of the individual to maintain backward ideas in Judaism without being read out of the fold on that account. The right to be wrong is the essence of liberty.

Nonetheless, it is clear that the spirit of medieval Judaism was far less hospitable to religious diversity than had been Rabbinic Judaism in the centuries immediately before and after the destruction of the Temple. Thus, while the Sadducees, who denied the validity of the Oral Law, were never excommunicated, the medieval Karaites, who rejected the authority of the Talmud in favor of the letter of Scripture, were excommunicated by various individual scholars. At the same time, other scholars refused to invoke the ban against them, and ultimately a more lenient attitude prevailed.

The excommunication of Spinoza in 1656, like the earlier ban on Uriel Acosta, by the Sephardic community of Amsterdam, though frequently cited, was actually highly exceptional and the result of specific conditions. Primarily, it was the reflex action of a community threatened simultaneously on two fronts. On the one hand, the Jewish community in the Netherlands was living on sufferance, so that harboring a heretic who attacked the fundamentals of traditional religion might well jeopardize its status in the country. Second, the historic tradition of Judaism, long isolated from the winds of modern doctrine, felt itself too weak to sustain the reasoned onslaught of secular rationalism.[16]

Excommunication was attempted again against religious diversity in the eighteenth century, this time against Hasidism, a folk movement, pietistic in character, which arose in Eastern Europe. The ban proved a total failure. Ultimately, the sect abated its hostility toward Rabbinical Judasim. Today the Hasidim and the *Mitnaggedim*, their rabbinical "opponents," are all within the camp of Orthodox Judaism.

In the nineteenth century, when the Reform movement first began to appear in Central Europe, some Orthodox rabbis in Central and Eastern Europe sought to stem the tide by invoking the ban against the innovators. It had proved largely ineffective in the field of ideas even in the Middle Ages; now it was completely useless. It served only to drive deeper the wedge between the traditionalists and the non-traditionalists and was tacitly abandoned.

In sum, religious liberty within the Jewish community exists *de facto*. It is recognized *de jure* by all groups in Reform and Conservative Judaism and by more liberal segments in Orthodoxy as well.

It need hardly be added that divergences among the groups—and within them— are often sharp, and the antagonisms among some of the advocates of different positions are, all too frequently, even sharper. The upsurge in some quarters of "religiosity" which followed in the wake of the irruption of Nazi savagery and the mass bestiality of World War II had powerful impact upon Jews as well as upon Christians.[17] It has strengthened the tendency to withdrawal and insulation against the world among many survivors of the Hitler Holocaust and exacerbated their hostility to all those outside their particular group. This spirit is very much in evidence today, but it is a mood of the day, if not of the moment, and it will pass. If history is any guide, these attitudes of isolation and hostility will be softened with time under the impact of gentler experiences. The harrowing event of the last three decades cannot abrogate the tradition of three millennia.

An observation is here in order with regard to the status of religion in the State of Israel. The Israeli Cabinet includes a Minister of Religions (in the plural), who is charged with the supervision and the maintenance of the holy places of all the three great religions and with the support of their institutional and educational requirements. It is paradoxical, but true, that at present there is full freedom of religion in Israel for everyone—except for Jews! Catholic and Protestant Christianity, Islam and Bahai, all enjoy the fullest freedom of expression, including the right to worship and teach. In addition to the Minister of Religions, Israel has two (or three, or four) Chief Rabbis who are of unimpeachable Orthodoxy, except for those Orthodox groups who deny their authority. In accordance with the legacy of Turkish and British law, the Chief Rabbi (like his Christian and Islamic counterparts) has authority in the fields of personal status, notably marriage, divorce, and conversion, and, to a lesser degree, in the maintenance of religious observance in the army and public institutions, and in the supervision of religious education.

At present, the religious Establishment is supported by the State of Israel. To be sure, the effort is made to invest the contemporary situation with the halo of tradition. The historical truth is, however, that the very existence of the office of the Chief Rabbi in Israel represents not a return to Jewish tradition, but an imitation of non-Jewish models, and its value is highly debatable.

With the Chief Rabbinate as its symbol, Orthodoxy is the only officially recognized Jewish religious group in Israel today. Yet here, too, the innate tradition of dissent finds uninhibited expression. Thus, when the new and magnificent headquarters of the Chief Rabbinate was erected in Jerusalem, many of the leading Orthodox scholars announced that it was religiously prohibited to cross the threshold of the building!

Side by side with these tensions within Israeli Orthodoxy are various other groups, Reform, Conservative (called *Mesorati*, "traditional"), and Reconstructionist, representing a wide spectrum of modernism. They are exposed to many legal disabilities at the hands of the state and to harassment and annoyance by militants in society. In the fall of 1979, the two Chief Rabbis of Jerusalem publicly declared that it was religiously forbidden to worship in Conservative synagogues on the High Holy

Days. The decree proved counterproductive and was greeted with embarrassment, even among the Orthodox. Today there are several scores of Conservative and Reform synagogues in the country, and their schools are growing as well. The official ban upon weddings performed by non-Orthodox rabbis is under increasing challenge. Ultimately, the various schools of Jewish religious thought will demand and receive full recognition.

No long-term conclusions may therefore be drawn from the present union of religion and state in Israel. It is partial and subject to increasing strain and stress. That the ultimate pattern of religion-state relationships will approach the principle of the separation of church and state as understood in the United States is rather unlikely, but the religious disabilities suffered by non-Orthodox Jewish movements—and by no one else—will not long endure.

The conclusion is unassailable that the nature of Judaism, buttressed by its historic experience, makes the freedom of religious dissent a recognized reality for virtually all members of the community *de facto*, even by those who would not recognize it *de jure*.

JUDAISM—ITS RELATION TO OTHER FAITHS

The attitude of Judaism toward religious liberty for those professing other creeds derives, in large measure, from another unique characteristic of the Jewish tradition, one which is frequently misunderstood not only by those outside the Jewish community, but by many who are within it. This trait, deeply rooted in normative Judaism, is the balance between particularism and universalism.[18] The Jewish conception of freedom of religion is the resultant of two superficially opposing forces: the retention of the specific, national Jewish content in the tradition on the one hand, and on the other, an equally genuine concern for the establishment among all men of the faith in one God and obedience to His religious and ethical imperatives.

It is frequently argued that with the appearance of monotheism, intolerance became a coefficient of religion. It is undoubtedly true that, in a polytheistic worldview, tolerance of other gods is implicit, since there is always room for one more figure in the pantheon, and the history of religious syncretism bears out this truth. On the other hand, the emergence of belief in one God necessarily demands the denial of the reality of all other deities. The "jealous God" of the Hebrew Bible, who forbids "any other god before Me," therefore frequently became the source of religious intolerance. So runs the theory.[19]

It sometimes happens, however, that a beautiful pattern of invincible logic is contradicted by the refractory behavior of life itself. An apposite illustration may be cited. The French Semitic scholar Ernest Renan declared that the monotony of the desert produced a propensity for monotheism among the ancient Hebrews, whereas the variety in the physical landscape of Greece, for example, with it mountains and hills, its valleys, rivers, and streams, necessarily suggested a multitude of divinities indwelling in them. This plausible theory enjoyed considerable vogue until it was learned that the pre-Islamic nomadic Arabs, who inhabited the vast monotonous stretches of the Arabian Desert, possessed a luxuriant polytheism, and that all the Semitic peoples whose original habitat was the same desert, also had very elaborate pantheons. Thus the list of gods in the library of King Ashurbanipal contains more than 2,500 gods, and modern scholars have added substantially to the number.

Now it is true that Judaism was strongly opposed to paganism. It insisted upon the uncompromising unity of God and refused to admit even a semblance of reality to other gods. Nonetheless, Biblical Judaism reckoned with the existence of paganism from two points of view. Though logicians might have recoiled in horror from the prospect, the fact is that Hebrew monotheism, the authentic and conscious faith in the existence of one God, did accord a kind of legitimacy to polytheism—for non-Jews. In part, this may have derived from a recognition of the actual existence of flourishing heathen cults. In far larger degree, we believe, it was a consequence of the particularist emphasis in Judaism. Dedicated to preserving the specific group character of the Hebrew faith, the Jewish tradition was led to grant a similar charter of justification to the specific ethos of other nations, which always included their religion.

Whatever the explanation; the fact is clear. No book in the Bible, not even Isaiah or Job, is more explicitly monotheistic than Deuteronomy: "You shall know this day, and consider it in your heart, that the Lord is God in heaven above, and upon the earth beneath; there is no one else" (4:39). Yet the same book, which warns Israel against polytheism, speaks of the worship of "the sun, the moon and the stars . . . which the Lord your God has assigned to all the nations under the sky" (4:19, compare 29:25). Thus the paradox emerges that the particularist element in Judaism proved the embryo of a theory of religious tolerance.

The second factor that helped to grant a measure of value to non-Jewish religion is one more congenial to sophisticated religious thinkers. A broad-minded exponent of monotheism would be capable of recognizing, even in the pagan cults against which Judaism fought, an imperfect, unconscious aspiration toward the one living God. Perhaps the most striking expression of this insight is to be found in the post-exilic prophet Malachi: "For from the rising of the sun to its setting, My name is great among the nations; and everywhere incense is burnt and pure oblations are offered to My name, for My name is great among the nations, says the Lord of Hosts" (1:11).

Centuries later, Paul, standing in the middle of the Areopagus, echoed the same idea in his words: "Men of Athens, I observed at every turn that you are a most religious people! Why, as I passed along and scanned your objects of worship, I actually came upon an altar with the inscription, TO THE UNKNOWN GOD" (Acts 17:22–24).

This is not the only instance of universalism in our biblical sources. The author of the Book of Jonah pictures the pagan sailors and the king and inhabitants of Nineveh in a far more favorable light than he does the fugitive Hebrew prophet. There is the warm compassion of the Book of Ruth for a friendless stranger.

Towering above all is the breadth of view of the Book of Job, which pictures the patriarch Job not as a Hebrew who observes the law of the Torah, but as a non-Jew whose noble creed and practice are described in his Code of a Man of Honor (chap. 31). [20] In this, the most subtle and exalted presentation of individual ethics in the Hebrew Bible, Job lists fourteen ethical and religious sins from which he has been free. The standard of conduct they reflect constitutes perhaps the oldest formulation of a body of natural law which is binding upon all human beings.

This Code of a Man of Honor includes also the first affirmation of the equality of all people:

> Have I despised the cause of my manservant,
>   or of my maidservant, when they contended with me?
> For I always remembered,
>   "What shall I do when God rises up, and when He examines me,
>   how shall I answer Him?
> Did not He make him in the womb, as He made me,
>   and fashion us both alike in the womb?"
>
> (Job 31:13–15)

All these biblical writings testify to the fact that it was possible to maintain the unity and universality of God while reckoning with the values inherent in the imperfect approximations to be found in the pagan cults.

Thus the two apparently contradictory elements of the biblical world-view—the emphasis upon a particularist ethos and the faith in a universal God—served as the seedbed for the flowering of a highly significant theory of religious tolerance in post-biblical Judaism.

At the same time, it was self-evident that a universal God who is Father of all men deserves the allegiance and loyalty of all His children. A steady and unremitting effort was therefore made to counteract the blandishments of paganism and to win all men for Jewish monotheism through the use of persuasion. The biblical Deutero-Isaiah, the apocryphal *Sibylline Oracles*, the lifelong activity of Philo of Alexandria—indeed the entire apologetic literature of Hellenistic Judaism—were designed to win the allegiance of men for the one living God of Israel.

Holding fast to their conviction that Judaism alone represents the true faith in the one God, the prophets had looked forward to its ultimate acceptance by all men: "For at that time I will change the speech of the peoples to a pure speech, that they may all call on the name of the Lord, to serve him with one accord" (Zeph. 3:9). "And the Lord will be king over all the earth; on that day shall the Lord be one, and His name be one" (Zech. 14:9).

This faith for the future did not cause Judaism to overlook the realities of the present. The ultimate may be, nay must be, left to God; the proximate is the concern of man. Since Judaism did not deny *in toto* the values to be found in the religious professions and even more in the ethical practices of many of their pagan fellowmen, it created one of the most distinctive concepts of monotheistic religion, a unique contribution to the theory of religious liberty—the doctrine of the Noahide Laws, which actually antedates the Talmud.

The original impulse behind the formulation of the Noahide code was not the desire to be "lenient" toward non-Jews as being "beyond the law." The purpose was not even to free the generality of mankind from the obligation to observe the complex of biblical ritual and law incumbent upon the Jewish people. The aim was to restrain the tendencies to lawlessness and violence deeply embedded in human nature by imposing the great fundamental norms of civilized behavior upon all human beings and holding them morally accountable for any infraction.

The Noahide Laws as an adumbration of natural law have been described above. They arose in a pagan world in which the worship of the Living God and obedience to His will did not prevail. But the logical consequences of the doctrine were ineluctable, and they were drawn with increasing clarity after the emergence of the two other great monotheistic religions, Christianity and Islam. If all non-Jews are as much obligated to observe the Noahide Laws as Jews are to fulfill all the precepts enjoined upon them by the Torah, it follows inescapably that the non-Jew who observes the Noahide canon is as worthy of salvation as the Jew who observes the entire rubric of Jewish law. Hence, there is no imperative need for the non-Jew to accept the Jewish faith in order to be "saved."

These Laws of the Sons of Noah, it may be noted, seem to be referred to in the New Testament as well: "We should write to them to abstain from the pollutions of idols and from unchastity and from what is strangled and from blood. . . . You abstain from what has been sacrificed to idols, and from blood and from what is strangled and from unchastity. If you keep yourselves from these, you will do well. Farewell" (Acts 15:20, 29).

This doctrine of the Noahide Laws, be it noted, was not the product of religious indifference. It arose among devotees of a traditional religion who not only loved their faith but believed that it alone was the product of authentic revelation. Yet they found room for faiths other than their own, as of right and not merely on sufferance.

THE DAUGHTER FAITHS OF JUDAISM

The principle of the Noahide Laws had originated in a pagan world. It obviously proved even more valuable when two monotheistic religions, Christianity and Islam, replaced paganism. Both "daughter faiths" sought energetically to displace the mother and deny her authenticity. The mother faith sought to repel these onslaughts as effectively as possible by calling attention to what she regarded as their errors. But she did not, on that account, ignore the elements of truth which her more aggressive offspring possessed.

The attitude of Judaism in the Middle Ages toward these two religions necessarily differed with the personality of each particular authority, his environment, and his own personal experience. The proximity of the Christian and the Jewish communities in Europe, and the consequent economic and social relationships upon which Jewish survival depended, compelled the medieval rabbinic authorities to reckon with reality. In the Talmud considerable limitations had been placed upon Jewish contacts with pagans, particularly at heathen festivals and with regard to idolatrous objects of worship. In the Middle Ages the rabbis could not maintain the position that Christians were pagans and that all the talmudic restrictions upon intercourse with idolaters applied to them. By and large, these modifications of talmudic law were originally *ad hoc* improvisations and limited to specific practices upon which the livelihood of Jews depended.[21] But what began as a practical necessity led to the rise of an appropriate theory.

Among the most painful features of medieval Jewish-Christian relations were the public religious disputations forced upon the Jews, often at the instigation of Jewish converts to Christianity.[22] Nonetheless, these debates led to one positive result. They gave the Jews the impetus to re-evaluate the general principles governing their attitude toward non-Jews and to recognize that there were significant differences between the pagans of antiquity, to whom the Talmud refers as "idolaters," and the Christians who were their contemporaries in the Middle Ages.

Thus the tragic disputation convened in Paris in 1240, involving the convert Nicholas Donin and four Jewish representatives, led to the public burning of twenty-four cartloads of Hebrew books. The chief Jewish spokesman was Jehiel ben Joseph of Paris, and he was assisted by Moses of Coucy. It is a tribute to the greatness of Moses' spirit that, in spite of this grim exhibition of fanaticism, he developed a new insight into the character of the dominant faith, an insight undoubtedly stimulated by his participation in the debate. Time and again he called upon his brethren to maintain scrupulous ethical standards in dealings with Christians, basing himself on broad religious and moral considerations.[23] Not expediency, but regard for the honor of Israel and the avoidance of *Hillul Hashem*, "the desecration of the Holy Name,"[24] became the fundamental motivations.[25]

The practical need of a *modus vivendi* between Jews and Christians could not be denied, since they lived in closest proximity with one another throughout Europe. Simultaneously, the outlines of a theory of religious tolerance were being laid by Jewish thinkers living in Muslim as well as in Christian countries. The teaching of the second-century Talmudic sage, Rabbi Joshua, "There are righteous among the Gentiles who have a share in the world-to-come,"[26] was slightly but significantly broadened by Maimonides into the generalization, "The righteous among the Gentiles have a share in the world-to-come."[27] Thus the principle that salvation was open even to those outside the Jewish fold remained normative and served as the basic principle underlying the Noahide Laws. The medieval poet and philosopher Judah Halevi wrote, "These peoples [i.e., Christianity and Islam] represent a preparation and preface to the Messiah for whom we wait, who is the fruit of the tree which they will ultimately recognize as the roots which they now despise."[28]

Rabbi Menahem Meiri, who lived in thirteenth-century France when several expulsions of Jews from that country took place, wrote,

> Those among the heathen of the ancient days who observe the seven Noahide precepts, i.e., refrain from idol worship, desecration of God's name, robbery, incest, cruelty to animals, and have courts of justice, enjoy the same rights as Jews; how much the more so in our days, when the nations are distinguished by their religion and respect for law! We must, however, treat equally even those who have no system of law, in order to sanctify the Name of God.[29]

He distinctly declares that "in our days idolatry has ceased in most places," and describes both Muslims and Christians as "nations disciplined by the ways of their religions."[30]

Moreover, even the trinitarian concept of Christianity, which Judaism emphatically rejected as impugning the unity of God, was not generally regarded as sufficient to deny to Christianity the character of a monotheistic faith. The twelfth-century talmudic commentator Rabbi Isaac the Tosafist set forth a legal basis for the view that belief in the Trinity was legitimate for Christians in his statement: "The children of Noah are not prohibited from *shittuf*, i.e., associating the belief in God with that in other beings."[31] This utterance achieved such wide scope and authority that it was frequently attributed by later scholars to the Talmud itself.

Maimonides, with his penchant for systematic canons of thought, was strongly critical both of Christianity and of Islam. Living all his life in Islamic countries, with few direct contacts with Christians, Maimonides tended to react negatively to the trinitarianism of Christianity and to its Messianic claims for Jesus as the Savior. On the other hand, the uncompromising emphasis upon the unity of God in Mohammedanism, with which he was in constant contact, gave him a greater degree of tolerance for Islam, although he castigated the sensuality of the Prophet Mohammed. Even the adoration of the Ka'abah, the black stone of Mecca, was regarded by Maimonides as a vestige of polytheism which had been reinterpreted in Islam—a remarkable anticipation of modern scholarship.

In a passage in his great code, *Mishneh Torah* (which appears mutilated in the printed texts because of the censor), Maimonides rejects the claim that Jesus was the Messiah on the ground that Jesus failed to fulfill the Messianic function as envisioned in Scripture and tradition. Maimonides then proceeds:

> The thought of the Creator of the world is beyond the power of man to grasp, for their ways are not His ways and their thoughts are not His thoughts. All the words of Jesus the Nazarene and of Mohammed, who arose after him, came into being only in order to make straight the road for the King Messiah, who would perfect the world to serve God together, as it is said, "Then I shall turn all the peoples into a clear speech, that they may all call upon the Lord and serve Him shoulder to shoulder."
>
> How is that to be? The world has already been filled with the words of the Messiah and the words of the Torah and the commandments. And these words have spread to the furthermost islands among many people uncircumcised of heart or of flesh, who now discuss the Commandments of the Torah. Some declare that these commandments were true, but are now no longer obligatory and have fallen into decline, while others declare that there are secret meanings within them, not according to their obvious intent and that the Messiah had come and disclosed their secret connotations.
>
> But when the true King Messiah will arise, he will succeed and be raised to glory, and then they will all return and recognize they had inherited falsehood, and that their prophets and ancestors had misled them.[32]

Maimonides elsewhere declares that Christians are idolaters because of their trinitarian beliefs.[33] In this regard, he goes further than the warrant of his rabbinic sources. Nor was his attitude shared by most of his contemporaries. Thus, his great predecessor Saadia (882–942), the first great figure in medieval Jewish philosophy and who also lived under Islam, declared that the Christians' belief in the Trinity is not an expression of idolatry, but the personification of their faith in life, power, and knowledge.[34] In his negative view, Maimonides not only ignored the talmudic passage quoted above, but was in sharpest variance with most Jewish scholars, such as Rashi and Meiri, who lived in Christian countries, knew Christians at first hand, and recognized their deeply rooted belief in the One God.

Later such rabbinic authorities as Moses Rivkes, Hayyim Yair Bacharach (1638–1702), and Rabbi Jacob Emden (1697–1776) explicitly recognized a common tradition linking Judaism and Christianity when they pointed out that Christians believed in God, the Exodus, revelation, the truth of the Bible, and *creatio ex nihilo*.[35]

In the eighteenth century, Moses Mendelssohn wrote a famous reply to the Protestant minister Johann Casper Lavater. Therein he expounded the traditional Jewish doctrine, speaking in the accents of the eighteenth-century Enlightenment.

> Moses has commanded us the Law; it is an inheritance of the congregation of Jacob. All other nations we believe to be enjoined to keep the law of nature. Those conducting their lives in accordance with this religion of nature and of reason are called "virtuous men from among other nations," and these are entitled to eternal bliss [*sind Kinder der ewigen Seligkeit*].

There was an obvious apologetic intent and a consequent exaggeration in his next statement:

> The religion of my fathers, therefore, does not desire to be spread. We are not to send missions to Greenland or to the Indies in order to preach our faith to these distant nations. The latter nation, in particular, observing as it is the law of nature better than we do here, according to reports received, is in view of our religious doctrines an enviable nation.

It is true that an active missionary campaign has not been carried on in Judaism ever since the pre-Christian centuries, when Hellenistic Judaism won untold pagans for "reverence for God" and thus helped lay the foundation for the rapid spread of Christianity. In the Middle Ages the external facts of history united with the inner nature of Judaism to preclude large-scale efforts to win non-Jews to Judaism.

Today, some voices are being raised in the Jewish community in favor of a more active effort to bring the message of Judaism to religiously uncommitted non-Jews, though without employing conventional missionary techniques.[36] A warm discussion on the question is now going on among Jewish religious leaders and laity. Officially such an outreach program has been adopted only by the Reform segment of American Judaism. Reform leaders have announced that their efforts will be directed primarily to persuading the non-Jewish spouses in intermarriages to study Judaism with a view toward conversion. Thus far, few if any concrete steps have been taken to launch the campaign for winning non-Jews for Judaism. It is therefore too early to judge the degree of its success. The other major groups, Orthodox and Conservative Judaism, have not undertaken such a program. The public posture of Orthodoxy is to oppose any Gentile conversion stimulated by the desire to marry a Jew as having an ulterior motive and not being "sincere." Privately, there are Orthodox rabbis who regret this attitude as burying one's head in the sand in the face of a major problem.

Conservatism is much more open to winning the prospective non-Jewish spouse for Judaism. It maintains, however, that the conversion should take place before the marriage ceremony, since only a marriage between two Jews has legal status in Jewish law. When the conversion takes place before the wedding ceremony, one may anticipate that the new home will be built on the foundation of a common tradition. To this end, Conservative Judaism is increasingly turning to institutes on Judaism for non-Jews interested in exploring the resources of the Jewish tradition, a practice in vogue in Reform Judaism as well.

However, both those who favor and those who oppose such an active effort are at one in recognizing the legitimacy of non-Jewish faiths, the availability of salvation to all who observe the basic spiritual and ethical principles embodied in the Noahide Laws, and the right of all men to the fullest liberty of religious practice and belief.

The attitude of Judaism toward religious liberty may now be summarized as follows:

1. Judaism insists on total freedom of religious belief and practice for itself, which will include full equality before the law and no extra-legal disabilities in society.

2. Judaism accepts the existence of differences within the Jewish community and accords to dissidents the right to their own viewpoint and practice. This right is recognized, at least *de facto*, by Orthodoxy and *de jure* by all other groups.

3. Judaism recognizes the existence of other religions and their inherent right to be observed *de jure.*

There is a measure of oversimplification in Albert Einstein's utterance, "I thank God that I belong to a people which has been too weak to do much harm in the world." But more than mere incapacity inheres in the Jewish attitude toward religious liberty. The balance between the universal aspirations of Judaism and its strong attachment to the preservation of its group character have impelled it to create a theory that makes room in God's plan—and in the world—for men and women of other convictions and practices.

Moreover, the deeply ingrained individualism of the Jewish character, its penchant for questioning, and its insistence upon rational conviction have made dissent a universal feature of the Jewish spiritual physiognomy. As a result, all groups within the Jewish community have achieved freedom of expression and practice. Efforts to limit or suppress this liberty of conscience have not been totally lacking and undoubtedly will reoccur in the future. But such attempts are invariably accompanied by a bad conscience on the part of apostles of intolerance, who thus reveal their weak roots in the tradition that they are ostensibly defending and betray their predestined failure to achieve their ends.

Finally, the millennial experience of Jewish disability and exile in the ancient and the medieval worlds has strengthened this attachment to freedom of conscience among Jews. In addition, the modern world has demonstrated that the material and intellectual position and progress of Jews, individually and collectively, is most effectively advanced in an atmosphere of religious liberty.

Thus all three elements, tradition, temperament, and history, have united to make religious freedom, both for the Jewish community and for the larger family of mankind, an enduring ideal and not merely a temporarily prudential arrangement. Undoubtedly Jews have fallen short of the lofty standards of their tradition in this as in other respects. Yet it remains true that, by and large, they have maintained their loyalty to the ideal of freedom of conscience for themselves and for all men.

Chapter 13

The Dimensions of Democracy

AS THE WORLD stumbles along toward the twenty-first century, its basic ideals collapsing everywhere and its mood combining cynicism, hopelessness, and terror, it is not easy to recapture the faith and optimism that characterized the American people during the first century and more of their history. One hundred years ago, the English political scientist James Bryce was writing his classic work *The American Commonwealth*. In order to justify his interest in the subject, Bryce wrote that American democracy was important because its institutions were regarded as those "towards which, as by a law of fate, the rest of civilized mankind are forced to move." Even the German philosopher Hegel, not particularly famous for his liberalism, described America as "the land of the future." For a long time thereafter, until well into the twentieth century, the feeling was widespread that democracy was the wave of the future. When World War I was fought, the great slogan of America was "make the world safe for democracy." Undoubtedly, both naivete and conceit entered into that affirmation, but idealism and hope were also present. Certainly the outcome of World War I seemed to justify the proposition, for when the war ended, the Austro-Hungarian, German, and Russian empires had all collapsed. In their stead stood an entire group of new democracies in the Balkans and on the Baltic. No wonder most Americans believed that the world was being made over in the democratic image.

How remote and unbelievable all these sentiments now seem to us! Today the question is not whether we can make the world safe for democracy, but whether democracy can be made safe anywhere in the world. It has been in retreat all along the line. The Balkan and Baltic democratic states have disappeared, all swallowed up in the Communist orbit, as have the German, Czechoslovak, and Yugoslav republics. Virtually all the newly established nations in Asia and Africa, as we have learned to our cost in watching the antics of the United Nations, have opted for dictatorship and totalitarianism, keeping the word "democratic" only for their official stationery. We have only to reflect on the events of the past half-century to see the evidence that democracy is on the defensive. It is Communism that has retained its hold on the European continent and is pressing forward in Asia, Africa, and Latin America. If we are to meet successfully the challenge confronting democracy, we need to comprehend the full content and implications of the democratic ideal. In this enterprise, we would do well to seek after the sources and try to explore some of the insights that the Judaic tradition can bring to bear upon the nature and the scope, the problems and the future of democracy.

It is a truism in contemporary thought that has become a cliché, repeated, incidentally, by no less a figure than Winston Churchill, that Athens was the cradle of democracy. "Democracy," to be sure, is a Greek word, as are the words "politics" and "economics." In fact, *Politics* and *Economics* are the titles of two treatises by Aristotle. But while the Greeks may have had a word for it, it was the ancient Hebrews who had the substance. In the Golden Age of Athens, scholars estimate that forty percent of the Athenian population was slaves. I am not referring to foreigners who might have been captured in battle and were impressed into bondage, but to native-born Greeks. If the word means "the rule of the people," there was no democracy in ancient Greece.

Biblical Hebrew, it is true, has few abstract terms and generally avoids theoretic formulations in favor of concrete practices. Nevertheless, if we seek after the genesis of democracy, we should look to its sources in the Bible and in postbiblical Judaism.

At least three factors were at work shaping the psyche of Israel and its ideals—the memory of the enslavement in Egypt, the nomadic period in the wilderness, and the heroic and tireless activity of the prophets, who never let their people forget their past.

Recent research by Oriental scholars has revealed that prior to the rise of the great Semitic empires, a primitive democracy existed in which all the males participated. The ancient Hebrews never established a great state, but the evidence of such a primitive democratic order is well attested in biblical sources, as the present writer has demonstrated elsewhere. The Hebrew terms *'edah* and *qahal*, generally translated "congregation," should be rendered correctly as "commonalty" or "assembly." In this early period, before the rise of the monarchy, the *'edah* exercised political and juridical functions. The "assembly" of all male members of the tribe determined issues of war and peace by a voice vote. There was no hereditary monarch or hierarchy of officials holding the reins of power. In the face of a crisis, a leader would arise, by virtue of his wisdom in counsel or his courage in battle; when the crisis was over, he would revert to his previous position as a member of the group. The biblical Book of Judges presents a picture of this temporary charismatic leadership in the lives of Ehud, Barak, Gideon, and Jephthah.

When, in the eleventh century B.C.E., a major national enemy, the Philistines, challenged the freedom of the Israelite tribes, Samson failed to repulse the enemy. It was clear that a centralized government, with a permanent officialdom was necessary. The people now came to the prophet Samuel and asked for a king, a request that was ultimately granted. Nevertheless, the prophet, representing the older tradition, declared that the demand for a human monarch was an affront to the kingship of God. In what is probably the oldest republican address on record, he described the future exactions of a king and warned the people against them. As will be noted below, the antimonarchical tradition continued to serve as a check upon the Hebrew monarchy.

According to biblical tradition, the Hebrews had wandered for forty years in the desert after their escape from Egypt. Though they were familiar with the institution of the monarchy in Egypt, no king or noble attained to power during the nomadic age. This period, incidentally, lasted considerably longer than forty years, since the tribes that settled in Trans-Jordan, the eastern bank of the Jordan river, retained their sheep-raising semi-nomadic economy for decades and centuries after the tribes west of the Jordan had progressed to agricultural and urban stages of development.

Throughout the period of the monarchy, the Hebrew prophets never permitted the people to forget its lowly origin as a pack of slaves suffering oppression at the hands of Egyptian taskmasters. The nomadic period that followed the enslavement was harsh and difficult in reality, but later generations and above all the prophets idealized the era, and declared that the period in the wilderness marked the ideal relationship of Israel and its God. Echoing the sentiments of his predecessor Hosea, Jeremiah said, "Go and proclaim in the hearing of Jerusalem, Thus says the Lord, I remember the devotion of your youth, your love as a bride, how you followed Me in the wilderness, in a land not sown (Jer. 2:2). The rough-and-ready egalitarianism, the absence of private property in any major sense, the practice of justice for all, and the feeling of mutual responsibility binding the individual to the group and the group to the individual—these were the ideals that the Hebrew prophets traced back to the nomadic stage and which the people were never suffered to forget completely, even in the later eras of sophistication, corruption, and class divisions.

The Jewish people is often described as *am haneviin*, "the people of the prophets." The epithet has a double significance. The nations of antiquity begat some great-souled individuals who cried out against injustice and hungered after righteousness, but they were few and isolated. Only the Hebrew nation produced a long line of prophets, from Moses to Malachi and beyond, extending over nearly a millennium, who created an indestructible prophetic tradition. In addition, the epithet means not only that Israel produced the prophets, but that the prophets produced Israel. They fashioned the Hebrew ethos for all time, which might at times be ignored but could never be completely suppressed. Hence the Talmud could declare, "Do not disturb Israel, for if they are not prophets, they are the descendants of prophets" (*B. Pesahim* 66b).

The people of Israel were never very numerous or powerful, boasting no great achievements in the arts and sciences, and clinging precariously to the eastern shores of the Mediterranean. Yet it was Israel rather than the great civilizations of Mesopotamia, Egypt, and Greece that created democracy, not the vocabulary, but the substance, and—what is more—embodied it in life.

Moreover, though it lacked words like "political," "economic," and "social," the Bible was able to make another essential contribution. It reminds us that democracy is indivisible, a lesson that both the democratic world and the Communist system have yet to learn. Political democracy cannot long live side by side with economic oppression or social and racial injustice, nor can true social justice endure in a police state, in a framework of political tyranny, the suppression of intellectual freedom, and the practice of terrorism. If today democracy is in retreat all over the world, it is not because people have become enamored of slavery; it is because they have become seduced into believing that they cannot have freedom if they wish to have security—and some of the actions of Western governments have done too little to refute the error. In the Jewish tradition, embodied in the Bible and in the Talmud, there was never this dichotomy between liberty and security, between justice and freedom, never a willingness to settle for one rather than for the other, because both were the imperatives of the Living God. There was always the understanding that *zedakah umishpat*, "righteousness and justice," included *hesed verahamim* "steadfast love and mercy" (Hos. 2:21). Hence the remedy for the ills of democracy is not less but more democracy.

Two preliminary observations are in order before we turn to the specific embodiments in life and law of the biblical concept of democracy.

With all the honor accorded the prophets and the important place they occupy in the pages of Scripture, their writings do not constitute the holiest section of the Hebrew Bible. In Judaism, the position of primacy is occupied by the Torah, the Five Books of Moses, which possess the central and fundamental authority in the Jewish tradition. The reason reveals a fundamental characteristic of the Jewish psyche.

Judaism has never been satisfied with the mere formulation of abstract ideals, however eloquently set forth. It has always been more concerned with specifics, with converting doctrine into deed. The teachings of the prophets, eternally valid as they are, nonetheless remain abstractions. The greatness of the Torah and of the talmudic rabbis who built upon it lies precisely here. The ideals taught by the prophets were translated by the Torah into specific enactments and institutions and were embodied in concrete practices. We have already cited the Golden Rule in Leviticus (19:28), "You shall love your neighbor as yourself," described by Rabbi Akiba as the greatest principle in the Torah. His colleague Ben-Azzai preferred another passage (Gen. 5:1–2), "This is the book of the generations of Adam. On the day when God created man he made him in the likeness of God male and female He created them"—the first half of the passage is a ringing affirmation of the unity of the human race, the second half, of the innate dignity of each human being, male and female.

To buttress the claim that the doctrine of love was a new revelation, the New Testament says, "You have heard that it was said, You shall love your neighbor and hate your enemy. But I say to you, Love your enemy and pray for those who persecute you" (Matt. 5:43–44). Now there is no commandment, "Hate your enemy" in Jewish literature, nor indeed is there a statement "Love your enemy." Instead the Torah commands: "If you meet your enemy's ox or his ass going astray, you shall bring it back to him. If you see the ass of one who hates you, help him to lift it up" (Exod. 23:4–5). This same pragmatic approach, less soul-stirring perhaps than "Love your enemy," but more realistic and by that token more likely to be put into practice, is exhibited in the Book of Proverbs: "If your enemy is hungry, give him bread to eat; if he is thirsty, give him water to drink," and because the author is aware of the weaknesses of human nature, he adds, "For you will be heaping coals of fire on his head, and the Lord will reward you" (Prov. 25:21–22). Always the stress is upon concrete actions rather than vague emotions, or, rather, the biblical spirit seeks to translate the emotions into attitudes and the attitudes into social and political institutions.

First in the area of *political democracy*. Basic to the Jewish tradition, and uniquely characteristic of it in the ancient world, was a *deep hatred of monarchical oppression*. The writings of the biblical historians and the speeches of the Hebrew prophets are filled with denunciations of the kings, the nobility, and the priesthood. Phrases like "the divine right of kings" and "the king can do no wrong" seem to have an aura of biblical language about them, but nothing could be further from the truth. Far from believing that the king can do no wrong, the basic message of the

Bible is that kings nearly always do wrong. Of all the kings of the Northern Kingdom of Israel, not one gets a good mark from the historian who wrote the Book of Kings. As for the Southern Kingdom of Judah, all the decent kings can be counted on the fingers of one hand.

Shortly before his resignation, a former President of the United States presumed to say that, as sovereign, the Chief Executive is above the law. Had the ancient prophets been here today, they would have laughed him to scorn. They would have reminded us that there is only one sovereign, who is God, and no one stands above the moral law—not even God, its source and guarantor.

The Book of Genesis, in an unforgettable passage, describes Abraham bargaining for the sinful people of Sodom, in the name of fifty, forty, thirty, twenty, or even ten righteous inhabitants. The basis of his appeal to God to spare the city is his declaration, "Shall the Judge of all the earth not act justly?" (Gen. 18:25). There is no teleological suspension of the ethical even for God.

Ancient Israel is the first instance known of a monarchy with limited power. In Deuteronomy (17:14–20), which Moses proclaimed to the Israelites before his death, regulations for the conduct of the king are set forth, limiting his powers in several significant respects.

While this legislation was undoubtedly utopian, its spirit was embodied in life, reflected even in the activity of the "evil kings" of Israel. There is the famous incident of the vineyard of Naboth, whose land adjoined the property of the wicked King Ahab. The king asked the peasant to sell him his holdings, but he refused. Ahab sulked in his palace until his foreign-born wife decided, as a good wife should, to make her husband happy. What did Jezebel do, or, rather, what did she not do? She did not take the land by *force majeure*, as any Oriental monarch would have done without hesitation. Instead she went through an elaborate scheme to suborn witnesses and have the hapless peasant tried on false charges of treason and blasphemy. Only then was she able to expropriate the vineyard (I Kings 21). Thus even the most "wicked" of the kings of Israel and his imperious foreign wife were restricted in the application of the royal powers in Israel.

The events of our century offer tragic evidence that the essence of democracy does not lie in the ballot box. The greatest masters of the ballot box have been Hitler, Stalin, and their imitators. The heart of democracy, as its enemies have always understood, is the *right of dissent*, the freedom to express opinions that are not in accord with the majority of the Establishment. This precious right, the very heart-blood of a free society, was maintained by the ancient prophets in the face of all challenges and threats, including imprisonment, exile, and even death. They never surrendered their God-given role "to tell Israel its sin and Jacob its transgression" (Micah 3:8), to call to book the royal court, the priests, the upper classes, and even the common people. Protesting against evil became part of the Jewish psyche and persisted through the ages.

Undoubtedly the right of dissent was often honored more in the breach than in the observance. The king, the nobility, and even the common people were often unwilling to hear the truth, and prophets paid the price in hostility, imprisonment, exile, and death, but the legitimacy of the principle could not be challenged. In the critical days before the final destruction of the Southern Kingdom of Judah, the prophet Jeremiah insisted on opposing the policies of the king and the nobility, who wished to rebel against Babylonia. His call to accept the foreign yoke could only be described as subversive, and accordingly he was bitterly hated by the "patriotic" party, who charged him with sedition. A record of the trial has been preserved in Jeremiah, chapter 26. In his defense Jeremiah cited the precedent of the earlier prophet Micah, who had also announced the doom of the state to an incredulous people. Jeremiah's case was undoubtedly helped by the presence of powerful friends at court, and he was set free. Another prophet, Uriah, who expressed the same views, but lacked the political support that Jeremiah enjoyed, fled to Egypt, but was assassinated by some hired gangsters (Jer. 26:24). But the principle of freedom of expression was never abrogated.

Freedom of dissent has not only a moral but an intellectual dimension. In the postbiblical period, as is indicated elsewhere in this volume, it became the bedrock upon which the entire system of rabbinic law was erected. The vast range of the Talmud and the Midrash is an impressive monument to the right to freedom of thought, including divergence from constituted authority.

However, freedom of dissent is not enough: it must be an *educated dissent*. Here, too, in the field of public education, the Judaic tradition makes a pioneer contribution. To be sure, textbooks on the history of education generally are silent with regard to the role of the ancient Hebrews in the field of education. The Torah itself commands every father to teach God's word diligently to his children (Deut. 6:4–7), which it sees as a prime example of the love of God. From several casual references in the biblical text, it is clear that literacy was widespread, even in the earliest period of Hebrew history (Judg. 8:14, Isa. 10:19).

In the postbiblical period, before the beginning of the common era, a system of schools in every community existed in Palestine. These were established, according to one source, by the High Priest Joshua ben Gamla, and according to another by Simon ben Shetah, one of the early sages of the Mishnah and a brother-in-law of the queen, Salome Alexandra.

This emphasis upon universal education may be contrasted with the words of Governor Berkeley of Virginia, who, in 1670, thanked God that there were no free schools or printing presses in the colony, "since they bring disobedience into the world."

There are other aspects of political democracy that can be adduced. Thus rabbinic law did not merely insist that a person was free not to incriminate himself, a right now guaranteed by the Fifth Amendment— it forbade a person to incriminate himself. Hence any confession to a capital crime was invalid as testimony.

Fortified by their conviction that they were speaking the word of God, the prophets could not be deflected from their task; "But as for me, I am filled with power, with the Spirit of the Lord, and with justice and might, to declare to Jacob his transgression and to Israel his sin" (Mic. 3:8). They denounced the oppression of the poor, the corruption of the courts, and the rapacity of the possessing classes which led to the establishment of great landed estates and the selling of the poor into slavery. The process of the concentration of wealth in the hands of the few, and the impoverishment of the many, was not limited to Israel; the trajectory was repeated in virtually every society.

The difference between ancient Israel and ancient Hellas is epitomized in the Greek philosopher and the Hebrew prophet. Plato dedicated two books of the *Republic* to defining the meaning of justice. But the Hebrew prophets did not engage in abstract speculation. They believed that any person of normal intelligence and decency would know what was right and what was wrong and the difference between just and injustice, between mercy and cruelty. The prophet Micah gave the greatest definition of religion ever spoken: "He has told you, O man, what is good and what the Lord your God requires of you, to do justice [*mishpat*], to love mercy [*ḥesed*], and to walk humbly with your God" (6:7).

The Hebrew term *ḥesed*, translated variously as "mercy," "loving-kindness," and "faithful love," occurs virtually on every page of the Bible. It flowered in the basic Jewish teaching of charity. It has often been pointed out that the Hebrew word *ẓedakah* literally means "righteousness"; the practice of charity is simply the performance of our obligation toward those less fortunate. The imposing structure of Jewish philanthropy in our own day, local, national, and international, is one of the outstanding Jewish achievements in history. The Torah and the prophets constantly enjoin the practice of charity toward the widow, the orphan, and the needy (Deut. 15:7–11, Amos 5:11, Isa. 1:17, etc.). In the greatest Yom Kippur sermon ever delivered, the prophet declares: "Is not this the fast that I choose, to loose the bonds of wickedness, to undo the thongs of the yoke, to let the oppressed go free, to break every yoke? Is it not to share your bread with the hungry and take the homeless poor into your house? When you see the naked, to cover him and not to hide yourself from your own flesh?" (Isa. 58:6–7).

The inculcation of the practice of charity over centuries made it "second nature" to the Jewish psyche. It also produced a unique human personality—the "schnorrer." A schnorrer is not a beggar at all; he is a colleague who helps one to perform the *mitzvah* of *zedakah!* In a charming novella called "The King of Schnorrers," the gifted and unjustifiably neglected Anglo-Jewish writer Israel Zangwill tells the tale of a commanding schnorrer who tyrannized over the entire rich Sephardic community of London. He would come into their homes and take whatever garments he needed, knowing that he was bestowing a great favor upon the man whose clothing he deigned to accept and making him realize it too!

As a matter of fact, there is only a little exaggeration in Zangwill's tale. In a much earlier period, the Talmud tells of a poor man who was a charity ward and explained to the rabbi that he was accustomed to eating a stuffed fowl and washing it down with old wine. Raba remonstrated with him, saying, "Aren't you ashamed to put such a strain on the charity fund of the community?" According to the Talmud, he was not in the least bit nonplussed. In impeccable Aramaic he replied, *Atu middideho ka'akhelna middideh ka'akhelna,* "Am I eating what belongs to them? I am eating what belongs to Him" (*B. Kethubot* 77b). Presumably, he kept on eating.

Thus the three sections of the Bible—the Torah, the Prophets, and the Writings—all strove to sensitize the individual conscience to human suffering. But they did not depend upon this alone to correct the ills of society. The biblical tradition recognized that suasion, exhortation and even education would not suffice to achieve a just society; communal action embodied in the legal system was required.

To grapple with the deep-seated malaise of poverty and inequality characteristic of all developed human societies, the Torah established a far-flung system of social legislation, and set forth a theoretical framework for its approach.

A brief survey of the biblical teaching may be presented under the following rubrics: (a) welfare legislation and social taxation, (b) the attitude toward slavery and free labor, (c) the status of private property.

SOCIAL WELFARE AND WELFARE TAXATION

The Jewish farmer was commanded to leave the corner of his field unharvested for the poor. Any sheaf of grain that was forgotten or any crop that had fallen to the ground or had been left in the field was no longer the property of the owner, but public property reserved for the use of the needy (Lev. 19:9–10, Deut. 24:19, Ruth, chap. 2). In addition, a tithe, an obligatory tax of ten percent, was placed upon the farmer for the support of the landless Levites who were the attendants at the Temple and were often destitute (Num. 18:21). In Deuteronomy (14:28) the provision was added that every third year the produce in the field was to be left for the stranger, the orphan, and the widow in addition to the Levite.

SLAVERY AND FREE LABOR

Even more fundamental is the biblical attitude toward labor. In the ancient world, where technology was generally primitive and productivity low, the only viable economic order had to be based upon slavery. Hence, slavery was universal everywhere. It is less than a century and a half since slavery was abolished in these United States, in Czarist Russia, and in the British overseas possessions. Slavery remained characteristic of human society virtually until the end of the nineteenth century. There are reports that even in this year of grace some of our honored allies like Saudi Arabia practice slavery pure and unalloyed, a situation prevalent in parts of Africa as well.

A poor, technologically underdeveloped people like the Hebrews in Palestine three millennia ago could not abolish slavery as such. But what the Torah did was to transform it radically, all but eliminating it. It set a limit of six years of service for any Hebrew slave, at the end of which he went free. Thus by a masterstroke, lifelong slavery was converted into limited bond-service. Even during these six years, the slave was safeguarded by the law. He had rights to his family relationships, and could not be physically beaten or maltreated, starved or underfed. Jewish law protected the slave with so many provisions that the Talmud declares that "he who acquires a Hebrew slave acquires a master for himself" (*B. Kiddushin* 20a and elsewhere). Non-Hebrew slaves did not enjoy the same limitation on the period of service; aliens in any society are far less privileged than citizens. Nevertheless, the basic physical protections of the law were extended to them as well.

The genius of Hebraism is perhaps best highlighted by noting that both Moses and Aristotle understood the importance of leisure for raising man above the level of the beast. Both knew that unless a human being has freedom from unceasing toil, he cannot develop his spiritual attributes and rise to his full potential. What were the consequences? Aristotle argued that since human beings need leisure to develop their highest capacities, slavery is justified, for the existence of slaves makes it possible for other men to be free. The Torah realized equally the importance of liberty for the unfolding of human personality, but it drew radically different conclusions. It established the institution of the Sabbath rest, one day in seven, which was applied not only to free persons but to slaves and even to beasts of burden.

In sum, in a variety of ways, biblical and postbiblical Judaism changed slavery into bond-service. Nevertheless, in spite of all these provisions, the thrust in the biblical tradition was antislavery. This is clearly evident in a remarkable law which had important consequences in American history. Twice before the Civil War the American Congress adopted a Fugitive Slave Law, according to which any black slave who escaped from the South had to be returned by every American citizen to his original master. Now at that time there were many law-abiding American citizens throughout the country who refused to obey that law. Through the Underground Railroad they helped speed these black slaves to freedom, either in the North or in Canada. These practitioners of civil disobedience were not scofflaws or enemies of the American system. They said that the law of God took precedence even over Congress; "You shall not give up to his master a slave who has escaped from his master to you; he shall dwell with you, in your midst, in the place which he shall choose within one of your towns, where it pleases him best; you shall not oppress him!" (Deut. 23:16–17).

Biblical Wisdom literature, as we have demonstrated elsewhere, emanated from the upper classes in Hebrew society. Nevertheless, it is in the Book of Job, which transcends limitations of class culture and ethnicity, that the all-embracing doctrine of human equality is enunciated.

In his great Code of A Man of Honor already discussed above, Job declares his probity and denies that he had ever been guilty of practicing injustice toward his slaves, because he was aware of God's seeing eye and the common origin of free man and slave.

> What shall I do when God rises up,
> and when He examines me, how shall I answer Him?
> Did not He make him in the womb as He made me
> and fashion us both alike in the womb?
>
> (Job 31:14–15)

Rabbinic Judaism went beyond asserting the equality of master and slave. According to an ancient law in the Book of Exodus, a slave who refuses to go free and prefers to remain in bondage has his ear bored through (Exod. 21:5–6). One of the rabbinic sages explains that this branding of the slave is a punishment: "His ear heard God proclaim, 'Unto Me shall the children of Israel be servants, for they are My servants' [Lev. 25:55]—and not servants to servants! Yet this man took a

human master for himself; he deserves to have his ear pierced through"
(*B. Kiddushin* 22b). For Judaism, freedom from slavery, is not merely a
God-given right; it is a divinely ordained command.

PRIVATE PROPERTY

Even more important for the ethos of ancient Israel is the biblical
concept of the status of property. The prophets did not limit their social
concerns to attacking individual cases of wrongdoing, such as the
defrauding of the widow, the oppression of the poor, cheating in
business, or the corruption of the judges. They recognized a major evil
that has threatened virtually every social system and has destroyed
nations and civilizations—the concentration of wealth in the hands of
the few and the impoverishment of the many. Isaiah thundered: "Woe
to those who join house to house, who add field to field, until there is no
more room, and you are made to dwell alone in the midst of the land"
(Isa. 5:8).

The Torah went beyond denunciation. As is nearly always the case in
biblical thought, it did not spell out an abstract theory on property. Its
attitude is expressed in concrete form in one of the most remarkable
institutions in the history of the world, the "year of release," or Sabbatical Year, a term which has become familiar with many modern connotations.

The "seventh year" had two basic provisions. The first element was
financial. In that year, all debts contracted during the previous period
that were unpaid were cancelled, thus preventing huge accumulations
of wealth (Deut. 15:1–6). The second element was agricultural. A farmer
was forbidden to plant or to sow his fields in the seventh year; he was
commanded to let his land lie fallow. Whatever grew on the land that
year was available to the poor, but not to its owner.

The Sabbatical Year is of the highest significance in three respects, as
has already been indicated. The first was ecological—the fact that the
land could not be sown gave the earth a chance to replenish its vigor, in
the days before modern chemical means were available. The second was
social—the fact that what grew that year was not the property of any
individual but belonged to the poor in order to relieve their want. The
third, and most important, was cosmic—it was a periodic reaffirmation
of the fact that God, the Sovereign of the world, and not man, is the real
owner of the land.

Biblical law did not deny the legitimacy of private ownership, but it
saw man not as the absolute and permanent possessor of his property,
but as a temporary trustee. The principle is clearly set forth in connection with a related institution—the Jubilee Year. In every fiftieth year, all

land that had been sold in the previous half-century had to be restored to its original owner without payment. The purpose was clear, and so was the rationale: "The land shall not be sold in perpetuity, for all the land is Mine, and you are dwellers and sojourners with Me" (Lev. 25:23).

A historical aside may be of interest. For centuries the biblical law of the Sabbatical Year, or year of release, was regarded as purely utopian. However, recent research has drastically modified this judgment. Professor J. J. Finkelstein of Yale University has published the Edict of Ammisaduqa, a Babylonian king of the seventeenth century B.C.E., which indicates that at the accession of the king to the throne and on the seventh, fourteenth, and twenty-first anniversaries, as well as on other occasions, unpaid debts were cancelled. It seems too, that those who had been sold into slavery for debt were set free. Finkelstein believes that the sources also indicate that land sold in the previous period reverted to its original owner. These enactments are described as being enjoined by *misharum*, "equity."

It is noteworthy that the Babylonian edict does not rest upon any fundamental ethical or theological principle, as does the biblical law. But obviously the Babylonian and the Hebrew enactments are related, probably deriving from a common Semitic background. It seems clear that both systems of law were grounded in reality.

To revert to our theme, biblical thought did not share Proudhon's dictum, "Property is robbery." It regarded private ownership, properly administered, as entirely legitimate. Hence robbery, theft, and the forcible appropriation of the possessions of another are criminal acts. Biblical law made provision for the legal transfer of property by gift, sale, and inheritance.

But property does not occupy the highest rung in the hierarchy of values. Since mankind is created in the image of God, human life is sacred, while private property is legitimate, being a custodianship from God. Hence, when a conflict arises between the two, property rights must give way to human rights. When this principle is suffered to fall into decline, democracy is in mortal peril, a potential prey to tyrannies of the right and of the left.

This cosmic principle, that God is the owner of the world He created, serves also as the basis of the biblical teaching on ecology, discussed elsewhere in this volume.

This brief survey of the Hebraic roots of democracy can easily be amplified. It should be sufficient to demonstrate that the Bible is the fountainhead of a very rich social and ethical tradition, far from irrelevant to our times. Judaism reminds us that political democracy cannot survive unless it is joined to the quest for social and economic justice, that liberty cannot endure unless it becomes a highway toward security, and that if we settle for one as against the other, we shall lose both.

Obviously, the specifics of ancient biblical and rabbinic law are not applicable to the incredibly complex technological society in which we live, but the spirit of Hebraism speaks directly to modern man, his problems, his perplexities, and his potentialities.

These living values in the Hebraic tradition may shed light upon a phenomenon upon which men and women have pondered for centuries—the miracle of Jewish survival and the mystery of Jewish existence. The affinity of the Jewish tradition for democracy seems to be validated by the history of our own times. The democratic idea, the concept of the innate dignity of all human beings and the inalienable right to life and liberty of all individuals and nations, has been under major challenge three times in the twentieth century, first by Nazi bestiality, second by Communist tyranny, and third by Arab piracy. All three enemies of democracy have encountered a common symbol of resistance upon which to vent their hatred—the Jewish people. The State of Israel is an embodiment of its indomitable will and right to live, in spite of all its errors, problems, and difficulties. Confronting the would-be tyrants and oppressors of mankind the Jew stands, determined not merely to survive, but to help fashion a world foretold by the prophet in which "men shall do no evil and work no destruction on all My holy mountain, for the earth shall be filled with the knowledge of the Lord, as the waters cover the sea" (Isa. 11:9).

It is hardly necessary to add that there is no intention here of identifying political democracy, as it is currently being practiced, with the Kingdom of God. On the contrary, as Winston Churchill declared, "Democracy is the worst possible form of government, except that all others are worse." The ills of democracy are all too evident today— inefficiency of operation in all echelons of government, unabashed greed and widespread corruption reaching up to the highest levels of society, and worst of all, the polarization of groups intent upon furthering their special interests. All these phenomena are the result of the erosion of the sense of the common weal, which, to be sure, never conquered human weaknesses, but helped keep them in check. Indeed the purpose of the present volume is to discover a basis for individual and group ethics that can save our civilization before it destroys itself.

It should, however, be kept in mind that all these defects of democracy are at least equally evident in the various versions of authoritarianism both of the right and of the left that are challenging the free world in our day.

The saving grace of the democratic order as against its enemies lies in its possession of a built-in mechanism for peaceful change and improvement. The ballot box affords a free electorate the power to express its will at regular intervals. The vote is a matchless instrument for self-correction, through the replacement of policies and personnel, the adoption of new strategies, and even the reversal of a given course in order to meet unsolved problems. However simplistic the formula "Throw the rascals out!" may sound, it confers upon the majority the power to work its will in society, while the rights of the minority are protected against the tyranny of the majority by the Bill of Rights, whether in a written or in an unwritten constitution. The safety valve of the ballot box makes possible a peaceful dialectic of change and holds out the promise of better things to come. Hence the defense of democracy is more than an expression of local patriotism; it represents the safeguarding of man's last best hope on earth.

Chapter 14

World Peace: Cornerstone and Capstone

THE SWIRLING MASS of discussions and controversies about the future of society are predicated upon the assumption that there will be a future for society. This comfortable notion can no longer be taken for granted today. While government leaders continue to intone the litany "A nuclear war must never be allowed to happen," both the foreign policy and the domestic economic activity of the federal government reflect a vastly different sentiment, articulated by one of its leading spokesmen, who in a moment of frankness has declared, "A nuclear war is thinkable, do-able, and win-able." The breakdown of negotiations for arms reduction, the escalation of expensive new arms manufacture, the stonewall opposition to a nuclear freeze, the scrapping of treaties already agreed upon—and our opponents are no less recalcitrant than we are—are all elements of a policy which Heaven forbid, may lead to the annihilation of the human race and the destruction of civilization.

The Judaic ethic, the major implications of which we have sought to explore, must speak to this issue of global war or peace, which is today both the foundation and the capstone of human survival. For without the abolition of war, all the putative contributions of the Judaic spirit and all else in our culture will be for naught.

In the past, many suggestions have been made with regard to the contribution of the Hebraic ethos to the modern world. Perhaps the most obvious, and surely the most frequently advanced, is the doctrine of ethical monotheism, the faith in a Deity whose goal for mankind is righteousness. The famous physician Sir William Osler declared that the greatest Hebraic contribution to civilization was the institution of the Sabbath, the idea of a regular day of rest for all living creatures, from which our entire system of limited hours of labor, vacations, sabbaticals, and retirement has developed. The American philosopher Morris Raphael Cohen stressed the concept of a philosophy of history, first articulated by the Hebrew prophets, the conviction that history is not a meaningless concatenation of unrelated incidents, but rather part of a pattern revealing a thrust and a direction to human events. The specific prophetic philosophy of history—that history is the revelation of a Divinely ordained process by which evil is used to destroy evil and usher in the good, and culminating in the establishment of the Kingdom of God, the universal reign of righteousness—may or may not be congenial to modern thinkers. However, all succeeding philosophies of history from Vico to Marx, from Spengler and Voegelin and beyond, are indebted to the prophets for the basic insight that there is meaning to history.

Generations of warriors for freedom, physical or spiritual, might argue that the concept of liberty, clearly implied in the Bible as God's will for all beings, deserves a position of primacy. As the medieval Jewish philosopher Judah Halevi pointed out, God introduced himself in the Decalogue not as "the Lord your God, creator of heaven and earth," but with the words, "I am the Lord your God who brought you forth out of the land of Egypt, out of the house of bondage." Thus biblical religion took its stand on the side of the oppressed against the oppressors, and declared freedom to be each man's duty as well as his right. Often obscured and denied, this basic ideal could never be expunged from Scripture and human consciousness. Hence the Bible served as a rallying point for the hopes of the exploited, the enslaved, and the oppressed for centuries everywhere.

In the final decades of the twentieth century, the cry for peace may well be the single greatest contribution of the Judaic ethos to the world. Today it is difficult to recapture the revolutionary impact of the idea of peace. No one in the ancient Semitic world or among the Greeks had ever conceived of peace among nations even as a utopian dream. As we have noted, for Plato the "Republic" of the future would always require a standing army against the barbarian hordes outside the gates. A millennium after the Hebrew prophets, the Roman poet Virgil, in his *Eclogues*, pictured an idyllic world at peace. We do not know to what degree biblical ideas were known to educated and sensitive Romans through the Greek translations of the Bible and other Hellenistic Jewish literature. What seems certain is that Virgil was giving an idealistic cast to the concept of *pax Ròmana*, which was, of course, preserved by the force of Roman arms and supported by the exactions of the tax-gatherers of the empire.

In any event, nearly a thousand years before Virgil, the concept of world peace had been articulated by the Hebrew prophets. Actually they made a threefold contribution. As has already been noted, for the first time in recorded history, they formulated peace among nations as a goal for human striving. Second, they regarded it not as a pipe dream or a beautiful vision, but as an attainable objective, indeed the inevitable destination toward which history was moving, because peace had been ordained by God, the Governor of history; in their words: "It *shall come* to pass," "all nations *will be* one," and "men *shall break* their swords into plowshares." The prophetic certitude is unmistakable. Third, for them, acutely conscious as they were of the weakness of human nature, they did not demand a transformation of men into angels as a prerequisite for international peace. What is required is the recognition of the sovereignty of the moral law and obedience to the judgments handed down by the tribunal of God.

On the one hand, the prophetic teaching on peace has been blunted by undue familiarity with the words, while on the other, its meaning has been ignored or misunderstood. It is therefore worth examining in some detail the three classical passages on this theme.

The first of these is in Isaiah (11:1–10):

There shall come forth a shoot from the stump of Jesse,
    and a branch shall grow out of his roots.
The Spirit of the Lord shall rest upon him,
    the spirit of wisdom and understanding, the spirit of counsel and might,
    the spirit of knowledge and the fear of the Lord.
And his delight shall be in the fear of the Lord.
    He shall not judge merely by what his eyes sees, or decide by what his ears hear;
    but with righteousness he shall judge the poor, and decide with equity for the meek of the earth;
He shall smite the earth with the rod of his mouth,
    and with the breath of his lips he shall slay the wicked.
Righteousness shall be the girdle of his waist, and faithfulness the girdle of his loins.
The wolf shall dwell with the lamb, and the leopard shall lie down with the kid, the calf and the lion and the fatling together, and a little child shall lead them.
The cow and the bear shall feed; their young shall lie down together;
    and the lion shall eat straw like the ox.
The suckling child shall play over the hole of the asp,
    and the weaned child shall put his hand on the adder's den.

They shall not hurt or destroy in all My holy mountain;
> for the earth shall be full of the knowledge of the Lord, as the
> waters cover the sea.

In that day the root of Jesse shall stand as an ensign to the peoples,
Him shall the nations seek, and his dwellings shall be glorious.

In the opening section (vv. 1–5) the prophet declares that a scion of the royal house of David will sit upon the throne, endowed with the ideal virtues of wisdom and understanding, counsel and courage, and knowledge and fear of the Lord. Hence, he will dispense justice, not on the basis of external appearances, but will judge on behalf of the poor and strike down the evildoers (vv. 1–5). Thus far a picture of a righteous king.

Now comes the famous passage: All the predatory animals will live in peace with the gentler creatures, and children will feel secure from harm (vv. 7–8). The next verse, 9, characterizes the new peaceful order as being universal. There will be no evil-doing or destruction on God's holy mountain, which is co-extensive with all the earth. The final verse, which may be an independent oracle, pictures the royal house of Jesse, David's father, serving as a banner for all nations, who will turn to him for guidance, while he would rest in glory.

The succeeding verses consist of several oracles foretelling the ingathering of Jewish exiles from the Diaspora (vv. 11–12). The Dispersion had begun before the destruction of the Judean state in 587 B.C.E. (and the passage may therefore be authentically Isaianic). Verses 13–15 look forward to the cessation of hostility between the Northern and the Southern Kingdoms, who will then unite against their common enemies (vv. 13–16).

It has been argued that the second section, which paints an idyllic picture of the lion lying down with the lamb, and which runs counter to the nature of the beast, demonstrates that for the prophet peace was a beautiful idea, but essentially a utopian fantasy which could come to pass only by a radical transformation of human nature. World peace, therefore, is "beyond history," achievable through a miraculous intervention by God into the natural order. Though this view of the passage is widely held, I do not believe it can stand up under examination.

In the first instance, God does not appear in the entire passage as an active participant in the establishment of peace among the animals. His name would be expected to figure prominently if the new order were directly dependent upon His supernatural intervention in the world.

Second, the passage does not contemplate any miraculous transformation of human nature. There will still be evildoers to be crushed and the weak to be defended. In the climactic verse 9, the prophet is clearly conscious of the persistency of evil and of the human propensity to destruction.

It is *possible* that the three verses describing peace and harmony among the animals may have been borrowed from some independent utopian oracle, though no example of this genre has reached us. Clearly, for the prophet, these lines are now a metaphor indicating that the brute instincts in mankind will be mastered in the future era. In sum, it is the real world as constituted at present that the prophet contemplates in his vision of the future.

Finally, even those who would insist on the otherworldly character of chapter 11 cannot deny that the two other passages in Isaiah are clearly this-worldly in content. A careful reading of the famous Vision of the End-Time, which occurs in Isaiah 2:2–4 and in Micah 4:1–4, with some minor variations, makes it clear that no ambiguity exists here, that it is the present world-order that will be rid of war:

> It shall come to pass in the latter days
> that the mountain of the Lord's house
> shall be established on the highest of mountains,
> and shall be raised above the hills:
> All the nations shall flow to it,
> and many peoples shall come and say:
> "Come, let us go up to the mountain of the Lord,
> to the house of the God of Jacob,
> that he may teach us his ways
> and we may walk in his paths."
> For out of Zion shall go forth the law,
> and the word of the Lord from Jerusalem.
> He shall judge between the nations,
> and shall decide for many peoples;
> They shall beat their swords into plowshares,
> and their spears into pruning hooks;
> Nation shall not lift up sword against nation,
> neither shall they learn war any more.

At the outset, the opening phrase *'aharit hayamim,* literally "the end of days" or "the End-time," should be understood correctly. Popular conceptions to the contrary notwithstanding, the biblical phrase does not *ipso facto* mean the far-distant, ultimate future, and it never refers to a new world order, the result of a supernatural cataclysm.

The idiom, which occurs thirteen times in the Hebrew Bible, is defined as "a prophetic phrase denoting the final period of the history as far as the speaker's perspective reaches."[1] Thus is it used by Jacob and in the speeches of Balaam for the period of the First Temple (Gen. 49:1, Num. 24:24). It is applied to the period shortly after Moses' death and to the near future, close to their own lifetimes, by the prophets Hosea and Jeremiah (Deut. 31:29, Hos. 3:5, Jer. 48:47, 49:39).

In our passage, the prophet is referring to a more distant future, but it is a period here on earth with all the constants of human nature unchanged.

The biblical term is not to be identified with the later rabbinic *'olam haba*, "the world-to-come." The rabbinic term that most nearly approximates the biblical meaning is the phrase *yemot hamashiah*, "the days of the Messiah." This is the meaning assigned to it by the third-century Babylonian sage Samuel: "There is no difference between this world and the days of the Messiah except freedom from subjugation by the great empires" (*B. Berakhot* 34a and parallels). The biblical "End-time" does not carry the connotations of a cataclysmic and miraculous intrusion by God or his appointed Messiah into the natural order. That belief developed in the Greco-Roman era, when it appeared impossible to overcome and destroy Roman oppression by purely human, natural means.

To revert to the prophet's message, he declares that in the End-time, God's house will be established in the holy city of Jerusalem on its highest hill, serving as the seat of God. Nations will have their differences, but all will come to the judgment seat of God and will accept the sovereignty of the moral law which He has promulgated, and by which He will adjudicate their disputes. They will therefore have no need of weapons of destruction, but turn them into instruments of peace, and no longer practice the art of mass murder.

Significantly, not only will clashing interests continue to exist among men, but national entities will also survive. Terms for "nation" and "people" occur five times in these four verses; clearly, the prophet does not anticipate the elimination of national loyalties and their submerging in "cosmopolitanism." Rather, he is a true "inter-nationalist," looking forward to an age when national distinctiveness will survive, not as an instrument of power, but as a specific ethos representing kinship and common culture characteristics of every human society. What will distinguish the future from the present is the universal acceptance of the hegemony of the moral law.

It is true that the prophet did not anticipate that peace, the consummation to which history was inexorably moving, would happen quickly and in his own time. Nor could he conceive how tortuous the road to peace would be. He could not imagine even remotely the convolutions and setbacks suffered nearly three millennia later by such institutions, officially dedicated to world peace, as the Hague Court of International Justice, the League of Nations, and the United Nations. Nevertheless, this vision was not to be relegated to a supernatural overturn of the natural order. Men would still be men and nations, nations—and yet peace would come.

For Isaiah, peace was surely not an immediate prospect. In his day, the center stage of history was occupied by two mighty empires, Assyria to the east and Egypt to the west of Palestine, battling for world mastery. His own country, the tiny kingdom of Judah, of which he was a passionate patriot, was being ground between these two millstones. In that critical juncture for his nation's future, the prophet was nevertheless able to declare:

> In that day there will be a highway from Egypt to Assyria, and the Assyrian will come into Egypt, and the Egyptian into Assyria, and the Egyptian will worship with the Assyrians. In that day Israel will be the third with Egypt and Assyria, a blessing in the midst of the earth, whom the Lord of hosts has blessed, saying, "Blessed be Egypt, My people, and Assyria, the work of My hands, and Israel, My heritage."
> (Isa. 19:23–25)

As the political and social condition of the Jewish people continued to deteriorate during the period of the Second Temple, and even more so during the long centuries of the Roman Exile, the hope for the establishment of a just order became increasingly remote, and belief that it could be achieved in the present world was more and more difficult to maintain. The faith in a supernatural Messiah, who would miraculously destroy the forces of evil, bring Israel to dignity and honor, and establish justice and peace, now became a basic article of faith in traditional Judaism. The daughter religion of Christianity had been born in a period of world crisis. For the new creed, the Jewish doctrine of the Messiah was now radically transformed in character and became the cornerstone of the faith in a Savior redeeming the individual sinner. The task of establishing a just world order was now deferred to the Second Coming of Christ.

Nevertheless, the prophetic vision of the establishment of the Kingdom of God on earth continued to live in both faiths. Rosh Hashanah, the Jewish New Year, celebrates the sovereignty of God, and the prayerbook has enshrined the prophetic hope in a hymn by an anonymous medieval author, *Veye'etayu:*

> All the world shall come to serve Thee
> And bless Thy glorious name,
> And Thy righteousness triumphant
> The islands shall acclaim.

And the people shall go seeking
Who knew Thee not before,
And the end of earth shall praise Thee,
And tell Thy greatness o'er.
With the coming of Thy kingdom
The hills shall break into song,
And the islands laugh exultant
That they to God belong.
And all their congregations
So loud Thy praise shall sing,
That the uttermost peoples, hearing,
Shall hail Thee crowned King.

The concrete ethical content of the Kingdom of God was spelled out in one of the greatest prayers in the Jewish liturgy for the High Holy Days, the *Alenu*, which Solomon Schechter called "the Marseillaise of the Jewish spirit." So important was this messianic theme for the Jewish consciousness that the *Alenu* also entered the daily service and is recited as a concluding prayer three times daily.

The *Alenu* was composed by the great scholar Rab, one of the chief architects of the Babylonian Talmud. It expresses the authentic spirit of the Jewish tradition, going back to the prophets, combining particularism and universalism and keeping the ideals of national loyalty and concern for humanity in creative tension with one another. The first section of *Alenu* offers thanks to God for the unique character of the Jewish people and its special destiny in the world. The second then declares:

We therefore hope in You, O Lord our God,
That we may speedily behold the glory of Your might,
   that we may remove the idols from the earth,[2]
   and the false gods will be utterly cut off,
That we may repair[3] the world by the Kingdom of the Almighty
   and all living creatures will call upon Your name.
That we may turn to You all the wicked of the earth,
so that all the dwellers of the world may recognize and know
that to You every knee must bend, and every tongue swear loyalty.
May they all bow and kneel and render honor to Your glorious name,
and may they all accept the yoke of Your kingdom,
May You rule over them soon, and forever and ever.
For the Kingship is Yours, and forever You will reign in glory.
as it is written in Your Torah,
"The Lord will reign forever and ever,"
And it has been said by the prophet

"The Lord will be King over all the earth,
On that day the Lord will be one and His name one."

In Christianity too, the prophetic faith in the Kingdom of God in the here and now never perished. It was kept alive in the Lord's Prayer: "Thy Kingdom come, Thy will be done, *on earth as it is in heaven.*" The example of the Exodus and the words of the prophets inspired many Christian groups in the Middle Ages and beyond to do battle for freedom and justice by direct action.

By and large, however, the prophetic vision of world peace was transferred from life to liturgy. As both religions became institutionalized, in a world in which war was endemic and virtually perpetual, the hope for peace became a formula, relegated to a distant day when it would be achieved only through a miracle. Now each tradition felt impelled to deal with the actual phenomenon of war, and each developed a body of teaching on the subject from its own vantage point.

In the Bible there are relatively few regulations concerned with war. They include a provision for the distribution of booty between the actual combatants and those guarding the supplies in the rear, which was apparently observed in practice (Num. 31:25–32, II Sam. 30:17–25). Almost surely utopian in character was the ordinance exempting from military service men who were newly married, or had freshly planted a vineyard, or had recently built a new house (Deut. 20:1–9).

Regarding the legitimacy and the conduct of warfare, Deuteronomy presents two contradictory injunctions. The legislator commands the total destruction of the Canaanites on the ground that their presence was a standing temptation to idolatry (7:2, 20:16–17). That this function was not carried out is clear from historical sources in the Bible and by the fact that immediately after the first passage commanding the destruction of the Canaanites, intermarriage with them is forbidden. Undoubtedly, the defeated Canaanites merged with their Israelite conquerors, so that the prophet Ezekiel could say of Jerusalem centuries later, "Your father was an Amorite, and your mother a Hittite" (Ezek. 16:3).

This ruthless policy of extermination does not apply to other nations, the cruel Amalekites alone being excepted (Deut. 25:17–19). In all other wars, overtures of peace were to be proposed, and only if they were rejected were hostilities to commence. Even then, the law commands that fruit trees surrounding a city were not to be cut down during the siege (Deut. 20:10–20)—a prohibition of the *Schrecklichkeit* and the scorched-earth policy characteristic of more civilized eras. The legislator offers a moving reason for sparing the trees: "For are the trees human beings, that they should come under siege by you?"

In the centuries following the postbiblical era, waging wars ceased to be a live option—if that is the term—for Jews. This last-named passage, as we have seen above, became the biblical basis for a far-reaching and elaborate doctrine on ecology.

This two-pronged approach in the Bible to war the Talmud developed into two categories: *milhemet mitzvah*, "commanded wars," against the Canaanites who were to be totally destroyed, and *milhemet reshut*, "optional war," which Israel was free to undertake against other nations when it felt it necessary to do so. The regulations on war in the Talmud and the medieval codes were purely theoretical, with no practical application.

On the other hand, for the Christian Church the problem of reconciling its teaching of love and peace with the harsh realities of medieval war was far more acute. Accordingly, Catholic theologians and legists elaborated the doctrine of the "just war." With meticulous care and great acumen they set down the characteristics of permissible armed conflict. The first criterion was a "just cause." A second element was "discrimination," distinguishing between combatants and civilians. Moreover the principle of "proportionality" had to be observed. Only as much force as was required to achieve the war's objectives was to be employed. The doctrine of the just war was worked out with great moral earnestness and intellectual brilliance in scholastic philosophy and canon law.

One would be hard put, however, to find any discernible influence from this body of teaching on the course of events, either in medieval or modern times. Wars have continued to be waged, their cruelty and horror being limited only by the escalating capacity of men to devise new forms of torment and death for their fellows. War has continued to remain a constant in history.

To be sure, few people would endorse Mussolini's sentiment, "War alone brings up to its highest tension all human energy and puts the stamp of nobility on the peoples who have the courage to face it." All would pay lip service to the ideal of peace, while adding the "realistic" observation that war is inevitable.

As each new weapon was invented, its discoverers confidently announced that the newly enlarged power of inflicting destruction would, of itself, serve as a deterrent. The invention of dynamite toward the end of the nineteenth century seems idyllic by the side of the more horrible weapons of destruction, conventional, chemical, bacterial, and above all, nuclear, which are being perfected by the best brains of our age, and have made armament manufacture the most lucrative of all industries. It is a horrifying truth, being converted into a truism by dint of repetition, that the two great superpowers, the United States and the Soviet Union, have it in their power to destroy each other many times over, while dragging the human race with them to extinction.

Contemporary apologists, both covert and overt, for nuclear war try to pretend that contemporary armaments are the same as those of the past on a larger scale and that nothing has fundamentally been changed. To further this end, some ethicists and theologians seek to apply the criteria of the just war and to define its "rational" limits. They adopt a high moral stance and remind us that conventional war is also horrible— the clear implication being that there is no fundamental difference.

The citizenry and the local governments are urged to implement programs of "civil defense," but, by and large, Americans remain unconvinced and civil defense is a fiasco. The American people is assured on the highest authority that it is better to be dead than Red, and that nuclear conflict would be a just war because it would be waged against the "evil empire."

Now the scientists and the strategists come to the rescue of the politicians. The public is warned of the obvious truth that the subject of thermonuclear war is highly technical, and the conclusion is drawn that it had best be left to the experts. Since many billions of dollars are involved in the armaments build-up, ample funds are available for creating the vast smoke screen of words, in speeches, books, and articles, on the stage and on the screen, and above all, on radio and television. All are designed to permit the arms race to continue to escalate. Estimates are offered that a nuclear "first strike" would destroy only sixty million people and that our power to retaliate would inflict even greater damage on the enemy. Elaborate disquisitions, often couched in turgid Germanic prose or veiled in arcane technical jargon, are obviously beyond the ken of the ordinary citizen. Scientists present elegantly calculated "probabilities" and "reasonable countermeasures" as well as other "prudential" considerations—all ignoring the not-so-remote possibility of irrational action, human error, or momentary madness.

When this far-flung campaign finds itself unable to achieve its goals and the prospect of nuclear war continues to be unappetizing, the trillions being spent on armaments are justified as "deterrents." In fact deterrence is the favored rationale for stepping up the arms race or carrying it into outer space—all in the name of peace.

The idea has been advanced that if both the United States and the Soviet Union continue their massive nuclear build-up, the quantity of destructive power on both sides would serve as a deterrent, indeed a preventive, to war. Thus MAD (Mutually Assured Destruction) would deter either power from launching the first attack because of the certainty of instant retaliation. The MAD doctrine, it is argued, is a pragmatic "compromise" between the advocates of nuclear disarmament and the proponents of what is euphemistically called a "limited nuclear war." The principle of Mutually Assured Destruction, we are informed, also occupies a middle ground ethically between the idealistic morality of the former and the realistic practicality of the latter. Generally unexpressed is the additional advantage that under the MAD doctrine the trillions bracketed for nuclear and non-nuclear armaments would be safe against budget cuts.

The theory of Mutually Assured Destruction ignores all the irrational factors in human behavior, the possibility of accidents, the outbreak of hysteria among the masses or the leadership, the desperation after initial losses in a conventional war—all hazards that cannot be eliminated. The world cannot permanently be poised on the brink of nuclear war with only MAD as its shield.

The worldwide call among all peoples for a nuclear freeze is attacked as dangerous because "you cannot trust the Russians." Proponents for peace are derided as naive, as though there were no other plank in their platform for peace.

It is to the lasting honor of the Roman Catholic bishops of the United States that in the face of considerable opposition and calumny, they have spoken out against the perilous charade of nuclear armaments leading to nuclear war, in which our country has been playing a leading role. The bishops, in their historic 1983 statement, "The Challenge of Peace, God's Promise, and Our Response," declared that only resistance to armed, unjust aggression qualifies as a just war. While such a paradigm of a just war may be constructed in theory, it has little or no relationship to the complex realities of international conflict in the twentieth century.

In every major war that has bloodied our age, blame is not easily assigned to one side or the other, because of the multiplicity of causes that enter into the picture. Who was responsible for launching World War II? The answer is obvious: Hitler; it was absolutely essential to defeat Hitler and frustrate his plans if civilization was to survive. But what about the culpability of the Allies at Versailles and the vindictiveness and callousness with which the victors treated the democratic Weimar Republic during the difficult years following the First World War? What about the collusion of silence and inactivity by the Allied powers in the face of Hitler's demonic campaign of extermination against the Jewish people and millions of others?

Moreover, all the neat qualifications in classical just war theory regarding discrimination between combatants and civilians and proportionality in the use of force are meaningless in the context of nuclear war. It is entirely natural that the bishops would seek to save as much of

Catholic traditional teaching as possible. In the process they have come to recognize that we face a totally new situation, vastly more terrifying than any nightmare imagined in the past.

In the face of the far-flung campaign to legitimatize the mad armaments race of our times, four truths stand out—and they are simple, not simplistic. *First, nuclear war differs qualitatively and not merely quantitatively from previous conflicts, even World Wars I and II. Second, there is no just war possible in a nuclear age. Third, for the first time, the human race faces the specter of total extinction and not merely large-scale casualties. Fourth, despite the vast differences between them, both the American people and the Soviet population share one overriding interest in common—both have a powerful desire to remain alive.* A nuclear freeze, mutually agreed upon, is a dramatic and essential first step for setting into motion a variety of other steps needed to safeguard peace. The settlement of the issues dividing the two superpowers, the signing of agreements like SALT I and II already agreed upon, the negotiation of reductions in conventional as well as nuclear arms, the establishment of mutually acceptable inspection procedures, many of which do not require on-site verification, claims to the contrary notwithstanding—all these must be vigorously and promptly pursued. Those who hold the reins of power must be held accountable for imperiling the cause of peace. The alternatives today are not war or peace, misery or well-being, but the abolition of war or the extinction of mankind.

It required centuries for the ideal of peace to emerge in the human consciousness. Even then, only men of the stature of Isaiah and Micah had the temerity to insist that peace was not only beautiful but attainable. The dizzy march of what used to be called "progress" has far outdistanced the prophets; unlike their generation, ours cannot afford to wait. The abolition of war is no longer a beautiful or even an attainable ideal; it is a desperate and immediate necessity.

An ancient rabbinic legend tells that when God offered the Torah to Israel and they hesitated to accept it, He held Mount Sinai over their heads and said: "If you accept the Law, very well, but if you do not, I shall bring the mountain down crashing upon your heads. Here will be your burial place" (B. Shabbat 88a). Faced by an offer they could not refuse, they accepted the Law. This is our situation today. We face the challenge that Moses set before his people in the days shortly before his death: "I call heaven and earth to witness. Life and death have I placed before you this day, the blessing and the curse. Choose life, so that you and your children may live" (Deut. 30:19).

Afterword

Three principal motives have led to the writing of this book. The first was the desire to contribute, however modestly, to solving the manifold crises of our time, all of which are basically moral in origin. Ultimately they are traceable to the absence, the loss, or the abandonment of ethical standards in human conduct, individual and collective. To be sure, claims have been advanced that science and the scientific method, on the one hand, and dogmatic religion, on the other, can supply a basis for morality today. These claims are examined and found wanting.

A third time-honored option is then explored, the doctrine of natural law, going back to classical antiquity and the Middle Ages. However, in modern times natural law has been criticized, and justly, as suffering from major drawbacks that make it remote and irrelevant in the face of the major problems that convulse our age. The book urges a reinterpretation of natural law. It suggests that if natural law is purged of some of its historical weaknesses, and its basic concepts are reinterpreted in the light of modern insights, it can serve as the basis for morals in our age.

The second motive was to call attention to the contribution that the biblical and postbiblical Jewish tradition can make toward the necessary revitalization of natural law, through the infusion of the dynamism and the passion for righteousness characteristic of the Hebrew ethos. Its potential contribution is not limited to general principles, but is concerned with specifics as well. Whether ethics is an art or a science may be argued, but it is indisputable that it is concerned with human relationships. Elsewhere we have explored the authentic biblical teaching on race and racism and presented the Judaic concepts of love, sex, and morality, which are far from irrelevant to our deeply troubled age.[1] In the present volume four more relationship-areas are presented: the natural environment, religious liberty, the democratic order, and international affairs.

A third motive that served as a strong incentive for the writing of this book has been a deep concern for the spiritual health of our generation.

The malaise is most noticeable in the democratic, highly industrialized West, which flatters itself that it represents the vanguard of civilization. It is a sad paradox that precisely at the time that men have reached the highest level of technological progress, they have suffered a decline of faith in their capacity to solve their problems by the use of their intelligence and constructive activity. Fearful of the future, many try to take refuge in the past.

As a result, a marked reaction is making itself felt in all areas of national life, in politics and economics, education and culture. It has brought in its wake patterns of repression both physical and intellectual that have been outgrown, or so it was believed. Religion, which should have sounded the prophetic call, has proved all too willing to put the stamp of sanctity on the gospel of greed, naked and unashamed, that prevails on the contemporary scene. On the grass-roots level of populist fundamentalism and in the abstruse lucubrations of theologians, ethics has been severed from religion or attenuated beyond recognition.

Nor have the academics been far behind. The well-known phenomenon that has been called *la trahison des clercs,* the betrayal of moral values by the intellectuals, is evident everywhere. Scholars have been available to undertake a far-flung process of "revision" both in American and in Jewish studies. The American experience is reinterpreted as a defense of property as against human values. The biblical cry reverberating through the ages, "Justice, justice shall you pursue" (Deut. 16:20), is ignored, muted, or distorted, so that the Hebrew tradition emerges as a bulwark of conservatism. The present work has undertaken to help restore the fundamental ethical thrust of the Jewish heritage.

There is a special Jewish dimension to the current spiritual malaise. It is all too easy to understand the state of mind of the surviving victims of the Nazi Holocaust, their children and grandchildren, as well as their contemporaries who witnessed the most unspeakable cruelties in the history of the human race. A deep suspicion of the Gentile world has therefore been planted in many Jewish hearts and minds. In some quarters, the entire fabric of Western civilization, including its protestations of idealism, its claims to compassion, its affirmation of faith in a God of righteousness and compassion, is felt to be a spider's web of hypocrisy. The old biblical cry "To your tents, O Israel" (I Kings 12:6) is proposed as a guide for modern Jews, who are called upon to replace the other biblical injunction, "You shall be for Me a kingdom of priests and a holy nation" (Exod. 19:6). Xenophobia, widespread in general society, has also penetrated Jewish circles, both religious and secular. Its manifestations—fanaticism, hostility, violence—are not attractive. As Lawrence Hogben pointed out, "Persecution rarely makes for the improvement of character in its victims. That is one of the strongest arguments against persecution."

This volume is a modest attempt to underscore the basic ethical thrust of Hebraism and, by that token, inspire the bearers of the tradition to rededicate themselves to its quintessential spirit.

Modern Jews—and indeed all human beings—are entirely justified in concerning themselves first with their own survival. In the animal world, self-preservation may be the whole law of nature, but for humankind, it is only part, and here a part is worse than none. George Santayana declared, "A man must stand with his feet firmly planted in his own country, but his eyes must survey the world." Hillel put it more succinctly and more directly: "If I am not for myself, who will be for me? But if I am only for myself, of what good am I? And if not now, when?"

Notes

Chapter 5

1. See Rudolf Stammler, *The Theory of Justice*, trans. from the German by Isaac Husik (New York, 1925), and Richard Wollheim, "Natural Law," in *Encyclopedia of Philosophy* (New York, 1967), vol. 5, pp. 450–454.

2. It has been argued that the Hebrew verb *raṣaḥ* in the Decalogue means only "kill unjustly, hence murder," and that therefore the Sixth Commandment cannot be invoked as a biblical warrant for opposition to war or capital punishment. This contention is too sweeping. While the root in question generally means "kill willfully, hence murder," this is by no means its exclusive use. Thus in the passage regarding cities of refuge prescribed for the accidental murderer (Num., chap. 35), the same root refers to a willful killer ten times (e.g., v. 16) and to an accidental killer seven times (e.g., vv. 6, 11); the latter meaning also occurs four times in Deut., chaps. 19 f., and a half dozen times in Joshua, chaps. 20 and 21, all with reference to the same institution.

These semantic distinctions aside, it may be argued that while the Sixth Commandment in the Decalogue refers to murder, the meaning of the concept of unjustified killing has evolved through time and now includes a broader understanding of its scope, so that capital punishment and war may now be subsumed under the prohibition.

3. See his paper, "Ethics and Natural Law" written for the Center for the Study of Democratic Institutions in Santa Barbara, California in 1960.

4. For these categories, *debbarim hamesurim lalev, patur 'abhal 'asur* and *patur bedinei 'adam vehayyabh bedinei shamayim* see the relevant articles in *Encyclopedia Talmudit* (Jerusalem)

5. See *New York Times Book Review*, Feb. 12, 1961.

6. In his paper, "Comments on Natural Law" prepared for the Center for the Study of Democratic Institutions in 1960.

Chapter 10

1. Emil Fackenheim, *Encounters Between Judaism and Modern Philosophy* (New York: Basic Books, 1973).

2. See David Ellenson, "Emil Fackenheim and the Revealed Morality of Judaism," *Judaism* 25 (1976): 402–413.

3. See Jacob I. Halevi, "Kierkegaard and the Midrash," *Judaism* 4, no. 1 (1955): 13–28, reprinted in R. Gordis and R. Waxman, eds., *Faith and Reason: Essays in Judaism* (New York: KTAV, 1973), pp. 125–140. References in our text are to the volume.

4. See Marvin Fox, "Kierkegaard and Rabbinic Judaism," *Judaism* 2, no. 2

(1953): 115–124 (reprinted in the same volume, pp. 115–124). References in our text are to the volume.

5. Halevi, op. cit., p. 131.

6. Ibid., p. 138.

7. Ibid., p. 130.

8. Ibid., p. 131.

9. Fox, op. cit., p. 119.

10. Ibid., p. 118.

11. They are all collected and annotated in the magisterial work of Louis Ginzberg, *Legends of the Jews* (Philadelphia: Jewish Publication Society, 1909–1938), vol. 1, and the notes in vol. 5.

12. See the superb study of the theme in S. Spiegel, *The Last Trial*, trans. Judah Goldin (New York: Pantheon Books, 1967).

13. Thus J. H. Hertz, in *The Pentateuch and Haftorahs* (London, 1962), devotes an excursus (p. 201) to the thesis that "the story of the Binding of Isaac opens the age-long warfare of Israel against the abominations of child sacrifice." This is basically the view presented by J. H. Gumbiner, "Existentialism and Father Abraham," *Commentary*, February 1948. However, Gumbiner's strictures on the Kierkegaardian view as "ethically and religiously impossible from the Jewish standpoint" are well taken.

14. See W. R. Smith, *Lectures on the Religion of the Semites*, 3rd ed. with additional notes by S. A. Cooke, reprinted with Prolegomenon by James Muilenberg (New York: KTAV, 1969), pp. 370, 410, and 630, note 4, on mass child sacrifice in Gezer; G. A. Barton, *Archaeology and the Bible*, 7th ed. (Philadelphia: American Sunday School Union, 1937), p. 215; cf. also p. 242.

15. For a different view as to the nature of the rite, cf T. H. Gaster, *Myth, Legend and Custom in the Old Testament* (New York, 1969), pp. 586–588.

16. That the Hebrew term *'adam* used here applies to human beings of both sexes has been noted above.

Chapter 11

1. It is traced in R. Gordis, " 'Be Fruitful and Multiply': Biography of Mitzvah," *Midstream*, August–September 1982, pp. 21–29.

2. See their respective commentaries on the passage.

3. R. Ezekiel Landau, *Noda Biyehudah, Responsa, Yore De'ah* II, 10.

4. Naḥmanides, *Commentary on the Torah*, ed. Ch. B. Chavel, vol. 2 (Jerusalem, 1969), p. 448.

5. The debate of Job and his friends (chaps. 3–31); Elihu's speeches (chaps. 32–36); the Lord's two speeches (38:1–40:2 and 40:6–41:26).

6. This Egyptian text and several similar ones were edited by A. H. Gardiner, *Ancient Egyptian Onomastica* (London, 1947). G. von Rad, who calls attention to the Egyptians and the Hebrew text, does not recognize the vast difference between them in literary character. See A. H. Rad, "Job XXXVIII and "Ancient Egyptian Wisdom," in J. L. Crenshaw, ed., *Studies in Ancient Israelite Wisdom* (New York, 1976), pp. 267–277.

7. For a recent comprehensive survey of the current literature on the subject by a strongly committed advocate, see Peter Singer, "Ten Years of Animal Liberation" in *New York Review of Books*, vol. 31, nos. 21–22, January 17, 1985 pp. 46–52. His essay, "Animal Liberation," published in the *New York Review of Books* on April 5, 1973, followed by a book with the same title, was one of the earliest presentations of the case for the rights of animals in our society.

8. See e.g. Andrew Rowan, *Of Mice, Models and Men: A Critical Evaluation of Animal Research* (State University of New York Press, 1983).

9. The first treatment of the question of the ethical status of animals by an academic philosopher, according to Singer (*op. cit.* p. 47) was Roslind Godlovitch's pioneering article, "Animals and Morals" published in *Philosophy* in 1971. For a bibliography of subsequent publications on the ethics of animal rights, see Singer, *op. cit.* Notes 6.

10. See *Shulḥan Arukh of the Rav, Hilkhot Shemirat Guf Vanefesh*, sec. 14.

11. *Tosafot* on *Abodah Zarah* 11a; *B. Baba Metzia* 32a.

Chapter 12

1. On the Chazar kingdom, see A. B. Pollok, *Kahazaria* (Hebrew), (Tel Aviv, 1951); D. M. Dunlop, *The History of the Jewish Khazars* (Princeton, 1964). For a brief account, see M. L. Margolis and A. Marx, *A History of the Jewish People* (Philadelphia, 1927), pp. 525 f.

2. On the medieval community, see Salo W. Baron, *The Jewish Community: Its History and Structure to the American Revolution*, vol. 3 (Philadelphia, 1942). The impact of the Enlightenment and Emancipation is treated in all works dealing with modern Judaism. A recent study is that of H. M. Graupe, *The Rise of Modern Judaism* (Huntington, N.Y., 1978).

3. Cf. his provocative book bearing the same title, *Secularism as the Will of God* (New York, 1954).

4. We have developed the theme of the relationship of ethics to religious faith in *A Faith for Moderns* (New York, 1960).

5. Instances are to be found, even today, in every religious group. Thus, for several years a furor has been going on in the State of Israel, where members of the ultra-Orthodox community of Me'ah She'arim in Jerusalem sought to prevent vehicular traffic on the Sabbath by stopping and even burning the cars coming through the Mandelbaum Gate. When the police arrested the leaders of the group, their sympathizers in New York demonstrated in front of the Israeli consulate carrying banners in the name of the "Committee for Religious Freedom in Israel."

The *New York Times* (Dec. 18, 1964) reported that the Most Rev. Louis Alonso Munoyerro, titular archbishop of Sion and Catholic vicar-general for Spain's armed forces, gave an interview to the newspaper *ABC* in Madrid, in which he denounced full religious liberty for Protestants in Spain as part of an international conspiracy that was seeking "to make Catholic unity disappear from our fatherland." The archbishop urged Spaniards to learn from history to be "circumspect" and not to "join the chorus of those champions of liberty who judge the success of the Vatican Council by whether it produced the enslavement of the conscience of Catholic people, and among them the Spanish people."

Fortunately, these attitudes are not representative of Catholicism or Judaism as a whole. Nor is religious intolerance rare among atheists. It is, of course well known that the Soviet Constitution guarantees "freedom of religion and the right of anti-religious propaganda." This right to "freedom of religion" is felt to be entirely compatible with the heavy disabilities visited upon virtually all religious institutions and leaders, the prohibition of religious education, and the all-but-complete suppression of Judaism.

6. Cf. the judicious comments on the subject of the role of the Maccabees in Christian thought in T. K. Cheyne, *The Origin and Religious Content of the Psalter* (New York, 1895), p. 29.

7. Cf. Josephus, *Antiquities* XII, 9, 1; 11, 3.

8. In Exodus, chapter 20, Jews reckon verse 2 as the First Commandment, verses 3–6 as the Second, and verse 14 ("You shall not covet") as the Tenth. Roman Catholics and Lutherans consider verses 3–6 as the First Commandment and verse 14 as containing the Ninth and Tenth. Most Protestants count verse 3 as the First, verses 4–6 as the Second, and verse 14 as the Tenth.

9. Cf. our paper "Educating for a Nation of Nations," in *Religion and the Public Schools* (Santa Barbara, Calif.: Center for the Study of Democratic Institutions, 1961), and our volume *The Root and the Branch: Judaism and the Free Society* (Chicago, 1962), pp. 94–114.

10. Cf. A. B. Ehrlich, *Die Psalmen* (Berlin, 1905), p. vi.

11. The literature on the religious movements in the Judaism of the two centuries B.C.E. is enormous. For a brief presentation of some of the differences among the sects, see our *The Root and the Branch*, pp. 34 f.

12. Cf. *B. Sanhedrin* 88b, *B. Shabbat* 17a, *P. Shabbat* 1:4, 3c.

13. Cf. *Mishnah Eduyot* 4:8; *B. Erubin* 13b.

14. Cf. *Mishnah Sanhedrin* 10:1.

15. Cf. Maimonides, *Mishneh Torah, Hilkhoth Teshubhah* 3:7, and RABD, ad loc.

16. On the uses of the ban in medieval Judaism and the famous though atypical excommunications of Uriel Acosta and Benedict Spinoza, cf. our *Judaism for the Modern Age*, pp. 292–306. Spinoza's complex attitudes toward Judaism and Christianity are analyzed in Isaac Franck, "Spinoza's Onslaught on Judaism," *Judaism* 28, no. 2 (Spring 1979), and "Was Spinoza a 'Jewish' Philosopher?" *Judaism* 28, no. 3 (Summer 1979).

17. The tendency to extreme pietism reappears after major catastrophes with sufficient regularity, we believe, to be called a "law." See Chapter 9 above for the phenomenon of "religious return" in the past and the present.

18. On this fundamental aspect of Judaism, cf. *The Root and the Branch*, pp. 23–27.

19. This contention has been a staple in the thinking of Arnold Toynbee. The same view is set forth by Leo Pfeffer, who cites the same commandment (cf. his "Church and State: A Jewish Approach," in Jacob Fried, ed., *Jews in the Modern World* [New York, 1962], I, p. 210). This is astonishing, since, aside from Pfeffer's profound insight into Judaism, he himself cites Roger Williams, who utilized the Decalogue (which includes this commandment) as the foundation for his theory of religious tolerance. Cf. Pfeffer, op. cit., pp. 219 f.

20. For a detailed analysis of the structure and content of this important ethical document, as well as for the exegesis of Job 31:13–15 cited below, see "Job's Code of Conduct," in R. Gordis, *The Book of Job: Commentary, New Translation and Special Studies* (New York, 1978), pp. 542–546; and, more briefly, idem, *The Book of God and Man: A Study of Job* (Chicago, 1965), pp. 91–101.

21. On the history of Gentile-Jewish relationships in Christian Europe, see the excellent study of J. Katz, *Exclusiveness and Tolerance* (Oxford, 1961). On religious tolerance in Judaism, see A. Altman, *Tolerance and the Jewish Tradition* (London, 1957), and the writer's *The Root of the Branch*, chap. 3, esp. pp. 47–52.

22. The texts of many of these disputations are assembled in J. D. Eisenstein, *Otzar Vikkukhim* (New York, 1928). Cf. also Katz, op. cit., pp. 106 ff., and the bibliography there cited; O. S. Rankin, *Jewish Religious Polemic of Early and Late Centuries* (Edinburgh, 1956); F. E. Talmadge, ed., *Disputation and Dialogue: Readings in the Jewish-Christian Encounter* (New York, 1975).

23. The modifications of the talmudic laws by great legal authorities in the early Middle Ages are analyzed by Katz, op. cit., pp. 12–36.

24. Cf. ibid., pp. 102 ff.

25. Cf. the moving passage in his *Sefer Mitzvot Hagadol* (Venice ed., 1547), pp. 152c–d, cited by Katz, op. cit., p. 104.

26. Cf. *Tosefta, Sanhedrin* 13:2.

27. Maimonides, *Hilkhoth Melakhim* 8:11; *Hilkhoth Teshuvah* 3:5; *Harambam Iggerothav* (Leipzig, 1859), pt. 2, p. 23b.

28. Cf. his *Kuzari* 4:23.

29. Cited in Bezelel Ashkenazi, *Shittah Mequbbetzet* (1761 ed.), p. 78a.

30. His descriptive phrase, *'ummoth hageduroth bedarkhei hadathot,* means literally "nations restrained by the ways of religion." Cf. Katz, op. cit., pp. 114–115, for a careful and well-balanced treatment of Meiri's views.

31. Cf. *Tosafot* on *B. Sanhedrin* 63b.

32. Cf. *Mishneh Torah, Hilkhoth Melakhim* 1:4.

33. Cf. *Mishneh Torah, Abodah Zarah* 9:3; *Commentary on the Mishnah, Abodah Zarah* 1.

34. Cf. *Emunot Vedeot* 2:5.

35. Cf. Moses Rivkes, *Be'er Hagolah* on *Shulhan Arukh, Hoshen Mishpat* 525:5.

36. The standard treatments of the history of Jewish proselytism are B. Bamberger, *Proselytism in the Talmudic Period* (Cincinnati, 1939) and W. G. Braude, *Jewish Proselytizing* (New York, 1940). For a brief history of proselytism in Judaism and the issues involved, R. Gordis, *Judaism for the Modern Age* (New York, 1955), chap. 16. In that presentation thirty years ago, I urged the Jewish community to consider the advisability of a dignified presentation of the tenets and practices of Judaism to all who might be interested, whatever their religious background. Thus, the suggestion anticipated the current "out-reach programs" in Reform Judaism, directed to inter-married couples.

This project should be clearly differentiated from the practice of some Reform rabbis who officiate at mixed marriages, where no conversion has taken place. I regard this latter practice as a tragic error, giving the false impression that the marriage is Jewishly valid. The contention has been advanced that in many cases the non-Jewish partner is led to convert subsequently. In spite of repeated requests for evidence I have not seen any data to support this contention.

Chapter 14

1. See Brown-Driver-Briggs, *A Hebrew and English Lexicon of the Old Testament* (Boston, 1907), p. 31a.

2. The first of several mistranslations widely adopted in various extant prayerbooks occurs in this line, which is generally rendered, "Thou wilt remove the abominations from the earth." In the preceding line, the infinitive *lir'ot* obviously cannot have God as the subject, for the content would be nonsense: "That *you* may speedily behold the glory of your might!" Each infinitive in the passage must be construed as active in meaning, with "we" as its subject, as is universally recognized in all translations of the opening clause: "That we may speedily behold the glory of thy might." It has not been noted that all the succeeding infinitives, *leha'abhir, letaqqen, lehaphnot,* are parallel and are similarly to be construed in the active voice, with the subject being "we." The poet is expressing his faith that man will have the strength and the wisdom to perform his duty toward the world. As the first paragraph of the prayer stresses man's duty to worship God, the second underscores man's duty to act in the world.

In addition to converting the infinitives into passives, most translations render *gillulim* as "abominations." The noun is a common pejorative designation for "idols." Hence it is ideally suited to express the worshipper's determination to remove the idols of greed, pride, and war that are the gods in the modern pantheon.

3. The Hebrew verb *taqqen* means "improve, mend, repair," a usage that occurs in the rabbinic phrase *tiqqun ha'olam,* "the improvement of the world, the advancement of human welfare," and is the normal meaning in modern Hebrew. The common translation, "that the world be perfected," may have been influenced by the use of the term in later kabbalistic sources. Thus the great sixteenth-century mystic Rabbi Isaac Luria lays stress upon man's duty to "mend the [broken] vessels" of a sinful world that had been shattered by the evil in the world, and thus to restore the universe to its pristine perfection. This meaning could not have been within the purview of the second-century talmudic sage Rab in composing *Alenu.*

Afterword

1. See our *The Root and the Branch: Judaism and the Free Society* (Chicago, 1962) and *Love and Sex: A Modern Jewish Perspective* (New York, 1978) for treatments of these two areas in the Jewish tradition.

Index of Names and Subjects

186

Index of Sources

BIBLE (in the order of the Hebrew Bible)